Working
with People

NAOMI I. BRILL *University of Nebraska*

Working with People

THE HELPING PROCESS

second edition

J.B. LIPPINCOTT COMPANY
New York Hagerstown *Philadelphia San Francisco*

WORKING WITH PEOPLE: The Helping Process, Second Edition

Library of Congress Cataloging in Publication Data

Brill, Naomi I
  Working with people.

  Includes bibliographies and index.
  1. Social service. 2. Social workers. I. Title.
HV40.B83 1978   361   77-29163
ISBN 0-397-47382-6

Soon after the first edition of this book was published, a woman came to see me and asked if I would help her to live till she died and to die with dignity. She had just learned that she had advanced cancer of the pancreas and her time was short. We met once or twice a month, had lunch together, talked, shared readings, ideas, feelings. She worked as long as she was able, participated in seminars on dying and death, shared her life with her family and friends, died as she had wished.

When she said good-bye at the end of our first meeting, I asked her why she had selected me—we were only casual acquaintances and I was no longer in practice. She was one of those persons who believed in being prepared for any contingency. She rooted in a battered shopping bag holding a pair of boots, a collapsible umbrella, a sweater, a newspaper, brought up a copy of *Working with People,* and showed it to me with a smile.

I hope this new edition will say to others what that edition said to her, and I would like to dedicate it to her, who shall be nameless, and to people who rarely see clearly or understand wholly, yet face living with courage and gallantry and keep struggling for a better world.

Contents

In dealing with people it is essential that workers possess an awareness of themselves and of their own needs, of ways in which they satisfy these needs and of ways in which they use themselves in their relationships with others. This chapter focuses on the development of this essential self-knowledge and suggests ways to work toward those personal changes that contribute to more effective working relationships.

There are many theories about human nature, each of which attempts to explain why people are as they are and how they develop both as individuals and as social beings. Using an eclectic approach, this chapter explains life as a dynamic process characterized by continual growth in which individuals develop by adaptation to the changing demands of both their own inherent potential and the environment in which they live.

Throughout the entire life experience, beginning at birth and ending at death, the process of socialization and resocialization runs like a thread. It is primarily determined by relationships with other people, and the manner in which it evolves determines the ability of the individual to utilize the resources of the society to maximum advantage. This chapter examines the definition and content of socialization, the nature of the process, and the responsibility of the human service worker in this area.

4. DEVELOPING AND MAINTAINING
   COMMUNICATION WITH PEOPLE   50
   The establishment of meaningful and disciplined communication is the basis for all work with people. Workers need to know (1) what they are communicating; (2) how they are communicating it; (3) how their communication is perceived and responded to by others; and (4) how they receive and understand these responses. This chapter deals with the basic knowledge of communication and the ways in which workers can utilize it more effectively.

5. DEFINING THE HELPING RELATIONSHIP   65
   Through communication and shared experiences and feelings, people develop relationships that can either help or hinder them in the realization of particular goals. This chapter discusses the meaning and content of working relationships and the ways in which the worker can best utilize them as dynamic processes.

6. UTILIZING SOCIAL SYSTEMS THEORY TO
   UNDERSTAND HUMAN INSTITUTIONS   78
   The relationship between the individual and society is one of mutual rights and responsibilities. Each draws from and contributes to the other. Using concepts from social systems theory, this chapter is designed to develop greater understanding of the institutions people have developed to meet their individual and social needs, and ways in which the worker can most effectively capitalize on this knowledge in the interests of both.

7. UTILIZING THE SCIENTIFIC METHOD
   TO HELP PEOPLE DEAL MORE EFFECTIVELY
   WITH THE DEMANDS OF LIVING   89
   As rational animals, people have developed the "scientific method" as a way of looking at and working toward a solution of the problems of life. An individual proposes a theory, collects and tests data relating to it, evaluates the results in light of the

theory, and moves on from there in a repetition of this process. But, people are also irrational beings whose feelings and behavior cannot be understood or dealt with purely on a rational level. This chapter proposes a basic model for working with people that takes into consideration all aspects of human nature.

variously with helplessness, with rage. This chapter deals with ways in which human service workers can recognize and cope with some of the problems created by this situation.

12. DEALING WITH DEPENDENCY   191

By its very nature, society is interdependent and the myth of the independent person is just that—a myth. Nevertheless, relative independence is essential for effective social functioning as well as personal fulfillment. This chapter focuses on those elements in relationship and process that contribute to the achievement of a healthy balance in this area.

13. BEING ACCOUNTABLE FOR WHAT WE DO   200

As the organizations charged with providing the human services have increased in size and complexity as well as in the amount of financial support they require, there has been an increasing demand for "accountability." This chapter examines what is involved in this concept and points out ways in which workers, who are the vital link in the whole process, can effectively discharge the responsibility not only for what they do individually but also for what is done in the programs of which they are a part.

14. INTEGRATING THE PERSONAL AND PROFESSIONAL SELF   214

The gap between basic theory and practical application of that theory is one that is bridged by integration within the worker of values, knowledge, and practical skill. It is an ongoing process that takes place during the life experience of the worker. This chapter deals with some of the factors involved in this integration and comments on the role of the human service worker in modern society.

Preface

The quiet revolution in values that is taking place in the world today is nowhere more apparent than in the plea for knowledge that is relevant to basic human needs—knowledge of how to live together in peace; of how to achieve social justice for all; of how to find fulfillment and realization of personal and societal potential; of how to distribute more equitably the world's goods; of how to provide opportunity for a physically, emotionally, intellectually, socially, and spiritually meaningful life for the complex human entities who stand with their feet in the mud, their eyes fixed on the stars.

Echoing this demand, the various academic disciplines are striving to serve these needs by bridging the gap between theoretical knowledge and practical application. Driven by a conviction that human life is finite, they are seeking answers to the practical questions of how to better serve people and enable them to use more effectively the knowledge that their research has developed.

Biologists want to know how to retain the all-important and indefinable quality of human life under present social pressures; psychiatrists, psychoanalysts, and psychologists, struggling with the problems of patients for whom therapies of various sorts produce only limited results, seek new approaches; architects and planners want to know how to insure human values in steel and concrete; educators, desperately facing increased learning problems in schools, want to know how to look at themselves, their system, and their changing students more effectively; doctors, increasingly aware that

xi

the physical aspect of the individual cannot be isolated from the remainder of self and society, are reaching for knowledge of the practical aspects of relating to and working with people; political scientists and economists want to know how to make the systems about which they theorize adequately serve the political and economic needs of people; sociologists want to go beyond merely describing society and its groups, and use their knowledge to affect desired change; lawyers are searching for better ways to reach people who need their services; home economists, nutritionists, and other practitioners want to know how to relate to and work with people whose cultures and value systems differ from their own; social workers, who started a hundred years ago with a vision of integrating knowledge of the total human being into a basis for practice and then lost their way, are striving to rediscover their own beginnings.

In the five years or so that have elapsed since publication of the original edition of this book, major social changes have taken place that have had an inevitable effect on the planning and delivery of human services. These services continue to fall into two categories: (1) those designed to provide opportunities for maximization of human potential and prevention of individual and social breakdown, and (2) those designed to provide remediation of such breakdown and restoration of capacity for functioning.

The role of the human service worker who, of necessity, must relate to this duality of purpose within a rapidly changing society, is a dynamic one, posing demand for acquisition of additional learning in both theory and practice skills. While the fundamentals remain the same—the basic human needs, the importance of relationship, the ability to communicate on many different levels, the need to view people and society as inseparable totalities involved in a never-ending transactional relationship—the so-called knowledge explosion exists in the human services as elsewhere and provides opportunity for developing new ways of working with people.

In looking at the total picture, six areas of changing emphasis emerge that seem sufficiently fundamental and lasting to be included in a basic book such as this. These six areas are:

1. The developing emphasis on a pluralistic society and on what has been called the communal individual. Two basic values that have been a part of culture in America since its beginning are being challenged in light of the demands of living together in an increasingly larger, more complex technological society. These are the values related to the concept of the melting pot, wherein all people

blend their differences into one great whole, and the concept of the independent person, who "rides alone into the sunset," who is dependent on no one but self.

2. The emphasis on rights of all people to what has been called social justice and the expansion of the concept of rights to different groups of people such as children and women. People are increasingly seen as having the "right" to medical care, the "right" to good housing, the "right" to work that is meaningful, the "right" to be themselves and to participate in the decision-making process within the bureaucratic structures that we have created to plan and deliver human services.

3. The almost impatient demand for what has been called "accountability," for the development of better tools and knowledge about evaluation of outcomes of programs and services and evidence, insofar as is possible, on the basis of empirical research, of the effectiveness of what is being done.

4. The increasing emphasis on application of knowledge and skills from the discipline of management to organization and delivery of human services on both the individual and the institutional levels. Human services have become big business. In at least one instance, they have even been labeled an industry, and the problems of management have grown accordingly. The rank-and-file worker whose services are directly with the so-called consumer is a major part of this development, as well as is the managerial staff.

5. The impact of increasing social pressures on the individual in modern society and the need for human service workers to be better prepared to deal with both individual and group frustration, fear and anger. In the final analysis the buck stops at the worker's desk; workers are likely to find themselves the targets for the feelings of clients who are powerless to cope with the demands of the system.

6. The increasing need for workers to be competent to teach new ways of dealing with the demands of living and new knowledge that can be used by clients both as individuals and in groups. A major problem in peoples' inability to function is lack of socialization in knowing how to use the opportunities that exist in the society we have created.

Out of these concerns and questionings, painful as they may be, perhaps at long last will come realistic recognition of the intrinsic wholeness of the individual and development of the essential multi-disciplinary approach to working with people. Along with recognition of the need for such a comprehensive approach has come an awareness that there is no final solution to the problems of living, that the concept of cure is inapplicable because it is a fact of life that problems have no end. In this dynamic condition lie both the challenge and the opportunity.

However, all of our additional knowledge, all of our developing skills are limited by the capacity of the individual who uses them to relate meaningfully to other people. A recent study of the open classroom in English schools revealed that the major factor of teachers' success in enabling students to learn lay not in the design of the learning experience but in the personality of the teacher. The complexity of modern human services demands ability to relate differentially with people on many levels and in many roles—clients, co-workers, administrators, the general public. We all take the knowledge and the skill that we have acquired and filter it through ourselves as we use it. The basic self remains of fundamental importance, and it is there that we must always begin.

The ideas and thinking in this book had their origins in study, working, and living. It is not possible in this brief space to give credit to all those to whom it is due, and to attempt to develop a truly comprehensive bibliography would be to undertake an impossible task. This book represents the way it all falls into place for me. Each reader will, I hope, find his or her own way.

Therefore, at the end of each chapter there is a brief working bibliography which will serve as a guide for those who wish to know and think more about a particular topic. It is designed for all who wish to engage in that most exciting of games—pursuing an idea through literature—and to provide what any good hunter needs—a starting point. The references are applicable on a much broader level than merely the particular chapter where they are listed and periodicals have been deliberately excluded. One should become conversant with those in one's particular area of work—they represent the changing edge of thought in one's own field.

An effort has been made to select books on the criteria of availability, readability, and credibility. Those listed afford a wide range in both difficulty of comprehension and usefulness to the general reader but try to offer something meaningful regardless of the level on which the reader operates. I believe each says something significant, but there are many others that might say it equally well and even better for another. Readers may use them to point the way for their own explorations.

In addition to the more technical works, it would be a mistake to overlook the part creative writing can play in the understanding and sensitization of the reader to self and others. Such listing would be truly endless, however, for it would include much of the great literature of the world. Books such as James Agee's *A Death in the Family*, Pearl Buck's *The Child Who Never Grew*, Dick Gregory's *Nigger*, Robert Frost's *Collected Poems*, the plays of Shakespeare and many, many others bring an added dimension of well-fleshed humanity and nuances of relationship and feeling that are invaluable to the human services worker.

Thus, an eclectic approach, tempered with a respect for life and humility in the face of its nature, is the foundation of this book. I owe the impetus for it to my children, my clients, my students, and my colleagues from whom I learned much of this respect and humility—the hard way!

NAOMI ISGRIG BRILL
University of Nebraska

Introduction

This book is designed for people who work with other people. It is based on the assumption that although tasks and roles may vary, there is a foundation of attitude, knowledge, and skill that is basic to all such work, whether it is done by untrained aides or by the most highly specialized professionals. It deals with fundamental ideas and processes that, over a period of time, become so much a part of the individual worker that in some sense they constitute the professional self, which is increasingly inseparable and indistinguishable from the personal self.

The principles and processes covered here are weighed against the criteria of fundamental values, theoretical soundness, and pragmatic effectiveness. The questions asked are: (1) Do the ideas represent a constructive value system? (2) Are they based on valid theory? (3) Do they produce the desired results?

To answer the first requires an objective value judgment, always a difficult task. The latter two also present problems, particularly at this stage in the development of our knowledge of human beings. In working with people we tended to practice before we theorized as to why we chose to use a particular technique in working with a particular person in a particular set of circumstances. We proceeded on a trail-and-error basis, and if one thing did not work, we turned to something else. We will probably always proceed in this fashion, the human condition being what it is and human need such that it does not wait on theorizing and experimentation. Nevertheless, with the growing realization that our great need does not lie in learning to live with our technology but in learning to live with ourselves, we have begun to devote more of our time to slowly and painfully building a body of knowledge regarding people and their functioning based on sound research and experimentation. We have begun to construct the tools that will enable us to look at the results of our efforts critically and to achieve as objective and rational an awareness of ourselves as is possible. We have learned much already, but the more we learn, the more we know remains to be learned. This book is, at best, a very small beginning.

Although the author's social work orientation is reflected in the vocabulary, an attempt has been made to express the ideas in this book in the simplest, most direct, and, hopefully, most meaningful terms regardless of source or previous usage. Certain words tend to be loaded with meaning, and nowhere is this more true than with those used to describe emotionally charged interactions between people. However, the intent of the user is much more significant in interpreting a word's meaning than its standard definition. Owen Wister illustrated this unforgettably when he coined the phrase beloved of small boys a generation ago, "When you call me that smile!" "The letter means nothing until the spirit gives it life," says Wister.[1] Words themselves are not cold, hostile or impersonal; these qualities are imparted by the user. For the purpose of this book, the reader should therefore accept the vocabulary within the framework of the author's concepts.

Three words are essential when any act is being described: the noun designating the actor, the verb designating the action, and the noun designating the object of the action. Those used here, worker, help, and client, were chosen on the basis of standard meaning, derivation, and applicability to a broad spectrum of individuals, groups, and activities. In this context, the words may be defined as follows:

Worker—One who works, who performs an activity, who, by sustained mental and/or physical effort overcomes obstacles and achieves a result.

Help—To give assistance to, to aid, to further the advancement of, to supply what is needed to accomplish an end, with a strong implication of advance toward an objective.

Client—A person or group of persons engaging the professional services of another, a person who is under the protection of another, one who hears.

1. Owen Wister, *The Virginian* (New York: Macmillan, 1902), p. 20.

Upon encountering these three generic terms, readers can substitute for them other terms that fit the needs of their own particular role or activity. For worker, one may use teacher, doctor, lawyer, social worker, nurse, nutritionist, aide, technician, and so on; for help, teach, treat, advise and defend, advocate; for client, student, patient, individual, couple, family, group, neighborhood, community.

The reader should not be deceived by the apparent simplicity of the principles and processes described here. In the hands of a competent worker and in print, they look and sound so uncomplicated that the reader is impelled to think, "There's nothing to it—I can do that." For example, take the basic principle that the various disciplines which deal with people must use as the first step: "Start where the client (student, patient, and so on) is." This sounds simple and obvious, but in trying to understand what it really means and how to put it into operation, a multiplicity of questions immediately becomes apparent. How do you determine where the client is? What information is needed to make such a determination? Once having decided where an individual is, how do you relate yourself, your ideas, your knowledge and your efforts to this person? The whole problem of relevance that is causing so many furrowed brows in education, social work, law, politics lies in these questions.

The principles relating to human behavior are far more complex than is obvious at first glance. Once one is aware of this, one can take them for what they are—a starting point only, from which to begin one's search for more complete understanding. In an attempt to clarify these complicated principles, the author has used numerous case illustrations. But some students have a tendency to focus so completely on the specific examples used for clarification that they forget the concept being explicated. To get the maximum service from this book, one must avoid this trap, by using the case illustrations only as a means of enhancing understanding and then by applying the concepts to one's own field of endeavor.

The reader should be aware also of the danger of oversimplification that is inherent in the application of principles and processes on a broad multidisciplinary basis as is done here. In the effort to develop ideas that will be comprehensive in their application, specific nuances of meaning may be sacrificed. We must be aware of this and, in our own thinking, question and reconcile those differences that concern us.

In addition, the fact that this book is directed toward such a wide audience should not be construed as advocating that there should be no differentiation of responsibilities among workers or that one person can be all things to all people. Each of us brings to our task not only the uniqueness of ourselves as individuals, but also the uniqueness of our knowledge and skill. Having a medical degree does not necessarily qualify one to deal with the agonizing efforts of a young woman to decide whether to relinquish a child for adoption. A minister is not always competent or the best person to help someone to cope with moral issues. It does not necessarily follow that the indigenous worker—the alcoholic working with the alcoholic, the poor with the poor, the black, white, and brown with the black, white, and brown, the mentally ill with the mentally ill, is best capable of dealing with those who are in similar circumstances. Sometimes such a worker is actually the one with the most potential for destruction in that particular situation.

The decision as to what each worker does should be based in part on where the best capacity lies. If ever there was a place for individuals to "do their own thing," it is in the area of working with people. The disciplined and knowledgeable use of the uniqueness of the individual can be a tremendous asset in dealing with the diversity of people and their needs.

Along with this awareness of the value of differences has developed an awareness of the fact that all professional and nonprofessional people who work with people share basic knowledge and skill. It serves as a common denominator from which all can move in the direction of their own specialization. This book represents an effort to organize and present this basic material in a usable fashion. The impetus for it accumulated gradually over a period of years devoted to teaching and working with a wide variety of people in all walks of life, all of whom seemed to be asking the same questions:

The elementary guidance counselor spoke of the poor family who moved into an upwardly mobile neighborhood of young couples under the Subsidized Housing Program.

"No one will speak to them, or let their children play with those children. It carries over into the school. What can we do about it?"

The student stopped in after class.

"I can't tell the housemother, she'd flip her lid. And the alums would just kick her out. She's a transfer so we don't know much about her—but it really shook Mary Lou up when she sneaked into her room in the middle of the night and

started going through her things. So far we've kept it from the rest of the House but . . . what should we do?"

"What are we going to do with these people?" the personnel director queried grimly. "We train them, give them jobs, and they goof off. They're late—they don't get here half the time, they just can't seem to put in a good day's work. Even if you give them a chance, they can't use it."

"This institution for retarded is a hangover from the 'put them way out in the country and forget them' era," said the director bitterly—"and the whole town behaves accordingly. They're scared of the patients. Mad because they're here—but want to make as much money as they can out of them and their families. How can we change their attitudes?"

"Something's happened to schools," said the old teacher. "The discipline problems and chaos in this high school are so great there isn't any time for learning. It started before we integrated the classes but it's worse now, and I don't know whether that's cause and effect or not. How can we help these kids use their chances to learn?"

"I love my work and my people, the Indians, really need it," said the nutrition aide in her sober fashion "but they just don't seem to want to learn to feed their families better. How can I teach them to make use of what I know?"

Where and how should we begin? How do you understand other people? How do you talk with them? Communicate meaningfully with them? How can you help people to use their own strengths? To change ways of thinking, feeling, and behaving that they either are not comfortable with or are destructive to them and those around them? How do you deal with social systems so complicated that you don't know where or how to begin? How do you work with people?

No man can reveal to you aught but that
which already lies half asleep in the dawning of your
knowledge.
The teacher . . . . gives not of his
Wisdom but rather of his faith and lovingness.
If he is indeed wise he does not bid you enter
the house of his wisdom, but rather leads you to the
threshold of your own mind.

On Teaching from *The Prophet*
Kahlil Gibran

1
Understanding Ourselves

"Know thyself," said the Greek oracle over two thousand years ago, thereby earning for herself that reputation for sagacity which comes to those who give voice to a basic human urge. From the time when we first evolved far enough as a species to indulge in speculation to our present conception of ourselves as only one life form—albeit the dominant one—existing in essential relationship with all other life forms, people have been striving to do just this.

What kind of creature am I? Where did I come from? How do I function? How can I understand and control myself, my own behavior, my life and my future?

Although for centuries the study of the self and the universe was frowned upon—early students ran the danger of being burned to death, exiled, or forced to recant their theories—the curiosity that has moved us from the trees, the plains and the caves to our present technological society is an irresistible goad. With the development of more sophisticated methods of study, knowledge and understanding of people and society gradually accumulate. The importance of this learning cannot be overestimated. Answers to the major questions of our time can be reached only when we understand ourselves, our needs, and our potentials.

Workers who aspire to utilize self in a disciplined and knowledgeable way in relationships with other people must have a personal objectivity based on: (1) awareness of self and personal needs, (2) ability to deal with their own patterns of personality, and (3) resultant

1

freedom from placing limitations on their individual ability to perceive with clarity and relate with honesty.

EDUCATION FOR USE OF SELF

There is an old definition of education, the origins of which are
obscure but which is nonetheless valid and applicable to this process:
"Education is the progression from freedom, through discipline, to
greater freedom." People are endowed with both the need and the
capacity to relate meaningfully to others of their own kind. There is
no indication that this is not a free and open capacity with potential
for development and maximum use, provided the basic needs of the
developing individual are met and stultifying experiences can be
avoided. Unfortunately, few people develop under optimum conditions, and workers find themselves limited by the manner in which
they meet their own needs as well as by ways of thinking, feeling,
and behaving that are not conducive to the development of effective
open relationships with others.

To free themselves for better use of their innate capacity to relate,
workers face an experience in reeducation which may be difficult.
Initially they must be not only capable of accepting their own im-
perfections, but also convinced that they are capable of change. Few
people are so smug or so rigidly defensive that they have not, at
times, questioned their own contribution to relationships. However,
it is one thing to recognize this and another to change it. Often the
causes lie buried in the unconscious mind or are beyond recall in the
distant past but create difficulties in the present situation. Workers
who are successful in liberating themselves from them can then begin
to enjoy and utilize their full capacity for human interaction.

Attitudes and behavior are learned in response to a need for reaction to particular circumstances and tend to become internalized
and invested with an emotional component that may have little
relationship to their real significance. The progression moves somewhat like this:

1. Circumstance that demands a reaction from the individual.
2. Response on a trial-and-error basis or on the basis of precept.
3. Selection of a particular response that is effective.
4. Development of feelings that this is the "right" response because it works for the individual in this situation.

5. Development of feelings that other people who respond differently are "wrong."

Culture dictates patterns or ways of behaving in response to specific situations, and these patterns are imparted to the child through the family, the school, the church, and other social institutions. In this process, the reasons for selecting a particular response may be lost in the mists of history, but the response itself becomes invested with an almost ritualistic and emotional significance and becomes the accepted way for that particular culture. The person who deviates from the cultural norm is often punished, the form of the punishment being prescribed by the culture.

Attitudes and behavior may also develop in response to unconscious needs and drives—protection from pain, preservation of personal integrity, allowance for essential growth, and assistance with dealing with reality. These coping mechanisms, as they are usually designated—denial, projection, regression, fantasy, and so on—are related to the stimulus for which they are designed in an indirect way, and, therefore, the behavior they produce often appears irrational to the observer. Selection of a particular mechanism is strongly influenced by culture and setting. People universally use these mechanisms, and they can be an effective part of the process of dealing with the demands of living. They can also be ineffective when they are used rigidly or unrealistically.

Whatever the dynamics of origin of particular feelings and behavior, the worker must be aware of both their existence and the fact that they are so pervasive that one may not realize how deeply they affect one's attitudes and behavior toward oneself and others.

Mary was only five years old that summer when she sat on the back steps and watched me iron out on the terrace and hang the shirts on the trees in the sun and wind. After regarding me soberly for a while she commented, "My mother irons indoors." I replied that it was too pretty a day to stay inside and this way I could both iron and enjoy the beautiful day. She suffered my rhapsodies patiently, but when I finished, repeated, with emphasis and finality, "My mother irons indoors!"

At five there was for her already a right and a wrong way, and the right way was her family's pattern. The person who deviated was wrong.

Workers who begin by accepting that what they are will affect what they can do strive to develop a self-awareness that will enable them to understand and change their attitudes and feelings, and control their own behavior in working relationships. Before beginning to practice, neophyte psychoanalysts must first undergo analysis to enable them to develop this awareness. In social work, the role of the supervisor includes responsibility for helping workers to look at themselves objectively, both alone and in relationship with others. Few of the helping professions lack this aspect of education for practitioners. Today's sensitivity and encounter groups are designed not only to sensitize people to themselves and their own feelings, but also to increase their awareness of the need to change the destructive impact their feelings may sometimes have on others.

Short of these formalized efforts, however, there are some concrete steps that workers can take to help them to deal with themselves in what is, after all, a very personal struggle. They can ask themselves some very basic questions:

1. How do I think and feel about myself?
2. How do I deal with my own fundamental needs?
3. What is my value system, and how does it define my behavior and my relationships with other people?
4. How do I relate to the society in which I live and work?
5. What is my life style?
6. What is my basic philosophy?

HOW DO I THINK AND FEEL ABOUT MYSELF?

Probably the most important factor about all individuals is how they feel about themselves. One may be physically or intellectually handicapped or whole; old, young, or middle-aged; wealthy or poor; fat or thin; of any color or race, but if one likes oneself, one can usually succeed in life and relate well to other people. This self-image is developed from a variety of contributory factors, but it is principally a matter of feeling about oneself. While extraordinary sensitiveness may be a part of individual endowment, it is the life experience that determines people's attitudes toward themselves, and within this experience the attitudes of other individuals and groups are of paramount importance. Thus the acceptance of children as they are and not as people would like them to be is essential during their developmental years. Early experiences which enable children to value and like themselves can form a firm foundation upon which they can depend during the crucial life stages, particularly those of adolescence and old age when they tend to be most vulnerable to self-doubt.

Debbie is a good example of a child whose early years were fraught with unexpressed conflict. She was the first child of upwardly mobile middle-class parents. Her mother—the pampered only daughter of an older couple—had set her heart on a boy. Her tantrums, when the arrival of a girl was announced, were clearly audible throughout the maternity unit. Although denied no material advantage, Debbie always felt that she had failed her mother and that nothing she could ever do quite measured up to what was expected of her. Even though she was a bright achieving girl, she always felt inadequate and unsure of herself.

Just as with other facets of personality, self-acceptance is not static. It is a matter of degree and subject to change according to circumstances and situations. Adolescence with its questioning and search for identity is often a period of intense discomfort and self-deprecation. The child, who as a ten-year-old was fairly comfortable and happy-go-lucky, may find herself at fourteen at odds with parents who are having trouble accepting her growing up, and concerned and unhappy about herself as a person in a society that seems to frown on her, her ideas, and her feelings.

With old age, the negative social impact is often equally strong. It has been said that the adaptive mechanisms of aging are without status in modern society. Certainly the tendency to slow down, to be more conservative, to narrow the circle socially, economically, and physically are contrary to the values of the lively ones in our fast moving technological society. The impact of this impatience and disapproval may help to intensify the older person's feeling of lack of worth and importance.

Thus the all-important ability to be comfortable with oneself is based on the following actors:

1. Awareness of and ability to accept oneself as a fallible individual with strengths and weaknesses.
2. Development of a flexible adaptive pattern that does not de-

mand perfection of oneself and hence does not expect it of others.

3. Capacity to recognize and deal with the impact of negative attitudes and behavior of significant individuals within the life experience, either social groups or the society as a whole.

4. Acceptance of the fact that self-liking is not static or unchanging. Only the Babbitts of the world never question themselves.

Self-acceptance and liking involves a continuous process of awareness, assessment, and flexibility.

HOW DO I DEAL WITH MY OWN FUNDAMENTAL NEEDS?

There are certain fundamental human needs that must be met if we are to survive, and the way in which we meet them will determine how healthy we are and how we develop and function as total persons. These needs can be considered in two overall categories: (1) the need for security and (2) the need to accommodate the drive toward growth. Each of these categories encompasses five areas or aspects of living which are almost inseparable: the emotional, intellectual, physical, social, and spiritual. Theirs is a dynamic interrelationship in which each is continuously affecting and being affected by the others, and there is no real and complete understanding of what is happening in one without understanding what is happening in the others (see Figure 1).

Emotional refers to those feeling or affective aspects of the consciousness that are subjectively experienced and are often difficult for the outside observer to give credence to. It is only within the past hundred years that we have even begun to understand the significance of this part of an individual, particularly in its effect upon functioning in the other areas. Now we are recognizing the tremendous power of the emotions and beginning to understand the part they play in determining the individual's ability to utilize other capacities.

Physical refers to the material structures of the body and its organic processes. Although this area is easier to study because of its nature, much is yet unknown, particularly of the way it affects and is affected by the other aspects of the individual.

Intellectual refers to the capacity for rational and intelligent thought, the power of knowing. It relates to the ability to develop,

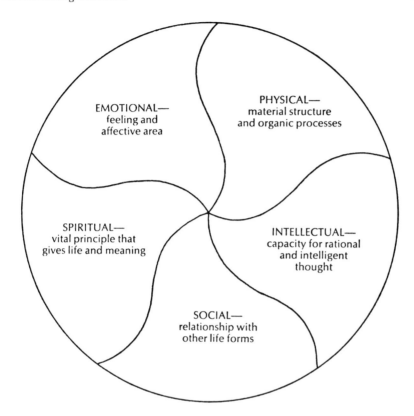

Figure 1 The Total Individual–The Continuous, Dynamic Interaction of Five Vital Areas

understand, and master knowledge and skill. One of the vital and as yet incompletely answered questions in this area is how people learn and how they can utilize this capacity to its maximum degree.

Social refers to the need and capacity for relationships with other people. It is becoming increasingly obvious that the word "people" is a limiting one and should probably be changed to a phrase such as "other life forms." We are more and more aware that not only must we exist in a state of balance with other vital elements in the universe and that these relationships can be meaningful and satisfying, but also that the attitudes and feelings that arise out of respect for self and other people also involve regard for the integrity of differing living mechanisms.

Spiritual is defined as the animating or vital principle which gives life to physical organisms. As such, its origin, function, and expression are not totally understood. It is obvious that people are more than a conglomerate of physical, social, intellectual, and emotional needs and drives, and that there is a spiritual aspect of each of these areas. Over the centuries, organized religion has attempted to provide a medium for expressing these spiritual needs, but unfortunately, particularly in its sectarian aspects, it has tended to compartmentalize rather than unify. To ignore or deny this aspect because of our incomplete understanding of it is to deny the totality of the individual.

The Basic Human Needs

Security, the first category of basic human needs, runs the gamut from the material needs to sustain life—food, clothing and shelter—to the less concrete ones for loving and being loved, for meaningful association with others, for a milieu that provides acceptance of ideas and feelings, regardless of whether or not they are in conformity with the cultural norms, and for reward for risk. Healthy security offers opportunity for a dynamic dependency. It provides the firm floor upon which individuals can stand with confidence and assurance as they grow. They can depend on this essential footing and can move from it to try new ways; they can return to it when faced with failure, to regroup and start again. This can be simply illustrated by observing children who are learning to walk—they pull themselves up, try, fall, weep with frustration over failure, try again, and eventually totter a few steps for the first time. How much simpler this task if the child has a solid surface on which to experiment, together with encouraging, supporting parents to provide a focus for these efforts. How much more difficult if the floor is slick or unsteady or the parents hostile, indifferent, or overprotective.

Growth is a continuous and essential concomitant of the life process. All individuals are endowed at conception with a maximum potential for growing and developing in every area of self and throughout their lifetime mature toward the point which is their maximum capability. Since genetic endowments and potentials differ greatly from individual to individual, the idea of equality has caused some problems. For our purpose here equality lies in the fact that each of us possesses the drive to grow, although maximum potentials may vary greatly. To illustrate this concept in its most apparent form, one individual may possess much greater potential than another for developing physical dexterity. While capacity for development in all areas may not be at equal levels, there is some evidence that the exceptionally well-functioning person tends to operate well as a total individual. Normally, however, individuals develop one area to its highest peak—perhaps at the expense of the others.

In a sense, one's potential lies dormant until it is stimulated by the impact of the internal impulses for normal growth and development combined with the external experiences that are taking place in the environment. It is important to remember that environment begins at conception and that what happens to the developing infant within the mother's body has major impact on present and future development.

People require stimulation to trigger development in all life areas, but it must be in a good balance determined by their needs at a particular point in time. Overstimulation, as is so often present in young families who are attempting to move upward on the economic and social scale, can be as inhibiting as understimulation can be stultifying. Timing is of great importance. There is some evidence, for example, that the child who is not stimulated to use the developing early coordination of muscles and nerves in even so simple a task as catching a ball will be unable, even with subsequent exercise, to achieve the peak potential for physical development. Growth and development take place in accordance with an internal timetable which follows a general pattern but which is unique to the individual.

There are many roadblocks in this process of developing potential, and the relationship between security and growth in any individual is seldom completely understood. Occasionally we see someone who flowers in conditions of adversity that are totally destructive to others, but such a person is the exception. The sad statistics on mental retardation in our enlightened society lend credence to this statement. Nine percent of all children in the United States are considered retarded, but only five percent are born that way—the others achieve this state by age thirteen as a result of their life experience. Three fourths of these children come from poverty areas.

In general we could say that in the physical area we need a basic minimum of material supplies, stimulation, opportunity for physical development at crucial points in the developmental timetable, and basic medical services that are one of the benefits of our modern society. In the area of intellectual development, we need stimulation and the opportunity to acquire and master knowledge, each according to his own capacity; in the area of emotional development, we need fulfilling relationships with significant other people and ability to accept and be at peace with ourselves; in the area of social growth, we need the opportunity to become socialized on an increasingly

wider scale with increasing capacity to relate meaningfully and effectively with people who are different from ourselves; in the area of
spiritual development, we need the stimulation and opportunity to
find a meaning in life that transcends the mere satisfaction of needs
and gives purpose and direction to the total experience (see Figure 2).

In summary, we can say that in looking at ourselves, our own basic
needs, and the ways in which we meet them, workers must keep in
mind the following factors:

1. Everyone has a need for security and dependency.
2. Everyone also has a need for growth and independence.

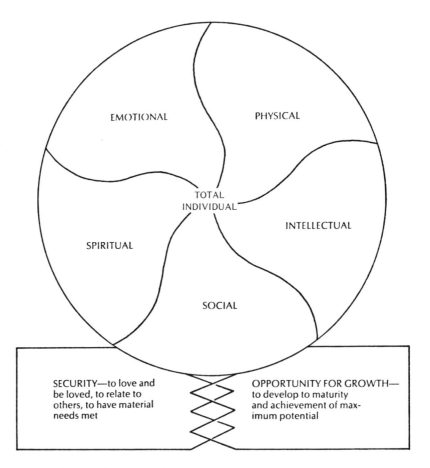

Figure 2 The Development of the Individual Rests Upon Fulfillment of Basic
Needs

3. Everyone is a unique individual and has a unique potential for development in each of the living areas.

4. The varying aspects of an individual's potential exist in a dynamic interrelationship that constitutes the whole, and no one aspect can be considered as separate from the others.

Workers who are aware of the existence of these needs within themselves can then look at the ways in which to meet them—for meet them they must. The drive for growth and expression will not be denied, and if it cannot be channeled in a positive and healthy direction, it will take an undesirable course. One's purpose in considering them is to avoid utilizing working relationships to meet one's own needs rather than those of the clients. While helping relationships can be a source of personal satisfaction that is normal and useful, workers whose personal lives do not meet their own needs may find themselves manipulating those with whom they are working, making them overly dependent, using them to satisfy needs for power, prestige, or self-fulfillment. This does not mean that workers get no satisfaction from their successes, no pleasure—and frustration!—from their working relationships. Rather it means that the satisfaction derives from the client's freedom to develop and to be successful as a person apart from the worker.

WHAT IS MY VALUE SYSTEM, AND HOW DOES IT DEFINE MY BEHAVIOR AND MY RELATIONSHIPS WITH OTHER PEOPLE?

Cultural groups tend to establish certain values and standards of behavior as significant and binding for their members. These values and standards are internalized and emotion laden, and become so much a part of one's attitudes, feelings, thinking, and behaving that one is often unaware of their existence. Effective workers must learn to avoid judging their clients' attitudes and behavior according to their own personal value system.

In Western society dominant values regarding people and society can be traced to four different sources: the Judeo-Christian doctrine with its concept of the integral worth of the individual and one's responsibility for one's neighbor; the democratic ideals, which emphasize the equality of all, and the right to "life, liberty, and the pursuit of happiness"; the puritan ethic, which says that character is all, circumstance nothing, that the moral person is the one who works and is independent, and that pleasure is sinful; and finally the tenets of social Darwinism, which emphasize that the fittest survive and the weak perish in a natural evolutionary process that produces the strong individual and society.

Even the casual reader will see that a dichotomy exists within this value system. We hold that people are equal, but that those who do not work are less equal. George Orwell says sardonically, "All animals are created equal, but some are more equal than others,"[1] and certainly this applies here. We hold that the individual life has worth, but that only the fit should survive. We believe that we are responsible for each other, but that those who are dependent upon others for their living are of lesser worth.

This dichotomy affects both workers and clients in their attitudes about themselves and each other and in their capacity to relate. We see physicians struggling to retain life while stating that both the individual and the society would be better off if the patient were dead. We see workers in public assistance programs administering financial aid to needy people with the grim conviction that their clients should not be supported if they cannot sustain themselves. We see legislators drafting legislation and voting funds to be used for programs to sustain the lives and serve the needs of people they are convinced are undeserving. We see teachers working with children they feel are unteachable. This dichotomy is particularly significant in helping relationships because, of necessity, there exist elements of dependence and independence, implications of superiority and inferiority, a need to give and to receive. Recognition and reconciliation of this value conflict is one of the primary personal tasks of the worker.

While these four constitute the major origins of values in our society, there are other significant sources. The development of this country from rural to urban, which has taken place with almost unbelievable swiftness within the past fifty years, along with the corresponding moves from agriculture to industrialization to technology, has resulted in changes in the basic institutions and structure of society. Old values and standards are questioned and discarded, new ones are not yet fully defined. For example, the end of the Russian Revolution and the establishment of the Soviet saw a development of group day-care centers for children of working mothers that was contrary to the cultural pattern of American society, which dictated that mothers should remain in the home and care for their own children.

1. George Orwell, *Animal Farm* (New York: Harcourt Brace & World, 1946), p. 148.

Today, fifty years later, day care is booming in the United States, mothers work outside the home in increasing numbers, and there is pressure to force poor mothers to leave their children and work with little consideration of whether this is the best solution in the individual situation.

To complicate matters further, there is no uniform pattern to these changes throughout the country, in spite of such developments as mass production of clothing, books, movies, and so on, which tend to push toward conformity. A value that is generally accepted and lived by in the urban ghetto may be completely intolerable in the neighboring suburbs or in the isolated, rural communities of the West and South. Differences in race, religion, education, economic standards, necessities for survival, all tend to work toward development of differences in values.

The comment has been made that America is a difficult country in which to practice obstetrics because of the many different ethnic groups with differing body builds and sizes. It is an equally difficult place for the helping person because of the many different value systems and norms for behavior that exist. In spite of the push toward uniformity and conformity, there remain differences in language that create problems in communication, differences in family patterns and customs, and differences in culture, as well as differences in physical appearance. The developing concept of a pluralistic society that tends to sanctify and perpetuate differences between groups of people faces the individual with the dual task of being a part of the "tribal" group and at the same time being a part of the larger society. It faces the helping person with the task of encompassing marked differences among people in order to understand and communicate successfully.

An additional problem arises from the fact that the helping people, in general, are of middle-class origin. And although in recent years people from all walks of life have been encouraged to enter human services work, studies indicate that the majority of these jobs are still filled by the middle class. This situation has given rise to the frequently heard accusation that workers tend to impose their own middle-class values on their clients. These are generally seen as values related to cleanliness, conformity, hard work, and sexual behavior.

Part of the responsibility of workers is to help their clients to be effective in the society in which they must live—and this calls for a certain degree of adaptation to the dominant value system, even while working to change it. We have seen this in the puerile conflict over male hair length, where a teenager has been forced to trim his locks in order to find employment. Such attitudes demand that the client who has been part of a group whose values run counter to those of the larger society must adopt a different way of living. The effective worker, however, cannot force or impose these changes. Society imposes the need for them—the worker's role is to help the client assess the nature of this imposition and decide how to adapt to it in a way that is not self-destructive.

An example of this is the value of time, punctuality, and regular consistent effort as characteristic of our whole industrial system. When concerted effort was made to include people from the hard-core poverty culture as employees, it was often necessary to make special provisions for getting them to work regularly and on time. Anglos often complain of the lack of time sense in blacks, Chicanos, and American Indians without recognizing the differing cultures and value systems within these minority groups.

The worker must have sufficient self-awareness to be able to differentiate between value changes that are essential for good social functioning, and those which are dictated by a personal value system, and that are so internalized that the individual is often unconscious of the reasons for adopting and using them as a basis for judging effectiveness of behavior. We see, for instance, the worker who believes that drinking is wrong, saying of the man who stops for a beer on the way home from work, "he drinks!" Social agency records are filled with notations of home visits in the morning where the mother "still in her nightgown with the breakfast dishes unwashed, is drinking coffee, smoking and watching television"—ergo, she is sloppy, dirty, and a poor mother.

Thus effective workers must:

1. Be aware that they are a walking system of values which is so much a part of them that they are scarcely aware of its existence and about the rightness of which they have considerable feeling.

2. Use all means possible to become conscious of what these biases are. One of the most useful tools in this struggle is becoming sensitive to one's use of the paranoid "they." "They" always wear bright colors and yell too loud; "they" don't mow their lawns; "they" don't support their families; "they" cheat on their income tax—and so on ad infinitum. Workers who are aware of doing this have taken the first step toward overcoming their biases.

3. Strive to evaluate themselves and their values objectively and rationally. Look at their origins and the purpose they serve and try to think about whether they will also serve this purpose for others.

4. Strive to change those values that, on the basis of this evaluation, need changing—to differentiate between those which dictate personal style of living, and those which leave clients "free to step to the tune of a different drummer" if such meets their need.

How do workers do this? If they are comfortable with themselves, and have sound, healthy resources for meeting their own basic needs, they will probably not find it too difficult to respect the differences of other people. They might begin by getting their own house in order. They might try to create and live within a climate of openness and honesty where questions and differences are not only tolerated but are an integral part of the richness of life. They might begin to know and appreciate, through literature, art, music, and personal experience, as many different kinds of people as possible and to understand and value the various approaches to life among them.

Rokeach proposes two classes of human values: terminal (those desired end states) and instrumental (those desired ways of reaching these end states).[2] He postulates that there is a limited number of basic values, and he reports a study that tends to substantiate the theory that people can and do change values as they perceive the dichotomy between what they profess and what they do in terms of implementing values. The importance of this kind of knowledge for human service workers is great, in terms of both their own personal equipment and the kind of personal and social changes they are attempting to implement. The role of values in human functioning is paramount.

Whitney Young, one of the great black leaders of the twentieth century, commented that children who grew up without knowledge of and ability to relate to and work with people different from themselves are handicapped. Many of us grow up bearing this handicap, but it does not necessarily mean that we must carry it with us throughout our lives.

There is no substitute for personal contact in learning to relate to people who are different from yourself—as all people are to a certain

2. Milton Rokeach, *The Nature of Human Values* (New York: Free Press, 1973).

extent. Such opportunity should be available to all children and young adults, who are usually more open to differences and not yet handicapped by preconceived ideas or by conscious and unconscious biases and fears. However, older people can also learn to see others differently.

> *Margaret, a fifty-year-old social worker, tells the story of attending a Quaker meeting where a young man rose and, identifying himself as a practicing homosexual, asked for the support of the meeting for a newly formed gay group. Margaret had been troubled for some time about her own feelings about her gay clients. The product of an orthodox religious background and a fairly conservative midwestern family, she had never known a person who was openly homosexual on a personal basis and was uncomfortable and unsuccessful with her work with them.*
>
> *She found herself liking the openness of the speaker and at the end of the meeting was able to talk with him about her own feelings. As she talked she realized that she was afraid of how he might feel about her and impulsively she asked if he minded women touching him. He laughed and put an arm around her shoulders. They became friends and through him she was able to deal with her fears, abandon stereotypes, and accept gay people all the way from the young men and women who flaunted their differences to the troubled middle-aged person with a spouse and children.*

HOW DO I RELATE TO THE SOCIETY IN
WHICH I LIVE AND WORK?

Workers, like all other people, hold membership not only in diverse small groups but also in the larger society. This group participation and these social relationships have a profound influence not only on the way that we see ourselves as individuals but also on the manner in which we see ourselves in relationship with other people. Workers must be conscious of the position they occupy in society and in the groups of which they are members. What roles do they fill and what status do these roles carry? With what particular subgroups do they identify? How do they relate to the power structure within the group and the society? How do they relate to people in general at levels different from their own. Do they relate effectively to people who are higher on the scale as well as with those who are lower?

We know that groups tend to relegate individuals to certain positions, to exert pressure for conformity, to punish the group member who deviates from group standards and norms. How do workers, whose task is essentially to act as a change agent when these pressures become destructive to people, deal with them in their own lives? Can they, if necessary, tolerate and deal with the disapproval of their own groups in order to attain important objectives?

WHAT IS MY LIFE STYLE?

In the process of living, we each develop our own style, our own tempo and rhythm, our own way of thinking, feeling, and behaving, our own set of personal values and sense of personal identity, our own way of life. Individual differences set us apart from each other and create a gap that must be bridged. Part of this arises as a result of our being endowed with a developmental pattern and a biological rhythm that is unique. Part is the result of those life experiences which establish certain ways of behaving and reacting. Not only does the worker react to this totality in the clients, they also react to it in the worker. The incompatibility that can result from this uniqueness derives from the difficulty in understanding and accepting people who are different from ourselves and from the transference of attitudes and feelings from previous experiences with persons who have displayed similar personality patterns. The client who brings to a helping relationship memory of a happy experience with a blunt, outspoken, dominating but warm and loving parent may have no difficulty in relating to a worker with similar personality patterns, whereas another client might shrink from such aggressiveness and never perceive the underlying warmth. Similarly, one might have trouble working with a questioning, querulous, complaining old lady if one's childhood had been scarred by such a grandmother. Another worker with a similar background may have carried over the memory of ways of relating to such a person that would help in the new relationship. The worker must be aware of both the assets and the liabilities that arise from personality and prior experience and learn to assess their effects on other people.

We must also learn to assess the impact of our personal life style on others and weigh its importance against the importance of the objectives that we wish to achieve. Sometimes it will be necessary to modify life style in order to even survive. Many long-accepted standards in areas of life to which deep emotions are attached, such as sex, the family, religion, are being challenged and workers who opt to be personally in the forefront of these movements will need to consider the possible impact on their effectiveness. In an isolated community, workers who flaunt accepted patterns of living will probably be unable to function.

Workers must develop a way of living that leaves them free to use themselves with others. A major problem for many workers is their inability to disagree, to present differing points of view, to refuse a request, to discuss an emotionally loaded issue, to say "no" in ways that are constructive. In part this arises from early training in the home, the school and the church which emphasizes not discussing painful issues, not questioning points of view or authority, not confronting differences honestly and openly. Because of these feelings workers may handle loaded situations with evasion, with attack, with false passivity.

Assertiveness training, which is one way that workers can use to develop the ability to deal with these problems, rests on the thesis that individuals have a right to be different, to express different ideas and points of view and to defend. They have the right to be heard (see box).

In assertiveness training differentiation is made among:

1. Nonassertiveness—in which people deny the right to be assertive to themselves and do not express their own thinking and feeling;
2. Assertiveness—in which people express their feeling and thinking in ways that show respect for the right of those with whom they are interacting to personal worth and to equal self-expression;
3. Aggressiveness—in which people exercise their right to express their own feeling and thinking but in a way that attacks those with whom they are interacting.

A young couple come to the door introducing themselves as members of a fundamentalist religious sect asking to leave literature and soliciting contributions. The householder, who does not support the group and thinks their beliefs are contrary to the beliefs of a free society, might respond:

1. Nonassertive—"Oh, all right, I'll take the literature and here's a dollar."

2. Assertive—"I don't agree with the aims of your movement and don't want to support it in any way but I'd be glad to explain my reasons for this stand if you wish."

BILL OF RIGHTS*

(From material taken from a workshop on assertiveness training by Patricia Jakubowski-Spector, July 1974, University of Maryland.)

1. You have the right to refuse requests from others without feeling selfish or guilty.
2. You have the right to feel and express anger and other emotions.
3. You have the right to feel healthy competitiveness.
4. You have the right to use your judgment in deciding your own needs.
5. You have the right to make mistakes.
6. You have the right to have your opinions and ideas given the same respect and consideration others have.
7. You have the right to ask for consideration, help and/or affection from others.
8. You have the right to be treated as an adult.
9. You have the right to tell others what your needs are.
10. You have the right on some occasions to make demands on others.
11. You have the right to ask others to change their behavior.
12. You have the right to be treated as a capable adult and not be patronized.
13. You have the right to not automatically be assumed wrong.
14. You have the right to take time to sort out your reactions— to use your time space rather than others' time space.
15. You have the right not to have others impose their values on you.

*There are almost as many Bills of Rights as there are people working in this area, each with its own particular emphasis. All emphasize the right of the individual to be oneself, to be different, to self-expression, to respect and consideration. Most of them emphasize an equally basic essential—the responsibility to extend the same rights to others!

3. Aggressive—"You people have got a nerve coming around here knocking on people's doors with that trashy literature. I've got my own church."

Assertiveness, by not attacking others and by expressing respect for their right, too, to be different does not mobilize hostility but creates an open climate in which differences can be discussed and compromises reached.

WHAT IS MY BASIC PHILOSOPHY?

The nature of the worker's beliefs about life, the individual, and society and their interrelationship forms a vital part of the capacity to work effectively with people. It provides the rationale and motivating force for these efforts and gives a personal significance to them—what we believe strongly we tend to try to put into practice.

The overall philosophical base of the human services lies in the beliefs that:

1. The individual is a social animal.
2. The individual exists in interrelationship with other people and with all other life forms. This relationship may be defined as one of mutual rights and responsibilities.
3. The welfare of the individual and of the group cannot be considered apart from each other.
4. Each person, and all living things, possess intrinsic worth.
5. Each person, and all living things, are characterized by a need to grow and develop toward the realization of a unique potential.
6. The individual and the society can be understood by use of the scientific method.
7. The individual and the society possess the capacity for change as a part of their intrinsic nature.

Workers who are committed to this philosophical base with a personal conviction that is both ethically and pragmatically sound will not only be motivated to search for ways to make it operational, but will also get maximum satisfaction from their efforts and in so doing greatly increase their capacity to achieve.

The personality of the worker in human services is probably the single most significant factor in determining effectiveness in dealing with other people. A recent study of the Summerhill school movement in England in relation to more traditional programs indicated that it is not the method of teaching—the highly structured or very free—that determines the ability of the child to learn, but the personality of the teacher. One who, as a worker, feels genuine warmth and concern for others and therefore can empathize with them, who is honest, open and loving, who can face the reality of living comfortably and be at peace with oneself will tend to be effective in enabling people to use the strengths they possess.

In summary, workers have a responsibility for knowing themselves both as individuals and in social relationships, being conscious of the way personality and behavior affect others, and being prepared to deal with those aspects of it that are destructive to the development and use of effective helping relationships.

RELATED READINGS

Alberti, Robert and Emmons, Michael. *Your Perfect Right: A Guide to Assertive Behavior.* San Louis Obispo: Impact, 1974. Practical guidebook for teaching assertiveness training.

Benedict, Ruth. *Patterns of Culture.* New York: Penguin Books, 1934. An eminently readable classic that sets a pattern for looking at social structures and the individual within them.

Erikson, Erik. *Childhood and Society.* New York: W. W. Norton, 1950.

———. *Identity, Youth and Crisis.* New York: W. W. Norton, 1968. Two engrossing paperbacks which present Erikson's thinking about the development of individuals in their infinite variety.

Fraiberg, Selma. *The Magic Years.* New York: Scribners, 1959. Interesting account of the first six years of a child's life.

Jourard, Sidney. *Personal Adjustment.* 2nd ed. New York: Macmillan, 1963. Examination of what goes into the development of the person as a healthy individual.

Klein, Alan F. *Society, Democracy and the Group.* New York: William Morrow, 1955. Stresses how family and culture affect group life and activity.

Kluckhohn, Clyde et al. *Personality in Nature, Society and Culture.* New York: Alfred A. Knopf, 1953. Anthropologists' view of the individual and the impact of culture on development.

Lidz, Theodore. *The Person: His Development Through the Life Cycle.* New York: Basic Books, 1968. Survey of the development of the person through the total cycle of life. Contains excellent bibliographies.

Maslow, Abraham. *Toward a Psychology of Being.* New York: Van Nostrand, 1968. Interesting exposition of a humanistic psychology, a theory of the drive toward health and creativity that is inherent in human nature.

———. *The Farther Reaches of Human Nature.* New York: Viking Press, 1971. Posthumous collection of Maslow's scattered writings.

Menninger, Karl. *The Vital Balance.* New York: Viking Press, 1963. A readable survey about the essential balanced life that constitutes health.

Perlman, Helen. *Persona: Social Role and Personality.* Chicago: University of Chicago Press, 1968. The development and significance of social roles written in Perlman's usual highly readable style.

Rokeach, Milton. *The Nature of Human Values.* New York: Free Press, 1973. Excellent and usable exposition of the development of basic values and how they can be changed.

Smith, Manuel. *When I Say No, I Feel Guilty.* New York: Dial Press, 1975. Good basic text in assertiveness training.

2

Understanding the Human Condition

There are almost as many theories of personality development as there are theorists considering the nature of people and of the human condition. These theories are tools that can be used to think about and understand people. Human service workers are best served by an eclectic approach which integrates ideas from many different thinkers. It is generally agreed that personality theories are also theories of behavior—personality is the individual's system that determines the unique adjustment to the environment, and behavior is the way in which this system is demonstrated. There are eight basic assumptions upon which such theories rest:

1. *People are knowable;* behavior is natural, and the mind enables us to know ourselves and our world.
2. *Cause and effect relationships exist;* nothing in nature is happenstance.
3. *Causation is multiple;* many causes operate simultaneously.
4. *Some causes are internal, some are external;* there is a constant interplay between the internal world and the external world to produce life functioning.
5. *Causes are both fundamental and precipitating;* that which is basic and ongoing and that which is immediate interact.
6. *Purpose and motivation enter into behavior;* these may be con-

Figure 3   The Three Faces of the Individual

scious, preconscious or unconscious and they may agree or be in conflict.

7. *The context of the total situation affects behavior* as well as the immediate circumstance.

8. *Reality is always more rich and accurate than our mental picture of it;* it is infinite in its detail and impossible to know in totality.

There are two major facts upon which modern personality theories agree: (1) life is a dynamic process; and (2) people develop by adaptation to the changing demands of both their own inherent potentials and of the environment in which they live. Viewed from this frame of reference, change is a categorical imperative, and once this has been accepted, workers will utilize the particular theories that will help to bring about the specific desired changes.

What is the nature of an individual? The worker can find a very useful yardstick for measurement in the statement credited to the anthropologist Kluckhohn, who sees the individual as a totality of three different sets of characteristics: (1) those shared with all other people; (2) those shared with some other people; (3) those which are shared with no one else (see Figure 3).

THE BIOLOGICAL HERITAGE

Our biological heritage is the result of centuries of evolutionary development and constitutes those characteristics which we hold in common with all of the members of our species, regardless of race, color, or various social and cultural patterns such as nationality or religion. Change in these characteristics comes through a long slow evolutionary process. Biological entities possess certain human needs that are common to all—the need to be nurtured and to have their basic physical needs met, to grow, to express their aggressive impulses, to realize the potential with which they are endowed, and to have meaningful relationships with others of their own kind. Biological existence is based on certain natural laws, disregard for which may lead to physical illness or destruction of the individual body and ultimately of the species. An overwhelming example of the results of such disregard is our present ecological dilemma which we have created through arrogance, ignorance, and the inability to perceive and accept the interrelationship of all life forms. By upsetting the delicate balances between them we have succeeded in creating an environment increasingly hostile to our own continued existence.

Once conception has taken place, the genetic endowment of the individual is set. The heritage of constitutional strengths and weaknesses is determined and from this point on, environment, both in utero and without, will be the decisive factor in how they are developed and used. Fashions in thinking about the relative importance of endowment and environment change from time to time. In considering these two aspects of our existence, the worker must be particularly aware of their interrelationship and cognizant of how environmental factors can help or hinder the individual in making maximum use of the potential for a good life.

THE SOCIAL HERITAGE

How we meet basic biological needs is dictated by the society and culture in which we live, and as a result we develop characteristics that we share with individuals from a similar cultural background. These characteristics develop in response to social laws laid down by the society which is interested in its own survival, and infringement of them is punishable by rejection and isolation. Change of these characteristics is a continual process that takes place with sufficient rapidity to be easily observable in a single lifetime. Culture provides a "blueprint for behavior" and this patterning occurs on several levels.

The primary, and probably the most significant one, is the family. Transmission of culture to new generations is one of its most important tasks. The very form that it takes—the position and role expectations of father, mother, and child, of aunts, uncles, in-laws, and all members of the extended family—is determined by culture. Throughout the world, geography, economics, population pressures, and so on influence the pattern of family life and cause variations in form which tend to perpetuate themselves. But because of the dynamic nature of people and society these forms become rigid only at great risk to themselves. Although they tend to change slowly, they do change. For example, in Western society we have been witnessing the contraction of the extended family and the increased importance of the nuclear family. The family tends to set the form of the adaptive patterns that the individual uses as a means of coping with both internal and external pressures, and of attitudes and ways of dealing with situations.

Rarely does the individual remain secluded within the boundaries of the family. As the pebble tossed in the pond creates widening circles of waves, so life experiences broaden, and individuals are exposed to new patterns, new ideas, new ways of behaving. As soon as a child develops a peer group, the second level of cultural indoctrination begins. At this point, where there are differences between family and peer group patterns, conflict ensues, and the individual is faced with the necessity of selecting the better way. The difficulties of this decision are intensified by the process of internalization—the emotional significance in ways of thinking and behaving which have been adopted and become a part of the individual. This is necessary conflict which, when successfully resolved, results in growth, but is nonetheless painful for all its necessity. The conflict is lessened when the cultural definition of the roles is an accepted one and is not in a process of great change.

This questioning is an integral part of the process of adolescence, but the growing individual is often caught between the need for and loyalty to the ways learned in the family, the ways of the peer group, and the drive of the developing individual self for creation of its own way. For the first time in one's experience, critical ability has developed to the extent that one can judge ways of thinking, feeling, and behaving and make one's own decisions.

Oscar Wilde, the writer and poet, has been quoted as commenting that "first we love our parents, then we judge them, and sometimes we even forgive them." This capacity for judgment comes at a time when the adolescent is striving to meet heavy developmental demands, physically, emotionally and socially. It is essential that young people exercise this capacity, but it can be a chaotic stage in the family, particularly if relationships are based on dishonesty, on a "do as I say, not as I do" rule, and if the child has not been left free to make appropriate decisions alone in earlier years.

The third level of indoctrination comes from the institutions that the society has set up. School, church, government instruct the person in expected ways of behaving. As long as a society is simple and composed of only one cultural group, life is fairly uncomplicated. Unfortunately, a society of any size tends to be a complex composite of many different cultural groups, each with its own value system, rules, and standards of behavior. The individual who is part of a small cultural group existing within a larger one must in some way adapt to the expectations and demands of both. When patterns of attitude and behavior of the two conflict, the individual is often in trouble.

This is the essential problem faced by members of the present so-called culture of poverty and of religious and racial minorities in all societies. The smaller cultural group, of which they are primary members, tends to set up certain patterns for behavior that frequently are nonfunctional in the larger society and tend to inhibit the capacity of its members to take advantage of what the larger group has to offer. A small group, as with the poor, tends to become self-perpetuating and locks its members in, so that they cannot move freely and benefit from what the larger society offers.

The basic purpose of current poverty programs has been to enable people to move from membership in a self-defeating culture to participation in the benefits offered by the larger one. As this movement progresses, evidences of conflict within the individual are often present in spite of relatively facile changes in outward appearance and behavior. The conflict faced by the student who has committed herself to return to work with her own people in the ghetto, but is tempted by the financial and social advantages of a job in another level of society, is only one example of this.

In considering human behavior from the cultural frame of reference, workers need to be particularly aware of the dangers of (1) stereotyping; (2) considering cultural groups as static and monolithic; and (3) forgetting that groups rarely exist without subgroups. Nowhere have these negative processes been more obvious than in our consideration of the poor, as Oscar Lewis points out so well.[1] We have tended to regard all the poor as being exactly alike and possessing all of the characteristics attributed to the group as a

1. Oscar Lewis has published extensively on poor families in varying cultures. See Related Readings at the end of this chapter.

whole. We have tended to consider the culture of poverty a monolithic entity embracing everyone without adequate financial resources. On the basis of these generalizations we have developed
remedial programs that have been ineffectual with many of their sup-
posed beneficiaries. Not all of the poor are members of the culture
of poverty, although the longer they remain poor, the more likely
they are to become so.

As long as one lives, one is mobile and changing, and always in the
process of both being and becoming. Equally, the social groups that
develop must remain vital if they are to serve the purposes for which
they were devised. When they cease to be, their members tend to
develop new ones or be assimilated into others. Cultural groups tend
to change slowly, but this change is ensured by the very presence of
subgroups and the differences that exist within them. The differences may be only a matter of degree, depending on the approach
used to interpret the strictures of the culture, but the fact that they
exist ensures change, even if it is only the expulsion of dissenters.
Such change is negative, however, for expulsion is often the crucial
step in ensuring the decadence of the culture.

In addition to the formal, expressed and accepted models of
attitude and behavior in cultural patterning which are found in the
family, the peer group, and the social institutions, there also exist,
on all three levels, nonformal values and standards of behavior. They
constitute an unspoken pattern that is often more effective in determining behavior than the officially accepted ones, and may frequently
contradict them, endorsing a way of acting that the group frowns on.
Orwell's comment regarding equality is an expression of this conflict.
The confusion created by these two opposing dicta is obvious. One
of the most difficult tasks faced by adolescents in growing up is
accepting and dealing with this tendency of families, groups, and
individuals to convey contradictory messages.

THE PERSON AS AN INDIVIDUAL

Finally, each person is unique. Each is the product of a unique
genetic heritage in continuous and dynamic interaction with a unique
life experience. Change within individual characteristics comes more
quickly than in either biological or social areas. While persons are
subject to the influence of both natural laws and social rules, the
element of freedom of individual choice in development cannot be
disregarded, and there is within each person a drive toward creativity
and self-realization.

"Genetic," "social," and "individual" factors combine to create the total personality, and if we are to understand the human condition, we need a way of explaining how it maintains itself. For this purpose we have chosen to utilize basic Freudian terminology which has become so much a part of the language of the times that its meaning is generally comprehended and accepted. Particularly useful for our purpose is the analytic division of the self (or mind) into the id, ego, and superego because it provides one means of understanding the interrelation of the various aspects of the personality. Lest the words themselves turn the reader off, particularly in light of the current attack on psychoanalytic theory as being inadequately grounded in research, we might add that it would be possible to use A, B, and C to designate these easily observable aspects of personality.

It is important to remember, however, that nearly a century has elapsed since Freud developed his particular tools for thinking. Some have been discredited in light of later theories, and some are being used in different ways than originally intended. This is the manner in which knowledge, which is a dynamic entity, develops. As are all people, theorists are products of their environment and, in spite of their efforts to be objective, their thinking must be weighed in light of both the current social reality and subsequent changes. One way in which Freud and most of the early personality theorists are being challenged is on the basis of the inherent sexism in their work. Almost universally they insitutionalized and perpetuated in their theories the sexual stereotyping of their times which, in light of current thinking, is viewed as destructive to personal self-realization. Freud's concept of the tripartite personality is an extremely useful one, however.[2]

2. Helen Perlman of the University of Chicago, a lively thinker and writer about why people are as they are, comes up with the following poem:

Lines Written After Prolonged Immersion in Freud, Hartman, Piaget et alii

Id
I never saw a person's id,
I hope I never see one.
But I can tell you if I did
I'd fashion me a heavy lid
To place on it to keep it hid,
Which is, I gather, what God did
When he first saw a free one.

Super-ego
That part of ego we can call super
Is part policeman and part snooper,

The Function of the Id

The id is conceptualized as the reservoir of basic, primitive impulses and the source of instinctive energy with the pleasure principle and impulsive wishing as dominant. This impulsiveness is controlled on an unconscious level by the superego, "the conscience of the unconscious," and by the ego, which operates on a conscious level, distinguishing the external world through the senses, acting as a mediator between the demands of environment and the needs of self, and developing the coping behavior necessary to create a balance between the two.

The Function of the Superego

While the id can be seen as the basic motivating force that moves one to action and achievement, the superego develops as a result of external social pressure, the "dos" and "don'ts," the "rights" and "wrongs," that society defines and imposes. It works to control the expression of primitive needs and drives in the individual. It defines acceptable outlets for this energy and attempts to channel it in a way that is not harmful to the individual or to others. Too rigid a superego inhibits action and achievement, too little leaves one prey to one's own primitive impulses.

The Function of the Ego

The role of the ego in individual functioning is of primary importance for the worker whose task is to enhance the client's capacity

---

It's super-cilious and haughty
And tries to catch you thinking naughty,
It warns you that you will get caught
For doing things you shouldn't ought.
Oh hell, if only Eve and Adam
Had left those apples where God had 'em!

Ego
As for that middle-man, the ego—
Ubiquitous, it goes where we go.
Derivative? autonomous?
A construct? or homunculus?
It tries to grapple, strives to see
The nature of re-al-ity,
Defending now, yet out to learn
It scarcely knows which way to turn,
It has so many functions, forms,
So many strategies and norms—
May heaven help us as we're groping
To grasp how ego copes with coping!

(*Social Work,* Vol. 19, No. 6, Nov. 1974, p. 697)

for a good life, for good social functioning. To achieve this good life, the person must strike a balance between individual needs and wishes, capacities and expectations on the one hand and the demands and opportunities of society on the other. The worker's role in helping the individual in functioning and in altering the society in order to provide greater opportunity for fulfillment will require that the worker understand and be competent to deal with this balance as it affects the functioning of the individual, both in one-to-one relationships and in groups. Let us look at what this concept actually involves.

The ego is essentially the reality-oriented aspect that enables one to perceive one's environment realistically and achieve this balance between one's own personal needs and the demands and opportunities of the setting. There are four steps in the operation of this process: perception, integration, adaptation, and execution. The initial step deals with how things are seen and understood. Reality can only be perceived through the eyes of the individual in terms of the self and its own needs. It can be truthfully said that everyone's reality is different—that even the psychotic's "unreal" reality is reality to the patient. This is graphically illustrated in the old story of the blind men and the elephant. None of these six men was completely right, none completely wrong from an objective point of view. Each perceived by touch a part of the elephant and hence the whole in terms of his own frame of reference. Thus the task of workers in relation to perception, is, first, to deal with and clear up their own myopia and then to try to understand what the client is seeing in the situation under consideration. The perception of reality as it is can be affected by lack of knowledge, by physical illness or handicap, by major or minor emotional disturbance, by previous experience, and by any of the social and personal pressures or inhibitions that predispose against clarity and realism. A good example of this is the attitude of some of the older American Indians toward the involvement of their grandchildren in the Head Start programs. Their previous experience with children being taken away by force to white schools on the reservations had not been a good one, and they perceived the Head Start workers and buses as similarly destructive.

The second phase of the functioning of the ego is the integration of or bringing together in an orderly fashion not only the perception of the reality in terms of what it means in relation to the individual, but also the integration of what the adaptation requires in order for the individual to live with or to attempt to change demands of this reality.

The process of adaptation constitutes the third phase and is based on the previous two stages plus the final execution or putting into operation of the adaptive mechanism. We have perceived the reality in terms of what it means for us, have weighed the relative merits of various responses, have selected a response in terms of both thinking and feeling capacities and needs, and then adopt this as our own and act upon it. Our adaptation may not appear to be the most reasonable or desirable one to the observer, but it is the logical one for us and the only one that we can make under the circumstances. For us to make a different adaptation, there must be new and different factors involved. It is imperative that human service workers keep this fact in mind, because it explains "unreasonable" and "irrational" behavior that so often appears senseless and destructive to the observer.

There is much discussion as to whether this whole process of the functioning of the ego through perception, integration, adaptation, and execution is on a conscious or unconscious level. Certainly the unconscious carryover of previous feeling and experience, the all-powerful drive of the id impulses, the heavy weight of the internalized superego are significant determinants of adaptive capacity and form. However, these do not represent the totality of the individual. We are also thinking and knowing beings, and this is an equally important aspect of self. In its broadest sense, the ego can be seen as functioning with both conscious and unconscious determinants that combine to determine adaptation and life style.

Each aspect of the functioning of the ego involves both a cognitive and an affective element. It is very difficult to separate the rational and the emotional contributions, but the worker must be sharply aware that both exist, are a part of all aspects of human functioning, and as such must be dealt with. The reaction of the Indian grandparents was based partly on feeling and partly on knowledge gained from previous experience with the early reservation schools. Only as they were able to deal with their fears and angers on an emotional level, and to understand that this was a new situation on an intellectual one, were they able to take advantage of the opportunity offered to their grandchildren.

The Concepts of Balance and Stress

In understanding the functioning of the individual, the concept of balance, or homeostasis, is important. Borrowed from physical medicine and widely adapted by various branches of the behavioral sciences, this concept states that there is a tendency toward a relatively stable state of equilibrium between the differing elements of an organism or system. Although it could be considered a contradiction in terms, it is helpful to think of this as a dynamic homeostasis. The nature of life is such that while balance is essential for functioning, it is constantly in a process of being upset, is always shifting and changing in order to adapt to the new input from experience and to the demands of maturation and development. The significant idea here is that the organism or system that is thrown into imbalance will strive automatically to regain its steady state. Viewed from this frame of reference, people can be seen as having a drive toward remaining operational even though this operational state may appear dysfunctional to the observer. The drive is significant and, combined with the equally strong tendency toward growth and development that is inherent in humans, gives human service workers a running start in their efforts to help clients achieve fulfillment in life.

Another equally important concept, also from physical medicine, and closely related to that of homeostasis, is that of stress. Originally formulated by Hans Selye, a Swiss physician working in Canada, it postulates that the body makes a general adaptation to stress which involves certain overall processes, as well as a specific adaptation to specific stress. In so doing, one gears oneself to fight or run when one's balanced existence is threatened. This threat may be in any of the life areas—physical, intellectual, psychological, social or spiritual— and in any combination of them.

A certain amount of stress is essential to maturation and development. Life poses the challenges, and one's built-in system for self-defense and growth mobilizes itself to deal with them. The healthful process of coping with these threats and challenges fosters growth and development.

Unfortunately, there are increasingly frequent instances in modern life where one can neither fight nor run, but is trapped in situations where stress is continuous and ongoing, and healthy coping impossible. The pollution of the planet—foul air, impure water, noise, over-crowding—is an example of this. Another can be seen more and more in developing individuals whose maturational stage demands opportunity for meaningful occupation, but who are denied outlet for this need because of personal shortcomings or social conditions over which they have no control. The ongoing tension created by this inability to move must be dealt with and can be turned inward against the self, resulting in physical or emotional illness or sickness of the spirit, or it may be expressed outwardly in antisocial behavior equally destructive to the individual and to others. Selye's concept is a basic one that has strongly affected our thinking in all areas of knowledge related to human nature, and we are studying and developing new understandings of what it means in living, in the aging process, and in death.

Thus the individual can be regarded as possessing a strong drive toward living, growing, and surviving. This life and growth take place by a continuous and ongoing process of adaptation. The individual is presented with a continuing series of problem situations, and the solution of one merely moves one on to the next. The word *problem* is used here not in the narrow sense of something wrong that must be set right, but rather as meaning a situation demanding action or solution. This broad definition allows us to use the term in relation to normal tasks of living as well as those abnormal, unexpected, or tragic events which occur in every life experience. As such, problems present challenge and opportunity, and are the substance of which living is made.

Each of us, at birth, is immediately faced with a series of tasks or problems that we must solve in order to survive and grow. We must breathe, eat, eliminate, begin to relate to other people, and move toward an increasingly separate and independent existence. As we begin to perform these tasks, we learn how to deal with internal and external demands that are placed upon us and to develop the capacity to cope, or coping ability. As we learn to cope with the successively more sophisticated and complicated demands of living and growing, our coping ability is strengthened. We find ways to meet the internal needs that are a part of our innate potential and to satisfy the external ones that are a part of our surroundings. We learn to deal with frustration and to develop mechanisms that allow for growth and protect from pain and harm. By the very process of dealing with the problems that confront us, we develop increasing capacity to handle future, more complicated ones if we deal well and adequately with the original demands.

Just as everyone has a differing level of coping ability, so everyone has a breaking point beyond which one cannot go. This point is determined by the many different factors that contribute to the life experience—one's constitutional endowment in dynamic interaction with one's surroundings.

THE DEVELOPMENTAL STAGES OF LIFE

The individual can thus be seen as moving in life through a series of developmental stages, the overall pattern having been laid down at the time of conception (see Figure 4). This progression is not at a uniform rate within the person nor uniform among individuals, but is steady and continuous. It is particularly important that workers, in utilizing this concept, be flexible in considering a norm for development at any particular stage, because norms vary greatly. They must consider what is normal for each particular individual, in terms of

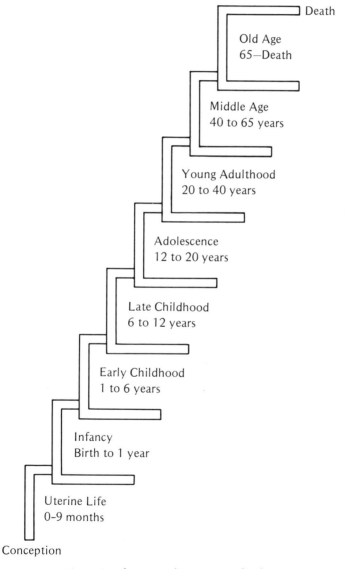

Figure 4 The Ascending Stages of Life

the particular heredity and the particular environment at this particular time in the individual's development. Consideration of the marked degree of difference in physical, intellectual and emotional maturity among any given group of thirteen-year-old girls will illustrate this point, and yet each of them will have her own norm and must be considered in light of it.

The stages in life are progressive and each is dependent on those which have preceded it. Given a healthy environment, children who experience an infancy healthy in all respects should proceed normally and easily through the preschool years, the school years, and into adolescence. When they have been unable to complete satisfactorily a developmental task in a given stage, they will move on into the next, carrying with them unfinished business that will create difficulties when a situation arises where maturity in that particular aspect of living is demanded. This is particularly obvious during the years of adolescence when the earlier unsolved problems in family relationships may explode into furious conflict, destructive to both individual and group. In marriage, where the formation of a new family calls for extra capacity to achieve on an adult level, early trauma may result in problems. The demands of the middle years and of aging, with their attendant losses and separations, call for a high degree of flexibility and capacity to tolerate change, the existence of which has been predetermined by earlier living and growing. The pattern for adaptation to the problems of later years is set in the early ones.

The concept of life stages, as with all knowledge, is dynamic—constantly in the process of changing. For example, at the present time, we are looking in more detail at what happens in the overall periods we call young adulthood, middle age, and old age. We are beginning to see phases within these periods that are predictable, and the more we understand them, the better able we will be to provide the essentials for healthy development within them.

It is increasingly obvious that old age is not a single condition, particularly if we define it as beginning at 65. Rather, with increasing life expectancy, it tends to fall into two distinct phases: the early years when the individual is able to work and to be, to a large degree, self-determining, and the later years when the debilitating diseases of extreme age require special care. Again, we cannot stereotype people— not all eighty-five- or ninety-year-olds are unable to manage for themselves.

In utilizing the concept of life stages as a tool in thinking, workers must guard against considering them as rigid or as stopping points. They might visualize them as plateaus that are so sloped upward that only by continuous movement can one retain one's footing. Once one begins to climb, there is no stopping until the end of life.

It is important to remember, also, that progression can be slowed or regression take place because of the life experiences of the developing person in any phase of this climb. Disturbances may be manifested in all life areas by physical growth problems, behavioral difficulties, social or intellectual abnormalities. Some of these are temporary, some become part of an ongoing pattern. Stresses of all kinds—accident, injury, illness, loss or separation from family, overprotection, addiction, abuse—can hinder normal growth.

Workers must be prepared to deal not only with these extraordinary crises but with the ordinary crises of living such as birth and death. The fact that these are universal and emotion-laden experiences means that the first task of workers is to deal with self and personal feeling before attempting to help others deal with both the facts and the emotions that surround them.

During the Vietnam War a former student was sent to a field hospital that took casualties directly from the fighting. In spite of the fact that part of her inservice training had been at a burn center, the impact of wartime suffering and death was great, and she wrote her old instructor, "Teach your bright young things about pain and death. If they do not know and cannot accept them as a part of life, they cannot be useful either to the suffering and dying or to those around them."

Fortunately there is an increasingly healthy emphasis today on facing these realities openly and honestly. Centers have developed where studies are being made of pain and how better to cope with it. The final crisis, death, has been the subject of intense study for the past decade, and a body of theoretical knowledge has been developed which, with accompanying practice skills, serves to better equip workers to help people make the necessary adaptations. This, again, is an area which workers in their personal lives need to learn to face without fear or evasion.

RELATED READINGS

Berelson, Bernard and Steiner, Gary. *Human Behavior: An Inventory of Scientific Findings.* New York: Harcourt Brace and World, 1964. Survey of studies of human behavior.

Hartman, Heinz. *Ego Psychology and the Problems of Adaptation.* New York: International Universities Press, 1958. An examination of life experience from the reference point of the role of the ego in adaptation.

Havinghurst, R. J. *Human Development and Education.* New York: David Mc-Kay, 1953. Learning as a part of the developmental pattern of life.

Hurlock, Elizabeth. *Child Development.* New York: McGraw Hill, 1956. Basic text, simply written, on the total development of the child.

Kubler-Ross, Elisabeth. *Questions and Answers on Death and Dying.* New York: Macmillan, 1974. Pioneer studies of work with people whose deaths are imminent. Excellent material.

Lewis, Oscar. *Vida.* New York: Random House, 1966. A significant, detailed study of the life style of a poor Puerto Rican family. Another book by the same author well worth reading is *Five Families.*

Maier, Henry. *Three Theories of Child Development.* New York: Harper and Row, 1965. Comparison of the theories of Erik Erikson, Jean Piaget, and Robert Sears.

Sheehy, Gail. *Passages.* New York: E. P. Dutton, 1976. A look at phases within the middle-age period of life.

Selye, Hans. *The Stress of Life.* New York: McGraw Hill, 1956. Readable and fascinating report on the development of Selye's theory of stress and its meaning.

Towle, Charlotte. *Common Human Need.* New York: National Association of Social Workers, 1957. Simple, direct, and usable report of how people's needs affect their behavior.

3
Learning to Live As a Social Being

The process of birth, by detaching the infant from the mother's body and establishing it as a discrete individual, poses the task of learning to live with other separate individuals. This learning takes place within a balance of freedom and restraint—freedom to be oneself within the confines imposed by other people's freedoms. Such learning begins immediately with the response or lack of response to the infant's cry; its arena expands with the expanding life of the child, who must acquire knowledge of self and others in social interaction. This acquisition must be accompanied by enough security to allow a high degree of personal experience, so that correction and adaption to change can be made almost constantly.

Basic to all theories about socialization is the concept of the self developed through social interaction with others; this core self possesses certain attributes that will determine the effectiveness of the person in transactions with the environment. The War on Poverty, which was characterized by an effort to enable people to use sources within the system, defined the outcome goal of socialization as "social competence" or the capability for full participation in society.

The major personal attributes contributing to socialization are:

1. A self-image that includes not only knowledge of self as a separate entity but also acceptance of self and conviction that one is competent to deal with the demands of life.

2. Respect for the integrity of others and knowledge of the boundaries of personal rights and responsibilities in relation to the rights and responsibilities of others.

3. Knowledge of and ability to subscribe to or coexist with the values and norms of society.

4. Knowledge of the rules that govern behavior in given social groups.

5. Ability to assess alternative behaviors and probable outcomes realistically and make choices in light of this reality.

6. Ability to deal with personal feelings constructively.

7. Ability to accept compromise and limitation.

8. Ability and flexibility to be active and self-motivating rather than merely reactive to social situations and to initiate and participate in change.

It is obvious that such a complex set of attributes in such an equally complex entity as a person requires learning from many different sources. This learning comes from the variety of social situations of which the individual is a part from birth onward. The major ones are (1) the family or family surrogate, (2) the peer group, (3) the social institutions such as the church, school, tribe or cultural group, and (4) the professional or work group.

Primary learning takes place within the family or the family surrogate (the increasing number of children who are not growing up within their biological families makes it essential to keep this in mind). Here individuals learn not only that they are separate persons but that they are separate persons who must, of necessity, exist in a give-and-take relationship with other people and that there are certain norms of behavior and rules that govern ways of expressing feelings, of thinking, and of behaving that must be taken into consideration. First children, however much they may wish, cannot destroy the second babies who have replaced them in that role. They learn that they must place limitations on their freedom if they are to survive.

Initially this learning is enforced by outside authority, but gradually external enforcement is internalized and a personal imperative develops, which to a greater or lesser degree dictates the importance and rights of self and others. The significance of the early years cannot be overestimated. The old saw, "Give me the child for the first six years and it is mine forever," is to a certain extent valid, but a great deal of important social learning also takes place outside the immediate and extended family and in later years. Growing individuals are seriously handicapped, however, if the early years have not left them with a good feeling about themselves and with the ability to define and respect the rights of others.

In modern society, children are early exposed to the tribe,[1] the religious group, and, at an increasingly younger age, the formal learning group. Here they not only learn group expectations and behaviors, they also continue to define themselves in terms of the expectations of others. This definition can be constructive or destructive depending on what these expectations are.

> *Bobbie is one of the Jones children, the fourth of eight. The Joneses are "no good." They "could at least keep themselves clean." That house "is just falling to pieces." They "don't even raise a garden." Mr. Jones "won't work if you offer him a job." Mrs. Jones "just sits on the front porch—doesn't even do the dishes, wash the clothes or cook a meal." "You should smell those children when they come to school—which isn't often!" "They just can't learn." "That ten-year-old is already fooling around with the boys."*

Bobbie has little opportunity in the social groups in the small town where the Joneses live to learn to define himself in a constructive manner. Unless there is an effective intervention, he will become what others expect him to become, and his potential for self-development will never be realized.

As children move out from the family into a peer group and become a part of various social institutions, they often find themselves confronted with cultures that differ from those that they learned in their family groups. The values and norms of these organized groups to which they are introduced are often rigid, strongly supported by rituals and demanding of conformity if the individual is to survive and to use the group. These norms deal with simple situations (such as what to wear to school) and complex situations (such as the relationship between student/teacher/parent); they are formal and openly stated (students must be in their classrooms by a certain hour) or covertly stated and accepted by the group (in spite of rules against

---

1. Tribe, as used in this context, means a group of people of common origin who feel strong cultural ties.

leaving the campus, the in-group sneaks off and goes for lunch at a nearby drive-in).

As part of socialization, the growing child must accommodate the differences between the family group and the peer or institutional group as well as between the subgroups within them. The school years and adolescence are marked by this accommodation. When, early in adolescence, children begin to sit in judgment on their parents, they are also judging the values, norms and supporting rules that they are being exposed to in the larger society. The importance of various groups changes according to the life stage of the individual. In contrast to the early years when the family is all-important, the school years and particularly adolescence are stages when the peer group is overwhelming in importance. (Young adults often "come back to the family" when they reach the age of nineteen or so.) Adolescent delinquency, for example, has been defined by Garrett and Rompler as a "a failure to comply with norms,"[2] and from this point of view such delinquency can rarely be effectively treated on an individual basis. The adolescent is responding to the norm expectations of the peer group which at that stage of development is of overwhelming importance. Many of our modern correction programs make maximum use of this group in working with such delinquency.

As developing individuals move through the formal educational world into the working world, they become a part of the profession, the trade, the occupation through which they will earn their livings. Each group is based on acceptance of a certain set of values and develops its own norms. These may be either formally or informally expressed. Most professions have a written code of ethics to which the neophyte must subscribe, as do many trades.

In addition, people tend to affiliate with so-called reference groups, which are formed groups of unrelated people developed on the basis of some common interest, such as a hobby, a recreation such as using campers for outdoor activities, a political belief.

Finally, people develop families of their own wherein a complex meld is expressed of all that has been integrated within the individual, in accommodation with the mate and other persons within the family group.

The capacity for group membership is essential to the healthy individual. Groups are not perfect but they are a source of strength and support for the individual that is essential to good functioning,

2. James Garrett and Peter Rompler, *Community Resocialization: A New Perspective* (Washington, D.C.: Catholic University of America Press, 1966).

particularly in our modern multifaceted society. They provide an antidote for what Slater calls *The Pursuit of Loneliness,* the title of a book in which he examines some of the more destructive aspects of current patterns of living. Research tends to indicate that the person who has no group ties, no feeling of belonging or being a part of a group of other people, is often a person who cannot function adequately.

Socialization prescribes role behavior, and one of the current uncertainties is that not only are roles changing drastically but we are conscious as never before of the limiting effects of role stereotypes. Major credit for this rests with the whole women's movement in all of its ramifications—urbanization, movement of women out of the home and into the paid labor force, development of alternate child-care plans, and the resultant awareness of the significance of sex role stereotyping as both a personally limiting thing and as undesirable from the point of view of building the strongest society possible. The implications of sexism are being perceived as equally valid for men as well as for women, and the total picture is changing gradually. The end result will undoubtedly be a freer and stronger society in which people can find their niche without being programmed according to sex, but being in the process only adds one more uncertainty to the many uncertainties with which human beings must deal during their developmental years.

Socialization is essential for survival and for social functioning, but this does not mean that the individual is a mindless conglomerate of conformity to existent patterns. Life itself is a process that demands innovation and change, and people who have these characteristics are generally highly regarded, although sometimes considered a little odd if they are too much in the vanguard. In addition, in a complex society there are many socializing agents; out of such conflict, change grows. The most effectively socialized people are the ones who are open to change, able to reconcile conflicting demands, but also able to conform enough so they can function.

There are many people whose socialization is such that they are either unable to function in society or function only marginally. It is with these people that workers in the human services are most frequently concerned. In order to more adequately define and meet their needs, they have been divided into three categories:

1. *The unsocialized.* This group includes those who have had minimal opportunities for learning how to live as social beings, who

have learned ways of behaving that are destructive to themselves and others. These are often people who have had inadequate nurturing during their formative years, who have had poor role models, who have little capacity for personal relationships or self-discipline, who have inadequate or erroneous knowledge and consequently serious health problems, who often, but not always, are poor, who live from crisis to crisis because they are unable to anticipate, to think and plan in an orderly fashion, or to make use of the resources of society to deal with the inevitable problems of living. If it is true, as has been said, that every solution contains two new problems, their every solution contains at least six new problems.

The Browns are a typical example of such a multiproblem family. Mrs. Brown is a third-generation welfare recipient who is slightly retarded and deaf. Sexually abused by her father at an early age, she was sent to an inadequate state institution for the retarded where she remained until she was 21.

Mr. Brown's parents died when he was three and he was raised in a series of foster homes. In his early youth he had a serious drinking problem, was brain-injured in a fight and developed tuberculosis. The Browns have five children, the oldest of whom has been removed from the family because he is a chronic runaway. The younger ones have a complex list of health problems including asthma. Mr. Brown gets disability payments as he can no longer work, and there is supplementation from welfare funds.

The home atmosphere at the first call was chaotic, the noise deafening. Both parents were in constant motion, attempting, unsuccessfully, to control the behavior of four hyperactive children. This consisted of rushing from child to child, screaming and slapping as a toy was broken, a sister teased, or a brother bullied. The house was overheated and the shades drawn despite its being a sunny June day. Piles of well-aged, dirty diapers presented a hazard to walking and breathing.

This family, which existed from crisis to crisis, resulted from the union of two people who had both lacked the basic nurturing experiences in a family group, who were unable to relate constructively to other social groups, who had not learned to use available resources to grow in ability to deal with their problems, and who were duplicating their own experiences with their children. They were unsocialized in the sense that they had not learned functional behavior in society.

2. *The inadequately socialized.* If socialization were considered to exist on a continuum from the unsocialized on the one extreme, like the Browns, to the totally socialized who are equally undesirable in their conformity and almost robotlike behavior on the other,[3] the inadequately socialized would probably fall somewhere just below the mean. They are rarely as personally or socially destructive as the unsocialized. They possess at least minimal abilities to relate to others and to make use of social resources but lack the ability to follow through or to appraise situations with sufficient realism to behave appropriately in order to achieve their goals. Frequently they are very unhappy people because they have trouble relating meaningfully to others and using themselves with others—they are good examples of Thoreau's people who "lead lives of quiet desperation" because they often try constantly but never make it.

An interesting study made of the turncoats of the Korean War revealed that these were people who had no group identifications. They had no history of membership on teams, in social or fraternal groups, no alliances with others that would give them experiences in use of group strength and support that would enable them to tolerate the otherwise intolerable situation of war.

3. *Those socialized in a specific subculture.* These are people whose social learning is perfectly adequate in the subculture in which they exist, but when some circumstance requires that they move into another culture, they find themselves unable to function. It is often present when people move from a constrained rural to a highly complex urban setting, and in minority groups—reservation Indians, the poor, the black, the brown, the yellow in the ghettos of the great cities, certain religious groups. Older people who have spent a lifetime in one kind of work experience or

---

3. An example of these would be found in the people who commit almost unthinkable atrocities with the justification that they are following orders. They are so completely socialized in a particular culture that the internal controls cannot censor inappropriate behavior.

living pattern may find themselves faced with the necessity of learning the role demands of new working and living groups.

Mary Lou was a statistic among the high percentage of freshman students who failed the first semester at State University. She had grown up in a deeply religious family who, on their isolated ranch, had maintained a pattern of living at variance with the larger culture. There was no television; Mary Lou never played cards or went to dances. She was not allowed to have her ears pierced, to wear shorts, or to go to parties except those related to church activities. She attended a small rural school where she was an outstanding student and valedictorian of her class. She was not allowed to have a boyfriend. Her decisions were made for her by her church and her parents.

As a freshman she lived in a dormitory that included both men and women, where every extreme of dress and behavior seemed present, where all of the things she had been taught were wrong were practiced. The final straw was that her small school had not prepared her adequately for the demands of college classes and she found herself unable to study and achieve.

Fortunately she was tough and young, and in the second semester, with considerable help from her adviser who worked with both her and her parents, she was able to pull herself together and make a successful adaptation to the demands of her new setting.

Socialization derives from learned behaviors—from becoming competent in roles (the sum totals of the behaviors necessary to sustain a particular position in a social group). Resocialization comes from learning new roles and new ways of behaving. Because this learning takes place in a social context, there are two major factors that must be considered: the people as individuals and the situation in which they have functioned and must function.

Individual abandonment of learned behaviors and adoption of new ones does not come easily. Personal patterns of living tend to become emotion laden and internalized—they are a part of the person who lives them, supported by a system of values and feelings as well as by a natural resistance to change. Also, people such as the Browns are often so badly handicapped by their own poor equipment and the seriousness of their early destructive experiences that socialization and resocialization are doubly difficult and can probably be attained only to a limited degree and with much help.

In addition to change, there must be supports within the social group for changed behaviors; this means that resocialization requires group change as well as individual change. It also means that group attitudes are subject to value judgments in terms not only of their effectiveness but also of their worth. Helping to socialize people for functioning in a destructive group might improve their self-image and make them more efficient in their living, but in the long run might be undesirable for the whole of society.

> *Wadsworth Junior High School is located in an affluent suburb. The most powerful peer group in the school made up of seventh and eighth grade boys and girls requires that the new students "rip off" the local drugstore in order to be admitted. This behavioral norm is strongly supported by the group and the child who does not conform is a rejected isolate. In order to resocialize these young people it is necessary not only to support them individually in changed behavior but also to work with the parents, the school and the culture of the neighborhood, which (outside of the local merchants) by its response gives tacit support to such delinquency with the attitude that this "is just a childish prank."*

The role of the human service worker in socialization and resocialization must be based on sound differential diagnosis as to the varying needs of people for specialized services. In general, however, workers will find themselves in the following roles:

1. *Supporter*—by understanding the feelings of bewilderment, depression and anger that people experience when their learned ways of functioning are inadequate, when they are forced to question not only their own selves but also others, when they are faced with the demand for change.

2. *Teacher*—by providing the data needed to evaluate what is happening in a form and manner that people can use. This could include such things as how to nurture children and develop a family life, how to adequately deal with the demands of a technological system, how to make career changes, how to use a complex educational system.

3. *Role model*—by providing a demonstration of a successfully socialized person with whom the client can identify. Role modeling is an effective way of teaching. Learning to use the problem-solving process, with its emphasis on expression of feeling, assessment of reality, identification of goals and consideration of alternatives, is one of the best ways to become socialized.

4. *Enabler*—by helping individuals and groups by concrete demonstration and by provision of resources to work toward change.

5. *Therapist*—by utilizing social learning theory and behavior modification techniques to set up controlled situations in which different behaviors will be learned through use of reward and punishment.

6. *Social changer*—by assessing the values, attitudes, norms, and behavioral patterns of the social group, by evaluating what it contributes to constructive functioning, and by helping to make changes if necessary.

The whole process of resocialization places the worker in the position of making a judgment as to the worth of the social situation itself. The example of Wadsworth Junior High School is typical of the bind in which society in general and workers and clients in particular find themselves. This school is in a neighborhood of upwardly mobile middle class families. They and their institutions—the school and the church—preach racial equality and personal honesty. They live in segregated neighborhoods, belong to segregated clubs, perpetuate institutionalized racism. They cheat on their taxes; on their frequent and extensive trips all over the world, they bring home "souvenirs" that they have stolen; they are sexually irresponsible, drink too much and often take both prescription and nonprescription drugs. Their values are reflected in their adolescent children, to whom the worst thing is not pregnancy, stealing, drinking, or cheating, but "getting caught." What then is the role of workers in resocialization? Do they subscribe to what Halleck calls "the lie of adult morality"[4] and teach a tongue-in-cheek attitude that does jibe with the reality of the social situation?

In reality, much of our social learning takes place in a schizophrenic situation, and the old axiom "Do as I say, not as I do" is as

4. Seymour L. Halleck, "The Impact of Professional Dishonesty on Behavior of Disturbed Adolescents," *Social Work*, 8(2): 27-50, 1963.

valid now as ever. This points out the tremendous importance of being able, as an individual, to make sound value judgments and on their basis to think and make decisions for oneself. Survival is vital, and without some degree of conformity to social values and norms, survival is impossible. For each of us then, workers and clients alike, the major problem is to learn to survive but at the same time retain our personal integrity and our commitment to the best possible life for ourselves and others.

RELATED READINGS

The literature in this area is vast, drawn from psychology, sociology, anthropology, social work, child development. The reader could begin with almost standard text in these fields, not forgetting the tremendous insights that can be attained by using fictional or biographical accounts of the growing up years, such as Willa Cather's *My Antonia* or the *Autobiography of Malcolm X*. Those listed below are a few that I found useful.

Bandura, Albert. *Social Learning Theory*. Englewood Cliffs, N.J.: Prentice Hall, 1977. Good basic text dealing with social learning theory and its use in behavior modification.

Bronfenbrenner, Urie. *Two Worlds of Childhood*. New York: Russell Sage Foundation, 1970. Comparison of childhood in two different settings and how they determine behavior and personality.

Elkin, Frederick and Handel, Gerald. *The Child and Society*. New York: Random House, 1972. Study of the process of socialization.

Garrett, James and Rompler, Peter. *Community Resocialization: A New Perspective*. Washington, D.C.: Catholic University of America Press, 1966. A view of delinquency as a response to norms and practical suggestions of ways it can be dealt with.

Gordon, Ira J. *Human Development from Birth Through Adolescence*. New York: Harper and Row, 1969. Simply written, explicit and valid—good beginning text.

Kennedy, Daniel and Kerber, August. *Resocialization: An American Experiment*. New York: Behavioral Publications, 1973. Useful presentation of ideas for resocialization of the "failures" in society. Good for practitioners.

Sex Role Stereotyping, Implications for the Human Services. Minneapolis: Minnesota Resource Center for Social Work Educators, 1973. Current manual on meaning and implications of sex role stereotyping and ways to deal with it.

Slater, Philip. *Earthwalk*. Des Plaines, Ill.: Bantam Books, 1975. Analysis of modern society and our place therein.

4

Developing and Maintaining Communication with People

When two or more people interact, communication takes place. It would be impossible to avoid unless all of the senses were destroyed. Basically, we communicate what we are. For this reason, awareness of and control or change of the destructive aspects of our personalities are essential if we are to work with people. The dictionary defines communication as "sharing that which is common, or participation." The concept is a dynamic one implying activity on the part of all persons involved. There is no communication without a receiver as well as a sender. One could, as poets do, communicate with the wind or the waves, but it would be a one-way street with a lone person sending and receiving.

The major initial task of human service workers is to develop and maintain communication with their clients. To do so they express themselves, their feelings and thinking through nonverbal and verbal channels, or they may use external symbols that have a commonly understood meaning such as the sharing of food or drink. In the final analysis, communication is the transfer of meanings from one person to another. Breakdown in meaningful communication is one of the great problems of modern society, and has resulted in a vast amount of study and research. Basically the problem seems to lie in the fact that we communicate ourselves, and our selves differ from each other (see Figure 5).

How are meanings transferred, and how do we arrive at that commonness of understanding and participation that Webster referred to? The process itself, in simplified form, is as follows:

We communicate what we are.

We communicate attitudes and feelings as well as ideas.

We communicate nonverbally, verbally, and through use of symbols.

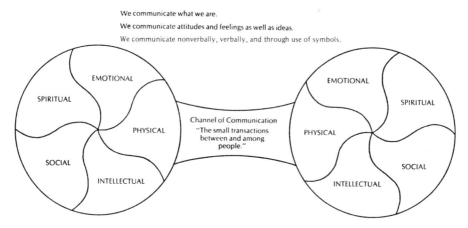

Figure 5   Communication Between People—A

A sender who wishes to establish communication evaluates the receiver with whom she wishes to communicate, and because she cannot transfer her ideas, attitudes, and feelings per se, encodes them in a manner that allows for their transmission. A receiver perceives the coded message and translates or decodes it into a form that he can understand and use. He then encodes his response and sends it back to the original sender. Both channels may be clogged by interference which disturbs and distorts communication of the intended message of the sender or receiver. This interference may range from attitudes and feelings, to group pressures, to reality situations (see Figure 6).

A black student came to see his adviser, a white, middle-aged, female professor. Observing that he was ill at ease, she commented as she searched the files for his records—"Are you a local boy?" He replied, with considerable dignity, "I resent that."

What happened in this communication? The faculty member, a parent with boys the age of the student, evaluated him in terms of her own experience, rather than in relation to his specific reality in a specific social situation. This created interference in both the encoding and the decoding, and the communication became a racial slur rather than the intended supportive interest.

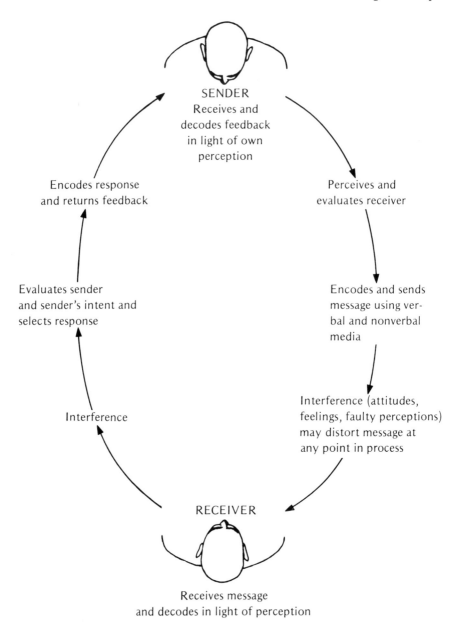

SENDER
Receives and
decodes feedback
in light of own
perception

Encodes response
and returns feedback

Perceives and
evaluates receiver

Evaluates sender
and sender's intent and
selects response

Encodes and sends
message using ver-
bal and nonverbal
media

Interference

Interference (attitudes,
feelings, faulty perceptions)
may distort message at
any point in process

RECEIVER

Receives message
and decodes in light of perception

Figure 6 Communication Between People—B

BASICS FOR CLEAR COMMUNICATION

Workers who wish to establish clear channels of communication with their clients must keep the following factors in mind:

1. Attitudes and feelings of both receiver and sender are vitally important. They affect all communication and can so distort sending and receiving that breakdown occurs.
2. An understanding of the similarities and differences between the people involved will determine the extent to which a common understanding and acceptance of modes of communication can be relied upon.
3. The capacities of the persons involved to use both verbal and nonverbal communication media and to interpret the symbols should be understood.
4. Workers should be able to use a variety of means of communication to meet the needs and capacities of their clients.
5. Workers should be able to evaluate the need for repetition and emphasis and ensure feedback to test comprehension.
6. Workers should use "loaded" words, gestures and symbols only as their meaning is commonly understood and accepted.
7. The tempo of communications should be geared to the client's level.
8. Workers should be aware of ways to eliminate interference both in their own communications and in those of their clients.

NONVERBAL COMMUNICATION

Nonverbal communication, or communication without the use of words, is the basic, primitive form of conveying information from one person to another. It has been estimated that in normal communications between two people, only one third of the meaning is transmitted on a verbal level and nearly two thirds on a nonverbal level. It was and is used when individuals do not possess command of a language, and the channels through which it operates are fundamentally affective rather than cognitive, although a cognitive element is clearly involved. Nonverbal communication takes place universally when two individuals meet for the first time, size each other up, and develop ideas of the kind of person with whom they are dealing, whether hostile or friendly, weak or strong, concerned or indifferent.

Infants who cry wordlessly, wave their arms, and pucker up their face are communicating feelings of discomfort. The response of the parents to these early attempts to say how the infant feels—usually in relation to how they feel—will determine the formulation of concepts related to these actions and the development of ways to communicate feelings of hunger, happiness, anger, and so on. Only later will come the words that will embody these feelings.

Nonverbal communication is continuous with or without verbal accompaniment. It is the principal means by which attitudes and feelings are conveyed, particularly in the initial stages of a relationship, but it goes on throughout any continuing contact between people. Because of this there is great danger that a worker may be communicating contradictory messages. One may say verbally, "I'm so glad that you stopped by," while at the same time conveying nonverbally, "I'm tired and harassed, it's late on a Friday afternoon, I'll be glad to see the last of you."

This kind of communication is confusing at best and can be extremely destructive to vulnerable persons. We see this with children caught in a situation where there is basic rejection of the child's needs and demands, and where the anger and frustration about this are communicated constantly by nonverbal means while the parents verbally profess love and concern. Such children are confused because they do not know which communication is valid.

Sensitive workers, who are aware of their own feelings, and recognize the impact expression through nonverbal channels has on the people with whom they are working, will attempt to deal with them in constructive ways. They can ventilate feelings of frustration with a fellow worker, hopefully one who will be healthy and knowledgeable enough to encourage ventilation rather than reinforcement of the negative feeling. They can use a good supervisor whose responsibility it is to help deal with these feelings. They can also in some instances acknowledge the existence of the feelings with the person with whom they are talking, try to understand their source, and decide whether it is possible to change the situation that provokes them. This can be done in a way that enhances healthy communication.

Over the years, our particular culture has tended to view expression of feeling as a sign of weakness or "femininity," so that very often deep and significant feelings can only be expressed nonverbally or symbolically. Even then, the expression may be so disguised that it requires knowledgeable interpretation. If there is feeling—and there always is—it will be expressed frequently by nonverbal messages. We are not always aware of nonverbal communications, but they can be potent influences in determining decisions and judgments.

Nonverbal messages are conveyed through the person and the setting. Personal appearance—physique, posture, body odor, dress, tension, facial expression, behavior, silence or speech, tone of voice, gestures or movements, eye contact, touch, body sounds—all convey messages to the receiver as does the physical setting—the appearance, aesthetic quality, comfort and privacy (or lack of them) and general climate. The ways in which we convey nonverbal messages about ourselves are endless. Once workers are alerted to where to look, what to listen for and to sense in both self and client, their sensitivity and ability to understand will increase.

Let us look more closely at some examples of these nonverbal media. Tone of voice is a frequently used one. From the carefully noncommittal tone designed to conceal, to the uncensored exclamation of pain, joy, anger, fear, grief, it is a revealing part of the whole process of conveying messages. The meaning of words can vary greatly according to the tone of voice in which they are spoken. The worker who wishes to test this need only select a simple phrase such as "I understand" and experiment with the many different meanings one can convey by altering one's intonation.

Facial expression is another important mode of conveying messages. To an extent faces tend to become "set" by the life patterns of the individual in expressions of apprehension, happiness, anger, passivity, friendliness, aggressiveness, and so on. Upon this lifetime foundation, response to the immediate situation will be superimposed. For example, the poker face, a man who traditionally plays it cool, is much less likely to express through his countenance the transitory feelings that are affecting him. However, the face that strives for bland concealment or negation of feeling—the mask face— conveys a meaning to the knowledgeable observer as significant as free change of expression.

Silence is a potent form of nonverbal communication and can express many different things according to the context in which it is used. It may be a companionable sharing, an expression of anger or despair, recognition of an impasse. Its use is influenced strongly by the cultural background of the individual; its meaning varies according to behavior patterns of the group. Silence can create great anxiety and be interpreted as an expression of hostility, so workers must be particularly aware of and knowledgeable about the needs of their clients if they choose to employ it as a means of communication or a technique.

Gestures and movements are time-honored methods of conveying attitudes and ideas. Relaxation or tension of the body, restless movement, biting the nails, shifting the feet, clenching or wringing the hands, drumming on the table—the list can go on ad infinitum. One of the most frequently stressed indices of communication in this mode is use of the eyes. "Eye contact" can be a significant factor in assessing the state of mind or feeling of the person with whom the worker is communicating. Here again, culture must be considered as well as individual patterns of behavior. The old beliefs about "the evil eye" are still prevalent among many people. Looking directly at a person or not meeting the gaze directly may be considered rude or taboo in a particular culture or family group. The eyes, "the windows of the soul" as they have been grandiloquently called, have special significance in relationships among people.

Physical appearance communicates definite messages about one's state of mind and feeling, as well as about one's ideas and general personality. Extremes say something about the impression one is striving to create, and one's feelings about oneself. Conformity or nonconformity with the generally accepted patterns of appearance carry a message. Cleanliness or lack of it can be significant.

Body sounds such as belching, sighing, cracking the knuckles, whistling, humming, eating noisily or quietly—all are ways of conveying messages about the individual.

Overall demeanor or bearing, the way one sits, stands, or lies down says many things to the observer. Individuals who are stooped and tired, slumping in pain or defeat, or carrying their shoulders straight and head high reveal something about themselves.

Physical touch is a particularly potent form of nonverbal communication. From earliest childhood the presence or absence and the kinds of physical contact are important factors in the emotional life of the individual. For infants it is a well-demonstrated necessity. Constructively used, it has a tremendous potential for strength and support, but it can also be destructive, as illustrated by the battered child, whose parents, by their actions, are certainly communicating something about themselves.

VERBAL COMMUNICATION

The ways in which we convey messages on a nonverbal level may be used either with or apart from verbal communication. Words allow for transmission of sophisticated concepts as well as of attitudes and feelings. The development of a written and spoken language has enabled us to build an extremely complicated society, to develop and retain exact knowledge, and to pass it along intact from one generation to another.

On the surface, once a language has been developed, verbal communication would seem to be a simple, straightforward, and satisfactory process. "I say what I mean and I mean what I say," someone has quipped, but actually we often do neither. It is an extremely complicated and difficult process to convey intended meaning through words. Differences in language, differences in patois within a given language, differences in meaning and usage of specific words, lack of knowledge or commonality of agreement as to exact meaning of words, limitation in vocabulary particularly in expressing nuances of feeling or meaning, all contribute to these difficulties, and the list could go on and on.

Frequently one uses phrases and words that are so much a part of oneself that one is unaware of what one is actually saying in words and what the impact of the message on the hearer is.

> *A white worker was involved in marriage counseling with a black couple. The husband was employed as the token black in an otherwise all white company. In talking with the wife about a quarrel they had enroute home from a company party the worker asked, "Did you feel uncomfortable being the only black woman with all those white ladies?" The worker was surprised and chagrined when what he was actually saying was pointed out to him.*

People may find it difficult to express an idea or feeling in words because they fear the reaction of the hearer, because their culture forbids free expression of it, or because they cannot accept the internal aspect that is struggling to find expression. When these factors are present, they may disguise what they are saying in such a way that the true meaning may be present, but hidden. If what needs expression is too painful or threatening, they may overreact and say the opposite of the true meaning.

> *In the current rush to find "field experience" for all students regardless of their suitability for this type of learning, Margaret was sent to live in a housing project where the tenants were predominantly welfare clients. Because she lacked adequate supervision, her increasing concern and anxiety went unnoticed. At the end of six months, she left school.*
>
> *At her final interview with her faculty adviser, she reiterated*

*almost hysterically that she "loved her neighbor" although it
was obvious that she disliked and feared the welfare clients. She
was unable to accept reassurance that she did not have to love
everyone and returned to the protected culture that had made
this an absolute for her.*

The worker who is faced with the need to interpret and understand disguised messages in truth needs the "third ear" of which
Theodore Reik wrote.[1] One should be cautious, aware of the high
possibility of error and schooled to attempt to validate one's interpretations through correlation with other behavioral clues the client
is presenting.

The effectiveness of efforts to speak honestly and clearly is dependent upon selection of words, perceived and understood meanings, the context in which they are used, and the specific meaning
ascribed to them by the culture of both sender and receiver. In addition, verbal communication requires agreement on the various
forms of language. Story telling, humor, the double entrendre, all
can be extremely useful forms of communication but are rife with
opportunities for misunderstanding. While they lend richness to discussion and often allow for expression of subtle feelings and ideas
that otherwise would be difficult to convey, they must be used carefully and only when accompanied by real sensitivity to reactions of
the participants in the communication experience.

COMMUNICATION BY SYMBOLS

The final form of communication to be considered is the use of
symbols. Although they are a nonverbal medium, their conscious
use is so prevalent in modern society that they should be discussed as
a separate form. They can be selected consciously or unconsciously,
to appeal variously to the senses, to the intellect, to attitudes and
biases, to fears and frustrations as well as to strengths and hopes.
They can serve a multiplicity of purposes—as attention-getters, as
creators of an atmosphere conducive to communication on another
level, as a medium for conveying ideas or feelings whose sophistica-
tion or subtlety makes expression and comprehension difficult.
"One picture is worth ten thousand words"—certainly the impact of

1. Theodore Reik, *Listening with the Third Ear* (New York: Grove Press, 1948).

cartoons or symbolic pictorial representation bears witness to the validity of this statement.

Symbolic communication takes place in various forms and on many different levels. Ideas of importance or status, feelings of confidence, consideration for individuals and their feelings, creation of an atmosphere that defines the function of the setting—all may benefit from the use of symbols.

It is rare to find communication confined to any one of the three modes—verbal, nonverbal, or symbolic. Frequently it involves a combination of all three. We plan a meeting or an interview in a setting conducive to creating a mood suitable for the business at hand; we serve food or drink—a universal and much used form for attempting to establish an accepting and nonthreatening atmosphere; we strive to be aware of what we are saying through ourselves; we use the spoken and written word; we fashion mobiles, pictures, transparencies and diagrams. We have probably the most highly sophisticated media for communication the world has even seen, and yet we have trouble with misunderstanding and breakdown in the essential processes.

INTERPRETING COMMUNICATIONS

Regardless of the medium of communication used, the receiver interprets the meaning of the message, and because people are different, these interpretations do not always result in comprehension of the intended thought or feeling. Thus, in interpreting messages, it is well to keep three factors in mind: (1) perception, (2) culture, and (3) context.

In this instance, perception is the way in which a communication is comprehended intellectually—how it is seen through the senses, how it is understood, and what it actually means to the person who receives it. We all perceive from our own frame of reference, and any communication can be perceived by the receiver as meaning something quite different from that intended by the sender. What could be perceived as a glare of rage might be merely the grimace of an anxious man, unsure of himself and what he is doing. The worker will be well-advised to check perception through other clues in the situation as a whole to test out understanding before acting on the basis of an assumption that channels are clear.

Workers must strive to attain sensitivity to the possibility that their words, phrases and attitudes may convey something unintended and may be perceived quite differently by their hearers. An outstanding example of this has become apparent through the questioning of values and attitudes which has accompanied the women's liberation movement. This has sensitized the society as a whole and human service workers in particular to the fact that the language as used is sexist, that it defines masculine and feminine roles in ways that make human roles secondary and limit realization of human potential. The language, of course, is merely a reflection of the value system of the culture; although the values are changing, the language lags behind. In this, as in all instances, workers need to develop a sensitive ear to what they are saying by the manner in which they are saying it.

In discussing perception, the formulation of the late Eric Berne about internal channels of sending and receiving can be very useful.[2] Berne, whose transactional analysis is currently enjoying wide popularity, particularly with workers whose major concern is dealing with faulty patterns of communication, sees all of us as having three levels from which we send and through which we receive—the adult, the child, and the parent within the self. Without stretching the point, we could call Berne's three channels the ego, the id, and the super-ego. When communications are received on the same level from which they are sent, the channels operate effectively and common understanding is achieved. When they are perceived and responded to on a different level, there is breakdown in communication.

> *Mrs. Winter, at sixty an obese, hypertensive, neurotic person, was advised by her physician to give up coffee. She responded indignantly, "You drink all the coffee you want—why shouldn't I?" The physician sent his message on an adult level, directed to an adult. She received and responded as a child. There was no real communication and the purpose of the exchange was defeated.*

Validity of perception is based on many different factors, some of which antedate the particular situation being perceived, some of which are part of that situation. Thus past as well as present experiences, attitudes, and patterns of communication affect the reality of perception. Perception is strongly influenced by the cultural background of the perceiver as well as by the present life experience, and the worker who would communicate clearly must keep both in mind.

---

2. Berne wrote about this in his book *Games People Play,* in a clear and understandable fashion. See Related Readings at the end of this chapter and Chapter 8.

In setting patterns for people, culture is a significant factor in determining how modes of expression are developed and used in both form and meaning. A brusque manner which may be perceived as rudeness or hostility may be merely the normal pattern of expression laid down by that particular culture for that particular situation. Laughter, which may be prescribed by a culture as a defense against fear or anxiety, may be perceived as an inappropriate, almost sick response by someone who does not share the same background. Eye contact, or lack of it, has a high cultural dimension. There has been some interesting research on reactions to pain, in which it was demonstrated that because members of certain cultural groups conveyed their suffering by free expression instead of the traditional stiff upper lip endorsed by Western social custom, they were considered ill and frequently referred for psychiatric consultation. There is probably no aspect of expression that does not have its cultural determinant, and because the patterns of attitude and behavior set by different cultures may vary greatly, they frequently constitute significant barriers to valid communication. We cannot learn all the cultural variations with which we will deal in our working capacity. Awareness of and openness to differences, lack of defensiveness about our own attitudes and ways of behaving, and an ability to say intellectually and emotionally as well as verbally, "I don't understand," or "Do I read you correctly?" will probably help.

The context, or total situation in which the messages are conveyed, is all-important in determining their meaning. The worker must look not only at the specific expression itself, but also at the whole both temporally and spatially. A message that may seem quite inappropriate in a specific frame of reference may be perfectly logical and understandable in the larger one. Every classroom teacher is familiar with the child who slams into the room in the morning making the maximum amount of noise and disturbance in direct contradiction to established ways of behaving. She knows that he may be reacting to something that happened before he entered the classroom and is sending out messages about it, just as another child, who may have left a similar family crisis at the breakfast table, slips silently to her seat and sits huddled with her misery. Both communications are understandable when considered in light of the total situation in which they take place.

Finally, we must look at the context in terms of the number of people involved in a specific effort at communication and the relationships among them. It is axiomatic that the larger the number, the greater the possibilities of complications and misunderstandings. Communication takes place not only between the original sender and the other members of the group, it also occurs among the members themselves, and the channels become many and diverse. The position of the worker in understanding and utilizing them becomes highly significant, and open discussion an extremely important tool in facilitating feedback and common understanding. Equally, the relationships among the people in the group will affect the meaning of the communication. For example, an adolescent boy usually communicates quite differently when his mother is a part of the group from the way he does when she is absent.

Workers in human service are increasingly in the position of needing to communicate with highly specialized groups such as legislators, councils, and committees as well as with the general public in order to change values, introduce new ideas, and secure support for different ways of doing things. Examples of this can be seen in the efforts of the Planned Parenthood program to ensure that children are born only to families capable of caring for them and wanting them; in the work of the expanded nutrition programs throughout the country toward improving public nutrition habits, particularly in families where there are growing children. In both of these instances, the underlying values that support present customs and behavior are strongly entrenched and have deep cultural roots relating to the sacredness of the family, the right to have children, the right to be free from outside interference in personal lives. Workers who undertake to change these need to be aware not only of the many factors that support the present behavior but also to have knowledge of ways to bring about acceptance and implementation of change. It is simply not true that if you invent a better mousetrap the world will beat a path to your door. You must know how to reach people, how to persuade them to see that the old mousetrap is not all that good, and how to encourage them to adopt new ways of thinking and behaving that will enable them to use the better mousetrap.

Such changes must occur at both the individual and the social systems level and, obviously, the two are so closely related that they are constantly affecting and being affected by each other. A special type of communication, labeled diffusion, has developed in order to facilitate such change. It is defined as "the process by which innovations spread to the members of a social system."[3]

    3. Everett Rogers and Floyd Shoemaker, *Communication of Innovations* (New York: Free Press, 1971).

This process involves five elements:

First is the *source of the new ideas*—the theoreticians, the inventors, the researchers who develop new ways of approaching problems but all too often are unable to sell their knowledge to the people who need it. Their specialized knowledge, skill, and language need translation into terms that outsiders can understand and relate to.

Second is the *message,* encoded and sent out by those who wish to make this new knowledge available to and used by the people who can benefit from it. This message is articulated in a way that potential users can perceive accurately; to point out the advantages of a different way of doing things and the rewards that can be expected to compensate for the pain of change.

Third is the *channel* through which these messages flow. Channels include the mass media, interpersonal communication or, most probably, a combination of both. Both have advantages and disadvantages. When faced with a new idea through the mass media such as television, newspapers, workshops, most people tend to try it out with their family and friends who can either reinforce or extinguish the idea by their response. There is a real advantage in having a respected teacher, leader, or professional sponsor an idea. When done on an interpersonal basis, the worker will need established credibility.

Fourth is the *receiver* of the new ideas, the potential customer for new ways of thinking and behaving, the member of the social system being influenced. It is particularly important that the innovator have accurate knowledge of the culture, the value system and the norms that support the attitudes and behavior that need to be changed in the receiver. The message that is not based on this knowledge will not be relevant to the receiver's experience and will probably go unheard.

Fifth and finally, *the effects of the innovation,* the "consequences over time," are seen as threefold: changes in knowledge, changes in attitude, changes in behavior. Time is of special significance in working with innovation. People who want to bring about change are often impatient and tend to forget that individual and social systems change slowly. The worker is always dealing with three aspects: the past, the present, and the future. Even in "revolutionary" change this is true. The burned-out hulks of buildings in the Watts area bear mute testimony to this fact in what they have been, in what they are, and in what they can be.

Rogers and Shoemaker visualize diffusion and acceptance of innovation as a four-step process: (1) knowledge, which involves awareness of the idea and some understanding of what it means; (2) persuasion, which involves the development of an attitude of acceptance or rejection of the new idea; (3) decision, which involves adoption or rejection of the new idea; and (4) confirmation, which involves seeking out support or rebuttal of the new idea. Once an idea has been accepted through this process, an underlying value system develops that will support and institutionalize it. The rapid development of complex innovations that characterizes our technological society requires that the human service worker, in order to be effective, be able to use diffusion theory.

In summary, we are only beginning to analyze scientifically and to understand the barriers to communication. The struggle for competence in this area, for clarity and honesty, is lifelong. Workers who never develop or who lose the capacity to "hear" what they are "saying" accurately through all media handicap themselves unnecessarily.

RELATED READINGS

Barker, Larry and Kibler, Robert. *Speech Communication Behavior*. Englewood Cliffs, N.J.: Prentice Hall, 1971. A look at what happens when people communicate by talking.

Berne, Eric. *Games People Play*. New York: Grove Press, 1964. Clear, readable, and interlacing formulations of the devious patterns of communications among people.

Campbell, James and Hepler, Hal. *Dimensions in Communication*. Belmont, Cal.: Wadsworth, 1965. Collection of readings in communication patterns and problems.

Fast, Julius. *Body Language*. New York: M. Evans, 1970. Communication through physical attitudes and behavior.

Goffman, Erving. *The Presentation of Self in Everyday Life*. New York: Doubleday, 1959. Human behavior in social situations and the ways in which we present ourselves to others. A second book by this author, *Interaction Ritual* (New York: Doubleday, 1967) is also worth looking at.

Hall, Edward T. *The Silent Language*. New York: Doubleday, 1969. An anthropologist examines the way cultures dictate the form of communication by modes other than direct speech.

McCrosky, James et al. *An Introduction to Interpersonal Communication*. Englewood Cliffs, N.J.: Prentice Hall, 1971. Practical and usable exposition of communication between persons.

Rogers, Everett and Shoemaker, Floyd. *Communication of Innovations*. New York: Free Press, 1971. An unusually clearly written and usable text in the whole area of introducing new ideas to people; numerous examples.

Zborowski, Mark. *People in Pain*. San Francisco: Jossey-Bass, 1969. Interesting report of research on cultural determination of ways of expressing pain.

5

Defining the Helping Relationship

Once communication between and among people has been established, relationships begin to develop. These relationships are the basis for meaningful contact with others. While they are probably one of the most important sources of satisfaction and fulfillment in the total life experience, they can also be extremely destructive and the source of great unhappiness and frustration. One of the first tasks of newborns is to develop relationships with the people with whom they must communicate in order to survive. This marks the beginning of a lifelong process toward socialization, the development of the capacity to give to and receive from others. While this capacity is inherent within the individual, its development and use depend to a large extent on the life experience. Infants whose natural reaching out to those around them is met with hostility, indifference, or misunderstanding will develop a reservoir of mistrust that will serve them poorly in later life. They are likely to develop attitudes and patterns of reaction that will inhibit others from approaching them, and make healthy relationships almost impossible.

THE NATURE OF THE HELPING RELATIONSHIP

In the course of an ordinary lifetime, an individual experiences many different kinds of relationships—parent-child, teacher-student, spouse-spouse, employer-employee, and so on. The one which concerns us here is the "helping relationship." It differs somewhat from other relationships but shares with them the common characteristic of being a dynamic interaction between two or more individuals. This interaction begins when communication first takes place and is a continuous process throughout the lifetime of the relationship. It is a reciprocal process, cumulative in nature, in which, once initiated, each successive response tends to be made in terms of those which have preceded it.

Accepting

The basis of any relationship is acceptance of the individual's right to existence, importance, and value. Indifference or lack of concern can completely inhibit the development of any meaningful interchange and can be more destructive than actual dislike. Like and dislike are dynamic states, usually precursors of action, but indifference is a static condition from which nothing grows. The violent racial confrontations, the marches and demonstrations of the 1960s, may have created a focal point for anger, but they also served to lessen indifference and create a potential for action. Out of acceptance should come freedom to be oneself—to express one's fears, angers, joy, rage, to grow, develop, and change—without concern that so doing will jeopardize the relationship.

Acceptance also involves recognition of the uniqueness of individuals as people who possess the need and right to participate in making decisions about matters relating to their own welfare. The extent to which a person is able to exercise this need varies among individuals, but the need is there. It is a vital part of the total growth process in life and a significant feature of the helping relationship, one purpose of which is enabling clients to exercise and increase their ability to participate in this decision making. The right and need of the individual to self-determination is an area in which we often get confused because of the social implications. When one person's exercise of self-determination adversely affects another, the necessity for some limitation becomes obvious. However, this necessity does not negate the existence of the need as a part of the relationship.

One of the major problems with the concept of acceptance is the fact that people tend to confuse it with "liking" the total individual and "approving" of that person's behavior. Thus the student who says, "I can accept anyone except the child rapist" has lost sight of the concept itself and is judging the behavior. We accept the reality of the individual's existence and place in the total scheme of things.

Like and dislike are products of this acceptance. The genuineness of acceptance of and concern for the client is a vital ingredient in the development of a meaningful relationship. Initially it is a regard for "people" but should be quickly developed into a regard for "this person."

Acceptance involves expectation. We not only accept people for what they are, we accept them for what they are capable of being, and this reality-based expectation assumes great significance in a helping relationship. Research findings indicate that the worker's expectation of the client's potential will influence the worker's attitudes and behavior and will have a bearing on the outcome of their joint endeavors. However, it cannot be too strongly emphasized that this expectation must be based on reality and arrived at without the influence of bias or stereotype.

Dynamic

The dynamic character of relationship demands that both or all of the significant individuals participate actively in the process. A one-sided reaching out effort does not constitute a relationship. The capacity to invest oneself with other people must exist within all participants, although the extent of this capacity may and does vary in degree among individuals.

A relationship is dynamic not only in terms of the activity of the people within it, but also in that as an overall entity it is constantly changing. Neither the individuals involved nor the relationship itself exists in a vacuum. People change and grow, new feelings and attitudes are constantly being integrated and fed into vital relationships which must in turn be able to encompass these changes if they are to continue to exist. An example of breakdown in the capacity to integrate change which occurs with distressing frequency in modern society is that of the student husband whose wife helps to put him through school but does not grow with him. When the changes in him are not integrated into the relationship between them, its vitality may be sapped and divorce may follow.

Emotional

The essence of relationship is emotional rather than intellectual. Primarily it is the give and take of attitudes and feelings that build a relationship and provide the channel through which ideas are imparted and decisions are reached. When relationship is faced with feelings or attitudes that it does not recognize or cannot or will not deal with, the channel becomes clogged and no longer serves its dual function of (1) being an end in itself by meeting the emotional needs of the client, and (2) serving as the channel through which rational endeavor can be made.

It is obvious that the importance of nonverbal communication in relationship can hardly be overstressed, particularly in the early stages. It is through this medium that emotional interchange most frequently takes place. Later, as words are added when necessary to describe feelings, it is equally important that the two levels of communication tell the same story—that one does not belie the other.

Purposeful, Time-Limited, Unequal

By definition, a helping relationship is purposeful and goal directed; otherwise there is no reason for its existence. It is directed toward enabling one of the participants—the client—to achieve a more satisfactory degree of functioning. As such, it is time-limited. When the purpose is served, the goal achieved, the specific relationship is terminated. It is also an unequal relationship in which the participants have differing roles and responsibilities, one to give and one to receive help. It is directed to meet the needs of one participant through provision of the needed help by the other.

In considering these three aspects of relationship, it is well to remember that they are not absolutes. While workers may hold as an overall goal the client's becoming self-sufficient, self-starting, self-determining, and independent of outside assistance, this, again, is a matter of degree. No one is ever totally self-sufficient. The very nature of life itself makes the concept of cure absolutely fallacious. Degree of functioning must be weighed in light of individual potential and social possibility.

The time limitation is subject to measurement by the same criteria. In a life experience characterized by continuous demands for adaptation or problem solving, it is impossible to name a date and say that from this time on no further help will be needed. However, an unnecessarily prolonged relationship tends to become sterile and meaningless. The worker's role demands teaching clients how to use help, how to use their own capabilities, and where to turn when future assistance is needed. A major task with many clients is to help them deal with a value system which implies that asking for help is a sign of weakness and inadequacy. In some instances this may be true but frequently such a request is an indication of adequacy and strength.

The recurrent need for help demands that new relationships be formed frequently. Here again, the worker's role demands striving to help clients achieve greater flexibility and understanding of people and a broader capacity to relate, so that they may be able to adapt to the different people with whom they must work in the future.

The fact that a helping relationship is geared to meet the needs of clients and not those of workers is basic, and yet if certain needs of workers are not being met, they probably will be very poor at their job. In their work they should be satisfying their need to be successful; they should be meeting the need to implement the basic philosophical conviction that the individual has worth, that the good of the society and of the individual are inseparable, that individuals have the capacity for growth and realization of their potential, and that while basic change comes from within, an outsider can provide help. Beyond this, workers' personal needs should not be involved.

Frequently a helping relationship is confused with a friendship. While friendships differ in purpose and time duration, the question of whose need is being met constitutes the major discrepancy between them and helping relationships. A friendship develops to meet the needs of both participants equally, although perhaps in differing ways. Workers who find themselves meeting their own personal needs in relationships with clients would do well to scrutinize themselves and their role very carefully. There may be elements of friendship that are appropriate but only as the worker is aware of them and of the purpose they are serving. From a helping relationship a friendship may grow but this is separate from the purposeful, goal-directed, working interaction.

In addition to confusing the helping relationship with friendship, workers frequently think that a relationship must be formal and structured. Actually the structure may only serve the purpose of bolstering up a shaky worker who is fearful of free and easy contacts with clients. There are definite uses for structure and form, but the basic relationship should not hang on these; it should exist and be usable in a crowded swimming pool, a hospital bed, or the privacy of a quiet garden or office.

Honest, Realistic, and Responsible

Finally, to be effective, a helping relationship must be realistic, responsible, and as honest as possible. Honesty (honor, integrity, sincerity, probity) between and among people is so difficult to attain that many people never experience such a relationship. Often we do not intend to be dishonest, hypocritical, or deceiving, but our defenses are such that we can only perceive ourselves as quite different from what we actually are. We all are familiar with parents, teachers, social workers who conceive of themselves as good in their roles—as warm, loving, giving people, but who are actually cold, rejecting, and often destructive. For this reason it is essential that workers strive to know themselves as they really are with their own unique combination of strengths and weaknesses. They must also perceive reality as it is, in terms of both people and situations. They must be aware of and deal with the distortion created by their own needs and desires, as well as their tendencies to see things as they would like them to be or to sit in judgment in terms of their own personal value system which may create a blindness all its own.

Exercising Judgment

There is a narrow line that honest workers must tread in exercising judgment as opposed to being judgmental. Their role will call for their making and using judgments, but these must be based on something more objective than their own personal value system unless that value system has been subjected to the most searching scrutiny and constitutes a valid standard by which to judge. This standard should be based on reality, a reality that is two-sided. In order to comprehend both sides, the worker must be able to see two views of the client and the situation. For convenience sake, we will call these the small and the large view.

The small view is the narrow one that workers see and understand because of their capacity to empathize with the client, to participate in the client's feelings and ideas without being a part of them, to understand how the client perceives self and situation, how the client thinks and feels about it. This small view is essential, for part of the workers' task is to understand similarities and discrepancies between these two views and to reconcile them. In short, workers must be able to hear the "sound of a different drummer" to which a client steps.

On the other hand, workers must also be able to perceive the larger view in all of its ramifications. They must understand the client and the client's behavior in the interrelationships of the total situation. How wide an area this view must encompass will depend on the situation workers must comprehend and deal with in order to assist the client.

Judgments arrived at on the basis of the correlation of these two frames of reference are much more likely to possess the quality of objectivity that is essential in order to avoid the judgmental and condemning attitudes that tend to inhibit the formation of effective relationships. The two sides of reality—the reality as it is and the reality as the client sees it—must be fully comprehended before the worker can make a valid judgment.

Judging is so confused with the assigning of blame that workers traditionally have been hesitant to make valid and appropriate estimations or form opinions about right and wrong, good and bad. It is, however, an essential part of the worker's responsibility, and to be effective, it must be done objectively and soundly based upon acceptance of the person.

In considering the uses and abuses of relationships the worker must guard against implicit promises which, while often not consciously dishonest, are unrealistic. These involve:

1. Implicitly promising more than can be delivered (trust me, reveal yourself to me, and all will be well).

2. Attempting to pretend a false acceptance that may or may not deceive but in either event is destructive to the client's capacity to be honest and to trust.

3. Implying that the relationship is permanent when in reality the worker may change many times in the course of a helping endeavor.

Overall, a helping relationship must be responsible in the sense that workers are worthy of the trust that the nature of their work places in them. While they are accountable to their clients, their superiors, and society as a whole, primarily they must be accountable to themselves, because only they can be aware of that which they invest in their helping relationships. While their own humanity and fallibility make it highly probable that they will err at times in this respect, they should develop sufficient self-awareness to know when they have done so, to resist the temptation to rationalize their own behavior, and to avoid its repetition.

Using Authority

By definition, a helping relationship is an authoritative one. Workers often have trouble in accepting and using this aspect of relationship because they do not know how to do so. They may retain personal conflicts about authoritative persons and situations with which they have been involved, they may lack commitment to its use, or they may lack the understanding that authority does not necessarily involve violation of another's rights and freedoms.

Two kinds of authority are appropriate in helping relationships:

1. The authority of knowledge. Workers who do not possess more and better knowledge about how to deal with the concerns of their clients than do either the clients or the general public have no right to intervene in people's lives. Teachers must know their subjects and know how to teach; doctors must know medicine and have skill in using this knowledge; social workers must know people and society and be able to use self in working with both; lawyers must know the law and be able to use it, etc., etc.

2. The authority of social sanction. In discharging its responsibility to provide maximum opportunities for its members to lead healthful lives in the broadest sense, society sanctions human service workers and charges them with the task of carrying out its mandates. This sanction requires that workers use authority to enable, to direct, to limit.

In reality, clients early become cognizant of workers' competence in this area. As one client remarked, "I know what's wrong—I need her to tell me what to do and how to do it." With the vast majority of clients, use of authority is only a problem if the worker makes it so. With those few who cannot accept any exercise of authority in relation to themselves, special practice skills are needed.

THE PHASES OF A HELPING RELATIONSHIP

A helping relationship, like any time-limited operation, can be visualized as having phases: Phase I—the beginning; Phase II—the middle; Phase III—the termination.

Phase I

Phase I is marked by uncertainty and exploration—a tentative feeling out, an attempt to evaluate the other person and determine what may be involved in this new situation. How trustworthy is this man? Will he harm me or can I let down my defenses with him? Will he like me if he knows what kind of person I really am? Will he lead me on and then kick me in the teeth like other people do? Can I safely push him around or is he likely to push me? Does he really know anything that will help me?

This is a sizing up and testing out period and should be accepted and acknowledged as such by the participants. Not all relationships flower or become significant. It is at this point, when meaningful communication is beginning to be established, when roles are defined, when needs are being expressed, acknowledged, and responded to that workers must be extremely sensitive to both verbal and nonverbal communication of feelings—fear, anger, uncertainty, lack of trust. They must be aware also of appropriate and inappropriate feelings, always remaining cognizant that this involves a judgment that may often be little more than an educated guess at this point in the relationship. They must convey acceptance to the client and the desire to understand what is actually being expressed.

The outcome of this testing out period should be an agreement— usually unspoken—between the worker and the client. In essence the terms are simple:

1. This is how we see each other.
2. This is the process through which we operate in this give-and-take situation.
3. This is the framework in which we will operate.
4. The first three terms are subject to change.

This agreement may vary, depending on the needs of the client and the capacities of the worker. With a person who has been severely traumatized by previous human relationship and cannot trust or reach out to anyone, the agreement would involve much more support and structure by the worker with repeated demonstrations of the capacity to be understanding, helpful, nonpunitive, and nonthreatening. With the client who can only be dishonest and manipulating, the worker may relate on the basis of "Okay, this is the way you want to play, but I'm not fooled." With yet another kind of person, the agreement may be for a good, fighting relationship characterized by aggressive confrontation and conflict. Phase I is the period during which definition of relationship, need, and type of relationship necessary in the initial stages are agreed upon, but always with the understanding that this is a dynamic process.

Phase II

Phase II—or the middle—is the working period of a relationship, although in the strictest sense Phase I is also a working period. The initial testing and questioning are completed, an agreement has been reached, and the "business" for which the relationship was established can take place. This should be a "comfortable" phase in that each participant has an adequate understanding of where each stands with the other and what to expect.

There is no justification for the establishment of a helping relationship unless there is business to be conducted. The fact that a relationship is in operation does not automatically deal with the problems at hand. It is necessary to stress this because of the current emphasis on feeling as being all-important. This exchange of feelings and attitudes must serve two purposes: it must meet the need of the client and it must provide a channel through which the work can take place. In the first phase, it may be a part of the work, but only a part. The middle phase, which begins when the initial agreement has been reached, is a dynamic one in which changes should be taking place, both in the feeling balance between worker and client and in the reality situations with which they are dealing. Thus it is a constant process of adaptation and readaptation to changes, but the underlying characteristics of acceptance and honesty must always be present. In a sense, meaningful relationships are constantly in the process of being redefined, but these new definitions are not the same as in Phase I. They are made against the background of knowledge of self and the other and of shared feeling, thinking, and experience.

Phase III

Phase III involves the process of termination. When we consider a helping relationship as being time-limited, we do not define the length of time involved. With some clients it may be a lifetime. There is nothing wrong with this, as long as the worker is cognizant of the reasons and they are valid ones, aware of the process involved, and conscious of the roles being played by the participants. Because the ending of any meaningful relationship has emotional significance for the participants even though they have been aware of its limited nature since its inception, it is necessary that the worker be aware of, and, if necessary, prepared to deal with this aspect. In recognition of this, society has set up certain rituals of farewell such as celebrations, sharing of food, giving of gifts which are ways of saying "remember me." The process of termination should be such that the client is able to (1) utilize the total experience as a constructive part of a lifetime of experiences, and (2) learn from it how to deal more effectively with inevitable terminations yet to come.

The depth of personal investment in a relationship is the most important factor in determining degree of pain and anxiety at termination. Superficial relationships in day-to-day experience are terminated lightly and easily. Our extremely mobile society tends to create immense numbers of these relationships, quickly developed and easily ended. It is a source of concern that the multiplicity of such experiences does not limit the capacity for deep personal investment of oneself with others. Yet each of us has a great need for relationships in which we are known as we are and accepted for ourselves. In this type of experience we tend to invest ourselves, often much more deeply than the busy worker realizes, particularly when the worker's investment is necessarily of such a different nature. With this in mind, the worker's role in termination is to provide an experience that will be constructive and pave the way for participation in and use of future satisfying relationships by the client, in both personal and outside life.

Any significant relationship contains within it elements of what psychoanalysts label transference and countertransference. People tend to relate in terms of how they have related to significant others in their past experience. In transference a client might see her domineering father in a domineering employer and react with the same helpless anger and frustration that she felt as a child. When this reaction is carried to extreme, the reality of the current relationship is lost.

The tendency to transfer feelings is not limited to clients; workers also experience it and have difficulty in controlling it. This is called countertransference. The manipulating parent who outwits the teacher in a conference may arouse the same murderous rage in the teacher that her childhood friend did under similar circumstances. We transfer not only feelings, but ways of responding to these feelings, and when we utilize them without awareness of their true origin and meaning, they are often self-defeating. Workers must recognize the reality of the current situation, be aware of the potential for transference, and capable of utilizing it in clients and controlling it in themselves.

One of the best tools for dealing with transference reactions is keeping the reality of current situations in view. When the client re-marked to her worker, "I can talk with you just like I did with my mother," he replied gently, "But I'm not your mother." This opened the door to consideration of how this relationship differed from the previous one and how things had changed from the past.

In no sense should the concept of helping relationships be con-sidered purely on the basis of one individual relating with another. Relationship is a basic factor in work with people in groups as well as on an individual basis. The intensity is generally diluted by the group situation, although it is the rare group worker who does not have individual contacts outside the group with clients.

There is no theory of working with people, no method of prac-tice that does not contain within it consideration of basic human re-lationships. In most theories the investment of the worker's self in the process is the essential and common ingredient. The extent of investment, the degree of intimacy and objectivity varies according to the demands of the particular mode of practice.

Helping relationships do not just happen. The worker is making conscious use of self in establishing a specialized kind of goal-directed connection with another person. While workers make use of what comes naturally, they also can learn and develop generalized skills in relating to people and then in applying them to specialized situations and persons. As workers do this they develop increased ability to em-pathize with clients, to perceive accurately and understand the clients' perception of self and situation. Carkhuff has visualized this as a three-stage process of attending, responding and personalizing.[1]

In attending, the worker, by use of self and the physical environ-ment, by use of listening, by use of observation, conveys intent and beginning understanding.

In responding, the worker gives feedback that reflects both the content and the feeling involved and offers opportunity to check accuracy of perception.

In personalizing, the worker helps clients relate to their own par-ticular situation and to the worker involved.

Like any other dynamic process, relationships will often need to be reworked to maintain maximum effectiveness, but the three skills that Carkhuff visualizes are basic at any point during the process.

---

1. Robert R. Carkhuff, *The Art of Helping*. Amherst, Mass.: Human Resource Develop-ment Press, 1977).

RELATED READINGS

Axline, Virginia. *Dibs, In Search of Self*. Boston: Houghton Mifflin, 1964. Beautiful and engrossing report on the skilled use of relationship between a therapist and a child.

Biestek, Felix. *The Casework Relationship*. Chicago: Loyola University Press, 1957. Simple, organized, and readable exposition of the meaning of a helping relationship.

Carkhuff, Robert R. *The Art of Helping*. Amherst, Mass.: Human Resource Development Press, 1977. Good training book with exercises that can be generally used. Simply written.

Frank, Jerome. *Persuasion and Healing*. Baltimore: Johns Hopkins Press, 1961. A study of various psychotherapies.

Fromm, Erich. *The Art of Loving*. New York: Harper and Row, 1956. A small and readable book that emphasizes the importance of self-love as well as learning how to care for others.

Hollis, Florence. *Casework: A Psychosocial Therapy*. New York: Random House, 1964. A presentation of the casework approach to the treatment of problems of interpersonal relationships.

Keller, Helen. *The Story of My Life*. New York: Dell, 1902. The story of a creative and enabling relationship between two people.

Kemp, C. G. *Intangibles in Counseling*. Boston: Houghton Mifflin, 1967. A consideration of the philosophical questions inherent in the helping relationship.

Loomis, Earl A. *The Self in Pilgrimage*. New York: Harper and Row, 1960. Emphasis on the meaning of relationship and communication among people.

Rogers, Carl. *On Becoming a Person*. Boston: Houghton Mifflin, 1961. A study of how persons grow and develop and of the relationship between therapist and patient.

6

Utilizing Social Systems Theory to Understand Human Institutions

Individuals do not exist in a vacuum. We are social animals and exist in relation with others of our own kind and with differing life forms. This relationship is a balanced one of mutual rights and responsibilities. The welfare of the individual and that of the group are inextricably bound up with each other, so that when the group does not meet the needs of the individual, it is in trouble; individuals who disregard the needs of the society of which they are a part are equally malfunctioning. Ensuring the rights of each becomes the responsibility of the other in a healthy society.

The society (individuals acting together) defines the position of the individual within it as well as the basic responsibility of the society toward its members. It creates institutions to meet the needs of its members as a pragmatic necessity to ensure its own survival. As a system of values develops (it is debatable which comes first—the position of the individual or the values) ethical as well as pragmatic considerations are involved.

THE SEARCH FOR A BROADER BASE

An appreciation of this vital relationship is essential for human service workers whose responsibilities call upon them to deal with the cutting edge of this interrelationship. The crucial part played by society, both through the physical environment and through impact

78

of other persons on individual social functioning cannot be ignored. It is difficult to understand how for many years we acted on the principle that an individual could be fragmented into parts that had no significant effect upon each other.

We saw the physician who prescribed a diet for a diabetic patient without regard for his limited income or his wife's reluctance or intellectual inability to comprehend her husband's condition or needs.

We saw the teacher who expected maximum learning by a bright child whose peer group did not accept her, or by a child whose familial values ran counter to the acquiring of academic knowledge.

We saw the psychiatrist, psychologist, or social worker who removed a child or disturbed patient from the family and neighborhood for treatment and then returned her to the pressures of an unhealthy or unchanged environment.

We saw the nurse or hospital worker who could not comprehend or accept her patient's reaction to pain and illness, which had been defined by a culture different from her own.

We saw the minister who counseled a couple with a large family about the tensions in their sex life without regard for the crushing reality of their poverty and debt.

We saw the group worker trying to help the adolescent find his own identity without changing the social situation that provided no opportunity for his employment.

We saw the employer who expected his employee to operate with maximum efficiency when his marriage was breaking down and his children were in trouble.

The list could go on indefinitely. Somehow, while we gave lip service to the necessity of dealing with the environment, we often neglected to do so in any significant way. We failed to see and deal with people the only way they can be realistically seen and dealt with, as total beings.

There are reasons, as always, for this emphasis on the part rather than the whole. This type of thinking is characteristic of countries as recently involved in their pioneer stage of development as our Western society has been, in which the concept of the strength of the individual is often all-important. It has also been greatly influenced by the puritan ethic with its emphasis on the importance of individual character rather than circumstance. We have believed that the individual should be strong enough to deal constructively with whatever the world demanded, perhaps because we would like to think that we are the total masters of our fate. It is only recently that we have begun to understand that while we may in truth make the circumstances, the circumstances will also make us.

We also have tended to deal with individuals because they are readily available, because we can isolate and work with them, and because we were only beginning to develop our knowledge of the ways in which individuals function both alone and in a social group. The development of psychological theory with its mechanistic emphasis tended to isolate fragments of individuals and their behavior without regard for their essential nature; psychoanalytic theory, with its emphasis on the internal life of the individual, seduced a whole generation with a promise of relieving personal trauma and thus providing a new chance for a satisfying life.

Social work, which had its roots in the concept of "the individual within the situation," its focus on work with the person and the surroundings, and its purpose as the improvement of social functioning, was strongly influenced by early psychological and psychoanalytic theory. In their search for causes and effective methods of working that would prevent and cure social breakdown, early social workers seized upon the insights into human development these theories provided and applied this knowledge without discrimination to all human problems. "How do you feel about this?" was the key question regardless of the situation, the implicit assumption being that if you "felt right" you could deal with anything. In addition, social workers adopted a medical model of study, diagnosis, treatment, and cure. This model posed an absolute contrary to the very nature of human beings, and this static concept and the dominance of psychological and psychoanalytic thinking tended to lock the youthful social work movement into a bind that took years to overcome.

The recognition that this method was no longer viable was hastened by the overwhelming social problems created by rapid social change and a yet ill-digested technology. Improvement of research methods also made it increasingly clear that effective work with people must take into consideration the totality of existence, the social as well as the personal reality, and the fact that this duality pervades every aspect of life.

Awareness of the need to be prepared to deal with the totality of the person is beginning to be seen early in educational programs for human service workers in the emphasis on interdisciplinary training, in the attempt to define a generic base for all human service, in the offerings of joint degrees. Nursing is developing a nurse practitioner with knowledge and skill in both nursing and social work; medicine is stressing the importance of the family practitioner who sees the individual as a person and as a part of family relationships; social workers are reaching out for courses or degrees in law in order to better serve complex people in a complex society.

The pendulum has started to swing, beginning noticeably in the last decade and gaining increasing momentum. We see greater and greater emphasis on group approaches and on manipulation of social change as offering opportunity for maximizing individual potential, for overcoming problems in functioning, and for creating a healthy society. Irving Buchan has said that "the real conflict we face now is a conflict not between the old and the new, but between the new and the futuristic, between what is known and what is emerging, between the individual and what might be termed the collectivised individual. The whole person is not and cannot be totally individual; part of the whole, today more than ever, must be nonindividualized, communal or collectivised. For we all live in a social environment with others. And that social environment, explosive with change, by continually impinging on us, becomes part of us."[1]

The great danger now is that we will again create an either/or situation. We are always searching for an easy, quick, and final answer to our problems. When a program does not produce immediate results, we abandon it and start another, often without retaining that which is valid. These abortive undertakings, often hastily conceived, poorly planned, and too quickly abandoned, cost millions of dollars and frequently create new problems without contributing to a solution of old ones. In our haste we tend to forget the long, slow process by which human beings make fundamental changes as well as the necessity of considering the total situation on a broad level. If we abandon what we have learned about understanding and working with the individual in favor of a total so-called social approach, we will not only lose that which we have painstakingly gained, but will also be disregarding the essential complementarity of the individual and the group.

Social change on a broad scale—through social planning, legislation, development of programs—can be achieved, but it is individuals who make use of the opportunities these developments provide. We build housing which individuals may or may not use to maximum ad-

1. Irving R. Buchan, "Humanism and Futurism; Enemies or Allies?" from *Learning for Tomorrow*, Alvin Toffler, editor (New York: Random House, 1974).

vantage; we offer employment; we create educational opportunities; in the final analysis the practical utility of these undertakings rests on the ability of individuals to take advantage of what is offered. We cannot separate the individual from the environment and the society. To be effective, we must understand and deal with both.

Faced with the necessity of evolving ways to deal more effectively with the individual as part of a group within an environment, workers look for ways to develop dynamic concepts that will (1) describe the nature of interaction between the individual and the social group; (2) ensure the integrity and well-being of both the individual and the group; (3) indicate where and how outside intervention can be most effective in producing constructive and socially desirable and acceptable results. A major problem is knowing where and how to "take hold." Probably the greatest frustration in modern life is our inability to deal effectively with the social institutions we have created. Each new development, theoretically designed to simplify, actually seems only to complicate matters further for the ordinary person struggling to control and live within society.

THE DEVELOPMENT OF SYSTEMS THEORY

One of the most useful of the recent developments is the utilization of concepts from systems theory.

Originating with a biologist around fifty years ago, systems theory has gradually been adopted for use in other areas of study. It attempts to set up rules defining the relationships among the parts of a whole. A system is defined simply as a whole made up of interrelated and interdependent parts. The parts exist in a state of balance, and when change takes place within one, there is compensatory change within the others. Systems become more complex and effective by constant exchange of both energy and information with their environment. When this exchange does not take place they tend to become ineffectual. A system is made up not only of interrelated parts but is itself an interrelated part of a larger system.

The utility of this concept as a way of thinking about a human being as a totality is obvious. It provides us with a dynamic point of view that stresses changing relationships and interrelationships rather than the static moment-in-time statement of classic diagnosis. The dynamic element in people creates a major problem in working with them and their groups. They are constantly changing, and a static description or prescription is often out-of-date before it is completed.

In addition to its dynamic nature, systems theory provides a yard-stick that can be applied broadly to the person as an individual; to the person as a member of a family; to the person as part of a small group; to groups in relationship to each other; and so on up to the most complicated social system (see Figure 7). This yardstick can be used in (1) assuring a unified view of the interlocking components; (2) assessing the relationships within the systems and speculating as to how they will be affected by change within any one part of the whole; (3) pinpointing the crucial point where attack is most likely to bring about desired change; (4) determining type and mode of intervention to be utilized; (5) anticipating probable results of intervention on each level.

Systems theory also tends to remove the onus of responsibility for all change from the individual and recognizes the importance of the situation in creating and maintaining problems in functioning that are often beyond the power of the individual as a part of the system to change. It removes workers from the central position as changers and emphasizes their role as enablers. This coincides with the basic principle that fundamental change comes from within the individual or the system; it cannot be imposed from without, although an out-sider can facilitate that change. It emphasizes the role of the natural mechanisms of adaptation. When changes are made in the system—as by rational agreement, legislation, program, disaster, and so on— people are faced with the necessity of adapting. We learn to live with the changes that occur in our surroundings, often slowly, but we have no other choice.

In looking at the nature of systems as wholes made up of interre-lated and interdependent parts, it is obvious that there are elements that strive to maintain the status quo as well as those which are ori-ented toward activity and change. These divergent tendencies are related to the two basic functions of a system: (1) its internal task to maintain the balanced relationship among the parts of which it is composed; and (2) its external task to perform the function for which it was devised and to relate to its environment. In addition, a system tends to move toward old age and death, particularly if it is closed and lacks the input of new energy. If too much energy is devoted to maintaining relationships which have become rigid, the system can accommodate little input and expends its whole energy in main-taining itself. It is unable to perform the task for which it was devised and becomes malfunctioning.

The family in trouble is an excellent example of this kind of sys-

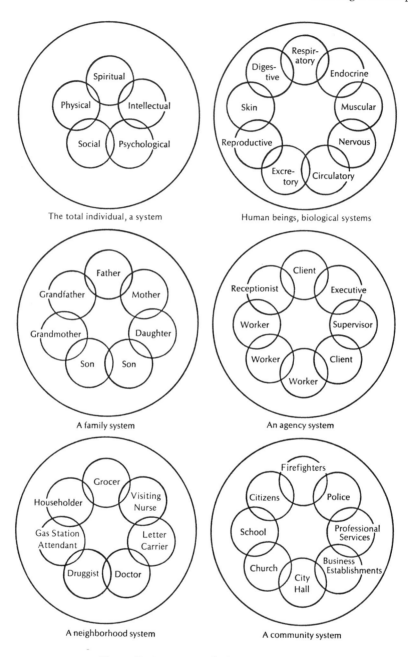

Figure 7 Systems and Their Boundaries

tem. The relationship among the members of the family has become rigid and constrained and based upon a destructive balance. The family is so involved in dealing with what is going on within itself that it cannot successfully fulfill the tasks for which it was devised — nurturing the young, meeting basic physical and emotional needs of its members, transmitting the culture.

On a larger scale, bureaucracies tend to become closed systems, spinning their wheels in order to maintain themselves, with very little energy left for effective performance of tasks and with no adequate provision for the input of new energy which, when processed, constitutes the vital output of the system.

USE OF CONCEPTS FROM SYSTEMS THEORY IN PRACTICE

What implication does all this have for workers whose task is improving the social functioning of clients, increasing the effectiveness with which they are able to perform various social roles? How can workers make practical use of it in approaching the job? They may well begin by asking themselves three questions: (1) What are the boundaries of the system or systems with which they are dealing? (2) What are the patterns and channels of communication both within the individual system under consideration and among the related external systems? (3) What are the explicit and implicit rules that govern the relationship among the parts, both internally and externally, particularly with respect to input (openness to new ideas or material), processing (working with these materials), and outgo (feedback or results of this work)?

Workers begin by defining the boundaries of the particular system with which they need to work. These will be determined by the focus needed for dealing most effectively with a particular area of malfunctioning. They may encompass a minute area or be almost infinitely extended. For example, in considering the problems of an individual, workers could choose differing frames of reference and define several different boundaries. These could encompass a neighborhood, a state, or a nation depending upon the level on which it was necessary to operate. As an example, we can take the specialized functioning of the physician. Using one frame of reference he sees his young patient with a venereal disease as a biological system composed of a series of specialized systems, each of which affects the other. He will intervene in the biological system with medication. He will operate in another system on another level by reporting the disease to the health department which will then attempt to reach everyone with whom the patient has had contact. On a third level he will intervene by participating in health education programs in the local high school. In so doing, he is working with three different service systems: (1) doctor, patient, clinic, paramedical personnel; (2) doctor, patient, paramedical personnel, health department people, patient's contacts; (3) doctor, school personnel community planners, lay people.

It is obvious in looking at systems that the concept of balance between parts is a particularly important one, and it is vital to remember that when a change is made in one part of the system there must be a compensatory change in the others. It is equally obvious that there is a factor of inertia to be considered—a push for retention of the status quo balanced by a push toward change. This delicate balance, this dynamic interrelationship, is a vital element in any system. Workers thinking in systems terms can see the total picture, the relationship between the parts involved and the type of change that is necessary to achieve a healthier balance. Hopefully they can select the level and mode of intervention which will be most effective, and they may work on several levels at once.

A family is a system characterized by intimate and specialized relationships. Usually the crisis that precipitates the need for help comes as a problem of an individual family member, a child failing in school or involved in delinquent behavior, a father who cannot hold a job, a mother who drinks heavily, an interfering grandparent, a marriage that is unhappy and deteriorating. The balance within this malfunctioning family is based on the behavior of the troubled family member, and the system will tend to pressure this member to continue in that role. Any change within the member apart from the system is extremely difficult to maintain. While the worker may help on an individual basis, focus should be on work with the family as a whole in order to change the family system and give the individual a fighting chance for healthy behavior.

Systems change becomes increasingly complicated as we deal with larger, more diverse and older social systems where the relationships, roles, and overall tasks of the system have become sharply defined and rigid. The worker who attempts to help change the system of a hospital unit or a school classroom to make it function more effectively may find the task one that can only be achieved by pressure for policy and administrative change on a very high level.

Workers are as much a part of many social systems as are their clients and as much subject to their controls and pressures. This becomes particularly significant and poses problems involving loyalties and basic responsibilities when the role of workers requires that they challenge and change the system of which they are a part and which they represent. Unfortunately, the systems responsible for human services have in many instances become rigid and inflexible, bureaucratized to the point where they are not adequately meeting human need. This is particularly sad in an area in which flexibility is such a vital necessity. In law, education, medicine, social work, nursing, we are witnessing great ferment as workers try to change their own systems. One of the most encouraging factors in this struggle is the presence of the no-longer-passive clients in the ranks of those striving for change.

However, these challenges to the status quo are often based on awareness that something is wrong without clear vision of what the goal of change is and what to substitute for the present system. The challenges themselves are an encouraging indication of vitality, and while they are a source of endless anxiety, frustration, anger, and fear, conflict, in some form, is essential to growth, and as such we should welcome it for the opportunity it presents.

In summary, systems theory compels the worker to keep in mind the totality of human experience as well as its volatile and balanced nature. It provides a set of consistent rules regarding relationships that can be applied across the board—to the individual, the small group, the institution, or the community. It gives specific indications for understanding and for intervention, and increases our capacity to predict outcome. It furnishes another tool for thinking, both specifically and generally, about the problems of people and their society. Like all tools, it is only as effective as those who employ it.[2]

RELATED READINGS

Ackerman, Nathan. *The Psychodynamics of Family Life*. New York: Basic Books, 1958. An examination of the family system and its interrelationships.
Bennis, Warren et al., editors. *The Planning of Change*. New York: Holt, Rinehart and Winston, 1966. Collection of articles on social change—see particularly that by Robert Chin, "The Utility of System Models and Developmental Models for Practitioners."
Cox, Fred et al., editors. *Strategies of Community Organization*. Itasca, Ill.:

2. See Appendix A for an illustrative case summary.

F. T. Peacock, 1970. Readings in work with communities as changeable systems.

Grinker, Ray, Sr., editor. *Toward a Unified Theory of Human Behavior.* New York: Basic Books, 1967. Well-rounded collection of various writings relating to general systems theory and its application in the behavioral sciences.

Hearn, Gordon, editor. *The General Systems Approach: Contributions Toward an Holistic Conception of Social Work.* New York: Council on Social Work Education, 1968. Collection of articles on application of concepts from systems theory to social work education and practice.

Merton, Robert. *Social Theory and Social Structure.* Enlarged ed. New York: Free Press, 1968. Classic text in the study of the institution of society.

Toffler, Alvin, editor. *Learning for Tomorrow.* New York: Random House, 1974. Collection of current writings dealing with the shape of tomorrow and the education necessary to deal with it.

Wilensky, Harold and Lebeaux, Charles. *Industrial Society and Social Welfare.* New York: Free Press, 1963. Classic text on the impact of society on the development of social welfare.

7

Utilizing the Scientific Method to Help People Deal More Effectively with the Demands of Living

No aspect of life is static. Evolutionary change comes so slowly that it may appear static, yet the process is continuous. Throughout a single lifetime, adaptations are, of necessity, made more swiftly. The individual, as well as the species, is involved in a constant process of change and adaptation both in the requirements of the normal growth and developmental pattern and in the essential adjustment to the demands of the environment.

People may be born with handicaps—physical, intellectual, or emotional—that tend to lead to the development of destructive patterns of living. Because of the pressures of their environment and social situation, they may adapt in ways that are equally destructive, although these may be the only adaptations they can make to ensure survival in their particular situation. The worker whose task is to improve the functioning of both the individual and society is concerned with ways of enabling individuals to alter the patterns of behavior that are destructive and with changing the unhealthy social situations that lead to their formation.

WHY AND HOW PEOPLE CHANGE

Therefore it is necessary to consider how and why individuals and social systems change, apart from natural development and maturational changes, and how this change can be facilitated.

1. People change as a result of rational decision in order to provide greater self-fulfillment and to avoid pain and discomfort.

2. People change when they learn, through facing and accepting the logical and inevitable consequences of their own behavior, that what they are doing is not really meeting their needs in a satisfactory and constructive way or contributing to their happiness and well-being.

3. People change through the development of relationships in which emotional needs are more adequately met and defenses accordingly need not be so rigid and constraining.

4. People change when, as a result of learning different ways of behaving, they provoke different responses from other people which in turn push them to respond differently.

5. People change when they are required to adapt to changing demands of the social systems of which they are a part.

6. People change when they have hope of reward for the risk they are taking in upsetting the status quo.

7. Systems change when there is change within the parts that comprise them and when provision is made for the utilization of new input.

Rarely do these conditions of change occur singly; frequently they are seen in various combinations. Together they encompass the rational characteristics of people, as well as their psychological, physical, social, and spiritual components.

One of the basic tenets of the philosophical foundation of human services is that "fundamental change must come from within" but that an outside force can help to facilitate it. This is true of systems on all levels, from individuals to the most complex social group. Basically they must be responsible for changing themselves.

Workers act as catalysts, setting into operation the conditions and forces that lead to change. To do so, they operate from another basic philosophical belief, that "people can be understood by utilization of the scientific method of study." This method provides a disciplined, orderly framework for workers' thinking and an overall pattern that can be learned and used to deal with the problems of life.

The classical "scientific method" involves recognition and systematic formulation of a problem, collection of data through observation and experiment, and the formulation and testing of hypotheses, or tentative explanations of the problem. The researcher hopes that a valid theory or law arises from this process. The orderly framework for working with people is an adaptation of this. It becomes a constant and ongoing process from the point at which the worker becomes involved in a situation until termination. While the words we use to describe the process are different, the process is basically the same.

STRUCTURE OF THE HELPING PROCESS

The structure of the worker's activities is as follows:

1. Engagement—involving oneself in the situation, establishing communication, and formulating preliminary hypotheses for the problem.
2. Assessment—appraising the situation on the basis of data—facts, feelings, persons, circumstances.
3. Definition of the problem—formulating the need.
4. Setting of goals—the end toward which the effort is to be directed.
5. Selection of alternative methods and an initial mode of intervention—looking at all the possible ways of tackling the problem and selecting the most propitious one.
6. Establishment of a contract—agreeing on a definition of the roles and responsibilities of the participants.
7. Action leading toward the desired goal—the work that is necessary.
8. Evaluation—weighing the outcome of action in terms of success or failure.
9. Continuation of working plan, abandonment of unsuccessful intervention and selection of a different approach, or termination—continuation and selection of a different interventive strategy are based on a repetition of this process.

In light of our basic belief that people have a need and right to be involved in decision making in matters that concern them, we must ask: what is the role and responsibility of the client in this whole process? First, we must remember that this is a description of the activity of workers—this is their working structure. Second, clients must always be involved in each step to the extent that they are capable of participating. This involvement is part of the total process, and workers who shortcut or evade—probably using the justification that it is a timesaving device—are contributing to failure, creating dependency, and making more work for themselves. This way of working should be a growth experience for clients; only as they are involved in it will they grow (see Figure 8).

Engagement

Engagement is that period in which workers begin to orient themselves to the task at hand. The initial involvement in a situation for which a worker has responsibility may come about in different ways.

a. Voluntary application for help. These clients are usually conscious that they have a problem; they have probably considered and perhaps tried various ways of dealing with it which have been unsuccessful, and they are sufficiently aware of their need for help to request it. They may or may not know what the real problem is, but they know that something is hurting, and they want relief from this pain and concern. They may or may not be prepared to do what is necessary to get this relief—as do most people, they probably want an easy, quick, permanent, and all-encompassing solution with little or no additional pain or effort on their part and probably as little real change in their life pattern as possible.

b. Involuntary application. Circumstances force some clients to secure help against their own wishes. These are critical situations that leave no alternative, such as extreme poverty, incapacitation,

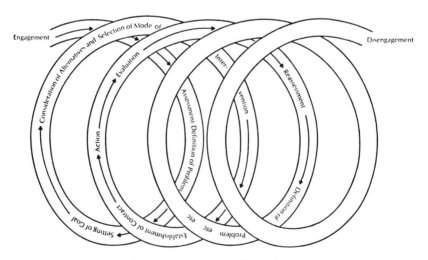

Figure 8   The Ongoing Process of Working with People

disasters, or social pressures from significant individuals and institutions (wife, husband, parent, employer, schools, military, legal, or correctional services) which enforce compliance with referral. While there is usually an element of reluctance in all requests for help, clients who feel that they have been forced into coming present an additional hurdle for workers, whose initial task is to recognize and deal with this reluctance.

c. Reaching out effort by workers. By the nature of their responsibility, workers will often reach out to involve themselves with other people who are not actively seeking or being referred for help. They may be conscious of the need but unwilling, unmotivated, or unable to do anything about it.

The task of workers in engagement is to: (1) involve themselves in the situation, (2) establish communication with everyone concerned, (3) begin to define the parameters within which they will work, and (4) create an initial working structure. Beginnings are important, and while it is always possible to go back and start over, the initial fresh impetus is gone forever. A second start involves reworking what has happened in the first. Beginnings in human services may be as simple as walking into a crowded waiting room, receiving a letter, a card or a phone call, or as complicated as attending a board meeting involving differences about a major company decision or going into a neighborhood in a state of crisis over some loaded issue such as school busing.

While not essential, it is helpful if the client can have direct contact with the worker during the engagement period. So much nonverbal communication takes place under such circumstances, so many feelings can be expressed and worked out, that whenever possible an effort should be made to ensure this type of interaction.

In this initial step, workers can only proceed from their general knowledge of people and social situations and their awareness of themselves, with knowledge that the clients involved will be judging them and what they represent at the same time that they are evaluating the clients. Preconceived opinions about the people and their situations, the problems and their solutions, emotional biases, prejudiced attitudes, anxiety, fear, and hostility on the part of both worker and client can operate to make honesty in engagement difficult. An essential part of workers' equipment is objectivity, open-mindedness, and capacity to be aware of and control these reactions in themselves. An equally important skill is the ability to be aware of their existence in clients and to deal with them either directly or indirectly. Workers may do this by encouraging their open expression and discussing them and by demonstrating through the shared working experience that they need not be the determinants of outcome.

In modern parlance, engagement involves a "selling" job. In a sense workers are selling themselves and their services, and the task is much easier when their position and status are clearly defined for the client. Today, when values are changing, when the human services are obviously not meeting many of the needs for which they were designed, when challenge and question of the status quo are the rule rather than the exception, workers who represent established social institutions may find themselves meeting with widely varied expectations and attitudes. Even teachers, physicians, and lawyers, members of the long-established helping professions, are subject to question concerning their motivation, their knowledge, their skill, and their attitudes toward their clients.

The prevalence of these attitudes makes the task of starting where the client is and presenting self and service in a manner that is relevant to the client's need a little more difficult. While it is the responsibility of clients—insofar as they are able—to make themselves and their needs understood, workers carry the greater share of the responsibility for enabling them to do so. Engagement can be achieved only in terms of the concern of the people involved; when the worker is sensitive to what this concern is and can communicate this sensitivity, engagement can begin on the basis of the worker's service being relevant to the client's need. The engagement process should provide opportunity for the client to express expectations of the worker and the institution that the worker represents. People see helping individuals and services differently and often will withdraw when they are disappointed.

The result of the engagement process should be: (1) the worker is part of the situation; (2) initial communication channels have been opened; (3) the worker and the client stand together in an approach to a common concern with some definition of the role of each based on expression and clarification of the client's expectations and what the worker has to offer; and (4) there is agreement on the next step in the process.

Assessment

Assessment is the appraisal of the situation and the people involved in it. This assessment has two purposes: it leads to a definition of the problem and begins to indicate resources for dealing with it. Workers move from operating on the basis of general knowledge to operating on the basis of specific knowledge of a specific set of circumstances and persons. They collect pertinent data, test and analyze these data, and arrive at conclusions.

Factual material (and we must always be aware that feelings are facts) about any one individual or social situation is endless. Therefore it is essential to apply the "principle of parsimony": the worker must collect only that information which has relevance to the situation at hand and is essential to the formulation of valid working judgments. But even in the provision of specialized services the totality of the individual must be considered, although emphasis will be on the particular aspect of individual functioning for which the service is designed. If, for example, the problem is a physical handicap, the worker will concentrate on this, but will also determine the cause-and-effect relationship between this difficulty and the other aspects of the client's self. A physical handicap has a marked effect on a person's self-image, and will affect one's capacity to relate to other people, perhaps one's capacity to learn, and one's ability to utilize one's potential for happiness and achievement. Effective service must take all of these relevant aspects into consideration.

Sources of data are many. The primary one is the client. What clients are and how they feel and behave should be given first consideration. After all, it is their needs about which we are concerned, regardless of whether the client is an individual or a total community. Historically workers have moved from the stance that demands checking of the client's statements and observations with a variety of outside sources; to that which considers the client's view to be the only information necessary; to the present attitude which considers the client's view to be of major importance but only one aspect of the matter. Above all, workers must be realists, and reality presents different faces to different people. These differences constitute a significant part of assessment. Clients know how they feel (but often not why), what they are concerned about, what they have done to try to alleviate the situation and the results of these efforts, that they want relief from discomfort, and, much of the time, how they would like to go about getting it.

The significant people in clients' life experience constitute a secondary source of information. These include both people with whom they have personal relationships, such as family and friends, and people within the more extended systems of which they are a part, such as school, church, job, and so on. In considering whether and how to use other people as sources of data for assessment, the ideas, feelings, wishes, and capacities of the client are of primary importance. The client has both a need and a right to know who is being involved and how to participate in getting the necessary information.

The final sources of data are records, test reports, studies, and evaluations of various kinds. In utilizing this material the worker must keep in mind that its reliability is based on the validity of the testing instruments used, on the competence of the persons who prepared the reports and studies and did the testing, and on the capacity for objective judgment by the person or persons through whom the results were filtered.

While the collection, testing, and analysis of pertinent data are listed here as separate steps in a process, they usually occur simultaneously. In talking with the client and others, in reading reports, in studying tests, workers are constantly assessing what they are learning and observing. They look for assets and liabilities within the individuals, the situations, and the relationships; they observe and weigh the important feelings and attitudes of the people involved; they contemplate the causes of the current situation and look at how such problems have developed and been dealt with in the past; they consider the availability of resources both real and potential within the client and the community which will meet the evident needs.

Definition of the Problem

Out of this process comes a definition of the problem. This can in no sense be considered a simple process. It has been compared to peeling an onion in its multi-layered composition and its effect on the participants, but its complexity must be understood if it is to be dealt with effectively. The concept of problem can be considered both horizontally in terms of its ramifications in the present, and vertically in light of past, present, and future etiology.

It is currently fashionable to decry the significance of causation, particularly in work with crises and in encounter groups. It is considered a copout, an excuse, a refusal to face the reality of the here and now. Consideration of causation can certainly be misused as a substitute for responsible action, but this does not justify ignoring it. Workers who do so are failing in a basic aspect of their role. We can understand the present only in light of what has happened in the past. We can interrupt the course of an ongoing event effectively without knowledge of basic causation, but we cannot assure effective prevention. For example, we can halt the course of an epidemic by closing the path through which the contagion is spreading, but the basic problem remains unchanged, the cause of the disease still exists. To prevent recurrence we must isolate, understand, and alter the causative factors.

Determination of how causation can be used to define a problem relates to (1) the wishes and needs of the client, who wants relief from the discomfort of the present situation; (2) the role of the worker, who may be charged only with responsibility for dealing with the current problem; and (3) the nature of the problem itself, which may be one that can be effectively dealt with in terms of the immediate situation or one that must be attacked at the root.

Often there is variance between what the client sees as the problem and what the worker sees. The original definition, however, must be based on what the client sees, as this is what appears relevant to the client at the time. Defining the initial problem differently often results in losing the client.

The concept of problem is not static, but changes as work progresses, just as in the total life experience coping with one demand leads to another. In addition, we rarely deal with a single problem, but rather with a constellation of problems, each related to the other. The worker's task is to focus on the primary one, which will open the way to consideration of those peripheral to it once an initial solution is reached.

It can be useful to think about problem in three frames of reference:

1. Immediate problem—that about which the client is most concerned, which is causing the current difficulty and in terms of which the client perceives the need for help. This is usually only one aspect of the whole. (For example, Willy Jones comes into juvenile court for breaking the windows of the Phillips' house when bouncing his ball against their wall.)

2. Underlying problems—the overall situation that created and tends to perpetuate the immediate problem. (The high density population area where Willy lives with inadequate play space for growing children, too little supervision from his working parents.)

3. Working problems—those contributory factors which stand in the way of both remedy and prevention and which must be dealt with if change is to take place.

a. The anger and frustration of Willy Jones and the Phillips family.
b. The absence of free space in the neighborhood.
c. The ignorance and apathy of the parents.
d. The inadequacy of service programs such as YWCA, park department, and so on.
e. The indifference of city officials and real estate promoters.

It is obvious that each of these working problems involves many smaller ones that must be dealt with as the process continues.

Setting of Goals

Definition of the problem should lead logically to the setting of a goal. Actually one is done in terms of the other. The purpose of a goal is to lend direction to efforts. Without such a focal point activity tends to become aimless, random, and often ineffectual. This does not mean that a goal is rigid and unchanging. Life being a dynamic process, a fixed goal, except in a large overall sense, can be stultifying. If we define health as the capacity for maximum functioning as well as the absence of disease, the overall goal of human services, a healthy society made up of healthy individuals, is too lofty to be pragmatically useful except in determining a philosophical base.

However, there should be a long-term goal to meet the expectation of achievement for the particular helping services undertaken. In addition, progressive subsidiary goals will lend focus to the ongoing work. When one has been realized, another will loom ahead. An example of this is the situation of the worker who was dealing with the problems of Willy Jones and his neighborhood. The overall goal would be the provision of adequate recreational facilities in the neighborhood. A subsidiary goal would be the involvement of community members in working toward the solution of their own problems. The immediate goal would be determining the point at which the worker could most effectively intervene in order to start the process that would lead to the achievement of these goals. Each step enroute would have its own small goal and be part of the progression toward a larger one.

Goal setting is most effective when it is a shared process, when the client has a major voice in deciding what needs to be achieved and how this is to be done. Motivation and independence are strengthened by this involvement. The goal should always be based on what is realistically attainable. Differences between the goals held by the worker and those held by the client should be based on logical differences in roles and tasks in the working partnership. The overall goals should be held in common.

Sometimes that which the client sees as a goal promises no solution to the problem. In marriage counseling, one partner will often want the worker to punish the other, to "straighten him (her) out"; this may be more important to the client than working out conflicts in the marriage. The worker's initial task in this instance would be to work toward a redefinition of the problem and the goal.

Selection of Alternative Methods and
an Initial Mode of Intervention

When the nature of the problem has been defined and understood, when the goal toward which the work is directed has been set, when the resources within the overall situation have been assessed, alternative solutions and interventions should become obvious. The most propitious should be indicated by the above procedures. Final selection should be based upon the following criteria:

1. Maximum feasibility—that which possesses the greatest chance of producing the desired results. The worker must think in terms of what is possible and attainable, which unfortunately is not always the most desirable. Compromise is an essential element, as we must deal with things as they are, not as we would like them to be.

2. Availability of resources to carry out the plan—either already present or capable of being created. Resources should be considered from various points of view. An important resource is the client's motivation and capacity for carrying out a share of the work in utilizing a particular method of resolution. The question of motivation, that "inner drive, impulse or intention that causes a person to do something or act in a certain way" can be a puzzling and exasperating one. All too frequently we see ourselves and others who possess the capacity and opportunity for change as lacking this essential ingredient. Happily this is an area where much research is underway, and we are beginning to understand better the part that general health, emotional satisfaction, basic drives, reward and punishment, and self-determination play in determining motivation. Therefore, we can appropriately consider whether it is possible to develop motivation in situations where it appears to be absent or limited.

We should be extremely careful not to use "lack of motivation on the part of the client" to cover failure in the worker or society.

The capacities, physical, intellectual, and emotional, that clients possess are basic resources. What physical health, strength, and stamina can they summon? What level of intellectual achievement are they capable of, what knowledge and skills do they possess, what can they learn? What capacity do they have for relating to other people in a useful, satisfying way, what stress can they tolerate, what emotional stability do they possess?

In addition, what resources to carry out a particular mode of intervention exist within the worker? What knowledge and skill does the worker possess in the type of service that is needed? Is the worker personally committed and competent to deal with the problem posed by this particular client? Failing this, can a referral be made to some other individual or program that can meet particular needs?

Community resources that can be drawn upon to implement a mode of intervention constitute the final category. Here workers should think broadly and flexibly as there are both informal and formal sources that may be enlisted. Frequently that which is most needed cannot be found within the framework of an institutionalized service, but is found within private individuals and groups. In isolated rural areas as well as some urban areas, services may be either nonexistent or inadequate, and workers are thrown back on their own inventiveness.

Initially the worker will need to determine the most effective level of intervention—with an individual, a family, a group, or a community. Frequently it will happen that all four levels should be involved. The worker will have to determine the breadth and depth of need on each level in order to decide whether the services of a specialist, through referral, cooperative, or teamwork, are needed, or whether a generalist, possessing more modest knowledge and skill in all levels of intervention, can adequately work with the situation at hand. On the basis of all these considerations—feasibility, workability and availability—the worker will select a mode of intervention designed to meet the needs of a particular client in a particular situation.

Establishment of a Contract

From the selection of a particular alternative for action and a particular mode of intervention arises the need to establish a contract between worker and client. This is an agreement that involves a common understanding of the goal of the work, an agreement on method of procedure, and a definition of the roles and tasks of worker and client. In essence, the contract establishes a partnership. Contracts may be as diverse as those between foster parents and a caseworker to determine how they should serve the needs of a foster child; between a public health nurse and the volunteer committee that sponsors a geriatric service; between a psychotherapist and the individual or group with whom he is working; between a street worker and a neighborhood gang; between an administrator and her staff; between an employer and employee; between doctor, nurse, or technician and patient. Contracts are often unspoken, may be formal or informal, should be flexible, and may need to be changed many times within the life of a specific helping relationship as goals, procedures, and roles change. The basic premise is always the same—that of a partnership designed to deal with a situation that needs attention.

Action Leading Toward the Desired Goal

Required action is determined by the specific mode of intervention, and roles and tasks are defined within this sphere. The emphasis is on working with rather than for people, but the capabilities of each person are limited, even on a participatory level. When the client's limitations have been reached, the worker's responsibility is to intervene elsewhere in the system in the client's interests.

The child whose learning problem is related to the presence of an inadequate or psychopathic teacher can do nothing to change the situation. The worker, with cooperation of the teacher, the parents, and the school administrator if necessary, will have to do this for the child.

The householder whose home is being taken for urban development without adequate compensation can seldom alone change the law or bring pressure to bear on officials and governments. The worker and the householder's neighbors will have to help.

Evaluation

Wherever there is action, there is possibility for error by both worker and client. It is the worker's responsibility to create a climate where an accepted part of the procedure is objective evaluation or appraisal of what is occurring. In such a climate, worker and client may see the results of what has been done in terms of movement toward immediate and ultimate goals. A review of what has occurred, an analysis of success and failure with an attempt to understand the factors involved and the reasons for results should point to continuation, reassessment, or termination.

Continuation or Termination

Continuation is indicated when the results of the action show movement in the desired direction which confirms the validity of the original assessment, problem definition, goal, selection of mode of intervention, and contract.

However, the action may not result in progress toward the desired goal. The fault may lie at any point in the process. In engagement, false understanding may have been set up between worker and client. The original data may have been either incorrect or misinterpreted. The problem may have been wrongly defined or an improper aspect selected for initial work. The goals selected may have been incorrect, unreachable, or irrelevant. The alternative selected for action may have been a poor one and the mode of intervention inappropriate. The contract may have been too demanding, too simple, or invalid, and the action either a failure or inconclusive. A reassessment then must take place which involves the familiar process of picking up the pieces and starting over again; not, however, at the beginning. There is the asset of what was learned in the initial phase, and the liabilities created by its failure.

Termination takes place when the goal has been achieved and the service completed; when nothing further is to be gained by continuing; when the client requests discontinuance; when referral is made to another source of help, and the original worker will no longer be involved. In termination, as in the other steps, the client's participation is of maximum importance. If the helping relationship is at all significant, the way it ends will be important in terms of self-image and capacity for future relationships. The reasons for termination should be clear in the minds of both client and worker and, whenever possible, feelings about it expressed and understood.

A part of termination is leaving the door open for future contacts. As we have realized that life is a continuous problem-solving process, we have come to know that people may need help many different times with many different concerns. The desired results of a good helping experience involve not only increased knowledge of resources, but also increased readiness to use them as need be.

On paper, such a model tends to look as unwieldy, cumbersome, rigid, and infinitely detailed as a good recipe for stollen or runza. The neophyte who has been working with people on an intuitive basis will be in the position of the centipede in the poem who "lay disconsolate in a ditch deciding how to run."[1]

Actually it is a simple, continuous process, one step growing out of another. Intellectually it can and does take place in an extremely limited time; it can also be extensive, depending on the requirements of the situations under consideration. The important things to keep in mind are that it is a dynamic ongoing process; that it is an inter-related totality in which omission of any one part tends to invalidate the whole process; and that at best it is a shared undertaking that can be understood, learned and used by almost anyone. If workers clutch it jealously to themselves, its greatest value, that of teaching a way to approach the problems of living, is lost.[2]

RELATED READINGS

Alinsky, Saul. *Rules for Radicals—A Pragmatic Primer for Realistic Radicals.* New York: Random House, 1971. A direct and down-to-earth exposition of one way of working for social change. Don't let the word "radicals" frighten you.

Bartlett, Harriet. *The Common Base of Social Work Practice.* New York: National Association of Social Workers, 1970. Defines a theoretical base for the methods that social workers use.

Carkhuff, Robert. *Helping and Human Relations—A Primer for Lay and Profes-sional Helpers.* Vols. I and II. New York: Holt, Rinehart and Winston, 1969. Research-oriented approach to selecting and preparing human service workers and to practicing in these areas.

Dunham, Arthur. *Community Welfare Organization.* New York: Thomas Y. Crowell, 1958. Basic text in organization and work with communities.

Hamburg, Jill. *Where It's At—A Research Guide for Community Organization.* Boston: New England Free Press, 1970. A practical guide to where to turn for know-how in working with communities.

Klein, Alan. *Social Work Through Group Process.* Albany, New York: School of Social Welfare, 1970. State University of New York. Updates and gives clear direction in group work from a social work point of view.

Konopka, Gisela. *Social Group Work: A Helping Process.* Englewood Cliffs, N.J.: Prentice Hall, 1963. Simply and clearly written basic text on social group work.

1. A centipede was happy quite until a frog, in fun,
    Said, "Which leg comes after which?"
    This worked him up to such a pitch
    He lay disconsolate in a ditch
    Deciding how to run.
"The Puzzled Centipede or the Perils of Thinking," by Mrs. Edward Craster in *Under the Tent of the Sky,* John E. Bruton, ed. (New York: Macmillan, 1937.)
2. See Appendix B for examples of this process in operation.

Lippitt, Ronald et al. *The Dynamics of Planned Change.* New York: Harcourt Brace and World, 1953. Explanation of the process by which change can be brought about.

Morris, Robert et al., editors. *Encyclopedia of Social Work.* Sixteenth Issue. New York: National Association of Social Workers, 1971. Excellent two-volume work of practical, well-written, and informative articles. A "must" starting point.

Overton, Alice and Tinker, Katherine et al. *Casework Notebook of the St. Paul Family Centered Project.* St. Paul, Minn.: Greater St. Paul Community Chests and Councils, 1959. Soundly and simply written report on reaching out to families in need of help.

Perlman, Helen. *Social Work: A Problem-Solving Process.* Chicago: University of Chicago Press, 1957. Sound and well-written text on social casework.

Richmond, Mary. *Social Diagnosis.* New York: Russell Sage Foundation, 1917. An antique classic that foreshadowed present developments in working with people.

8

Developing
an Eclectic Approach

Operating from many differing frames of reference and with many differing points of view and philosophies about the human condition, workers develop practice theories and related methods by which change can be implemented. These methods with their attendant techniques, should evolve through a logical progression as illustrated in the accompanying figures (see Figures 9 to 11). They must be consistent with the basic underlying philosophy, with the overall goal, and with the worker's own theory about human nature.

Variations in basic values, philosophies, and theories about life give rise to differing ideas about how people change and about the methods that can be successful in facilitating this change. Difference is an essential concomitant of a vital and growing body of knowledge and must always exist and be welcomed. The mind that is closed to question and change is moving toward sterility as surely as any closed system.

However, because of these differences, workers are faced constantly with a bewildering array of new theories that purport to carry either *a* or *the* solution to human problems. Because success in working with people is indefinite and difficult to achieve, workers tend to grasp at new ideas and approaches in an almost faddish fashion, often abandoning the old without adequate reason or without having an effective replacement. Rather than flying back and forth like a shuttlecock from one to the other with desperation born of concern and the desire and need to produce results, workers must:

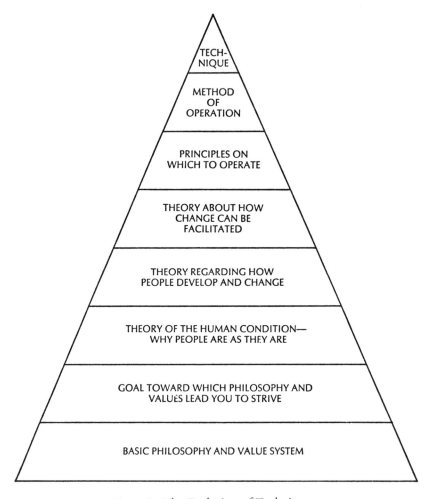

Figure 9   The Evolution of Techniques

1. Determine that there is no single way to deal with all of the problems of living.
2. Be open to consideration of new ideas and approaches.
3. Develop sufficient knowledge to evaluate such ideas, or reliable sources upon which to depend for this evaluation.
4. Decide:
   a. to select that which is useful from each to fit into a coherent overall working model, OR
   b. to focus on one particular approach geared to deal with one

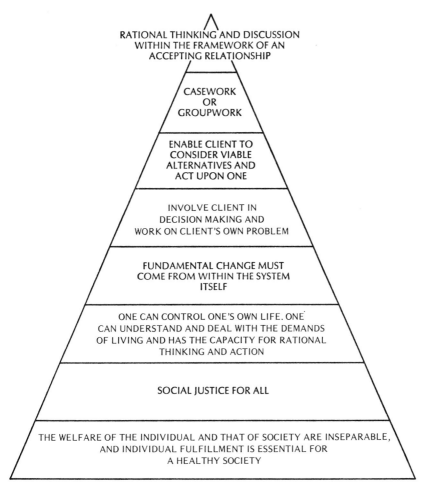

RATIONAL THINKING AND DISCUSSION
WITHIN THE FRAMEWORK OF AN
ACCEPTING RELATIONSHIP

CASEWORK
OR
GROUPWORK

ENABLE CLIENT TO
CONSIDER VIABLE
ALTERNATIVES AND
ACT UPON ONE

INVOLVE CLIENT IN
DECISION MAKING AND
WORK ON CLIENT'S OWN PROBLEM

FUNDAMENTAL CHANGE MUST
COME FROM WITHIN THE SYSTEM
ITSELF

ONE CAN CONTROL ONE'S OWN LIFE. ONE
CAN UNDERSTAND AND DEAL WITH THE DEMANDS
OF LIVING AND HAS THE CAPACITY FOR RATIONAL
THINKING AND ACTION

SOCIAL JUSTICE FOR ALL

THE WELFARE OF THE INDIVIDUAL AND THAT OF SOCIETY ARE INSEPARABLE,
AND INDIVIDUAL FULFILLMENT IS ESSENTIAL FOR
A HEALTHY SOCIETY

Figure 10   The Evolution of a Technique Based on Social Work Theory

particular area of need, learn all there is to know about it, integrate it with the self, and make it a way of working.

SPECIALIST OR GENERALIST

The role of the specialist is essential. Not only are we greatly in need of specific services, we also need the type of meticulous research and testing that can come from this emphasis on one way of working. However, the specialist can only be effective when the specialization derives from a body of basic knowledge of the individual as a whole.

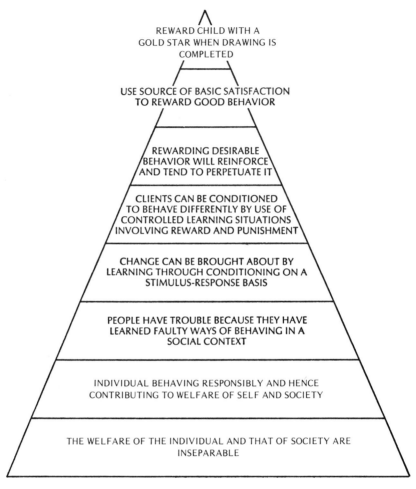

REWARD CHILD WITH A
GOLD STAR WHEN DRAWING IS
COMPLETED

USE SOURCE OF BASIC SATISFACTION
TO REWARD GOOD BEHAVIOR

REWARDING DESIRABLE
BEHAVIOR WILL REINFORCE
AND TEND TO PERPETUATE IT

CLIENTS CAN BE CONDITIONED
TO BEHAVE DIFFERENTLY BY USE OF
CONTROLLED LEARNING SITUATIONS
INVOLVING REWARD AND PUNISHMENT

CHANGE CAN BE BROUGHT ABOUT BY
LEARNING THROUGH CONDITIONING ON A
STIMULUS-RESPONSE BASIS

PEOPLE HAVE TROUBLE BECAUSE THEY HAVE
LEARNED FAULTY WAYS OF BEHAVING IN A
SOCIAL CONTEXT

INDIVIDUAL BEHAVING RESPONSIBLY AND HENCE
CONTRIBUTING TO WELFARE OF SELF AND SOCIETY

THE WELFARE OF THE INDIVIDUAL AND THAT OF SOCIETY ARE
INSEPARABLE

Figure 11   The Evolution of a Technique Based on Learning Theory

The majority of workers in human services are not specialists in the sense that they can focus on one particular aspect of need. By the very nature of the demands of their jobs, they are required to deal with the totality of individuals, either in helping them cope with the overall demands of living or in enabling them to make use of a more specialized service such as education, medical care, legal advice, psychotherapy, and so on. As such, workers must develop an eclectic approach to working with people, utilizing elements from many different practice theories. As long as these elements form a consistent whole, this seems justified. There is much duplication and overlapping in the various approaches to working with people, and the knowledge and skills developed through differing specialized research are not necessarily inconsistent when used in a larger context.

Out of this eclecticism has come a common core of knowledge and skills that specialists and generalists alike in all of the human services must possess if they are to be successful. This book represents one attempt to define the content of this core.

The significant point is that regardless of how eclectic it may be, the worker's approach must form a consistent whole, and be one which the worker believes in and is convinced can be effective. This conviction, combined with the worker's belief that each individual possesses the capacity for change and personal optimism about chances of success, are important factors in determining outcome. Without these, the worker is defeated before getting started.

DEVELOPMENT AND EVALUATION OF A WORKING MODEL

In determining what to incorporate from various approaches into a total working model, the worker will need to measure principles and methods not only by the yardstick of immediate results, but also in terms of their consistency with a basic value system, view of human beings, and theory of how change occurs. In human relations, the unresolved question of whether the end justifies the means is ever present. If philosophy and value systems are valid, however, they should help to dictate the means to achieve the ends. Means that are inconsistent with basic values are self-defeating if the values are valid. For example, we believe that people have a right and a need to be involved in decisions regarding their own welfare. If we choose to ignore this, if we arbitrarily make decisions and force changes, we may succeed on the surface but fail in the more important aspect: the promotion of individual growth and capacity to deal with life problems.

It is equally important that in their search for knowledge and skill from a wide variety of approaches, workers avoid faddishness and the swings of the pendulum from one extreme to another. When this occurs, we find overall approaches and techniques being used in situations where they are not applicable. The wide use of "insight therapy" to deal with poverty and its attendant problems is a tragic example of this. Overuse of the nondirective interviewing techniques of Carl Rogers is another.

Misunderstanding and misinterpretation of the theory and techniques of an approach can also lead to gross abuse. Nowhere can we find a more damning example of this than the way in which psychological test results have been misused in the public school system. The past two generations of schoolchildren have been classified, categorized, and frequently stigmatized by the misuse of an instrument that has limited utility. The tool is only as good as the user, and only the knowledgeable person who possesses a healthy skepticism can effectively utilize the wide range of knowledge being developed in the behaviorial sciences.

With these qualifications in mind, let us examine some of the outstanding approaches to working with people that have developed during the past century, and see which of the working principles of each can be used in the overall model proposed here.

Theories have developed principally under the aegis of five different disciplines: psychiatry, psychoanalysis, psychology, social work, and sociology. Anthropology has contributed significant additional understandings.[1] In addition, theories of management from business administration have increasingly become an essential part of the modern human service worker's preparation. These disciplines have worked independently and together in these knowledge areas; knowledge developed by one has been adapted and used by the others. We will consider only some relevant developments in these areas.

Psychiatry

Modern psychiatry, the study and treatment of disorders of the mind, is generally considered to have originated with the work of Kraepelin in Germany a hundred years ago, although Hippocrates in 60 B.C. attempted to describe mental illness on a scientific basis. Early treatment was mainly symptomatic and involved use of electroshock and hypnotism. Psychotherapy or "the talking cure" developed with the work of Breuer and Freud in the late nineteenth century, and focused on the internal conflicts of the individual.

The psychiatrist today is a physician, and psychiatry is recognized as a medical specialty. It has developed a classification of mental illness and various physical therapies as well as psychotherapy. Within the past two decades, drugs have been used extensively to control the various behavior manifestations that accompany emotional distur-

1. See Related Readings at the end of this chapter for the basic texts in each of these subject areas.

bance. The medical training of psychiatrists enables them to work with the interrelated totality of physical and emotional problems, and increasing interest is being demonstrated in social psychiatry. There is currently an interesting splinter group in psychiatry which holds that mental illness does not exist. Present research also emphasizes the roles of body chemistry, biology, and nutrition in mental health and in the overall ability to function.

Psychoanalysis

The contribution of psychoanalysis to the understanding of and work with people holds a very special place in the development of behavioral science. Firmly rooted in the medical profession, it attempted to define and understand the emotions and the inner life. Sigmund Freud, who is generally conceded to be the father of psychoanalysis, and those who have followed him—Adler, Rank, Rappaport, Allan, Erikson, and many others—developed theories of personality and related practice theories that have greatly influenced all the human services. The present day psychoanalyst frequently, but not necessarily, has a medical background and extensive training in the theory and techniques of psychoanalysis.

Classic psychoanalysis, as originally visualized by Freud, sees the origin of an individual's malfunctioning in one's efforts to deal with unconscious drives, related to traumatic experiences during the developmental years. From this frame of reference, a practice theory was developed which was characterized by (1) acceptance, (2) permissiveness, (3) transference, (4) catharsis and interpretation, and (5) insight, with resultant control of impulses. The techniques of free association and interpretation of dreams were widely used. We need only glance at these to realize how profoundly they have affected all subsequent work with people. Even the clinical psychologists, who attack psychoanalysis for its lack of a research base, utilize these techniques, and they are clearly reflected in the overall techniques listed elsewhere in this book. As always, when techniques are adapted for use in a different situation, with different problems and often in an oversimplified way, results have been problematical. Attempts to use this sophisticated verbal approach with nonverbal clients has caused problems. Because of its long-term nature, some workers who utilized it tended to adopt a leisurely approach not necessarily suited to all of the problems to which it was applied.

Those who followed Freud made various changes in his theories before adopting them. Adler developed a "rational" approach emphasizing the importance of the total family rather than just the parents. While he also stressed the significance of early experience, he originated ideas about an individual life style in which a person either compensated or overcompensated for early deficiencies. He was much more active and reassuring than Freud and used a rational or commonsense approach with his patients. His theories on (1) activity, (2) reassurance, and (3) rational consideration are widely used techniques in all of the present day helping services.

Otto Rank made a fairly radical departure from the teachings of Freud when he introduced the concept of separation anxiety resulting from birth trauma and saw life as a continuous recapitulation of this separation. His practice theory emphasized: (1) analysis of current rather than past problems; (2) control of the client's tendency to become dependent upon the worker; and (3) development of the will of the client to live a constructive life. These techniques are also being widely adopted.

Hartman, Anna Freud, Erikson, and the other "ego psychologists" emphasized the role of the ego in adapting to the demands of the environment. One of their most significant contributions was the concept that the "ego" possesses "free" energy that is not involved in dealing with unconscious drives but which can be conceived as constituting a push toward health. They saw this part of the individual as the mediator between individuals and their needs and the environment and its demands. They divided the functions of this aspect of the individual into the perceptive (that which discerns) and the adaptive (that which adjusts); the integrative (that which incorporates) and the executive (that which acts). This led to the concept of the individual's possession of coping ability, and hence to the concept that by this process one's ability to deal with the demands of living grows and develops by stages. Along with this came emphasis on the significance of environment and culture. Some current thinkers are questioning the concept of stages as being too rigid, emphasizing instead the constant fluidity of people and their capacity for change.

At present, the practice theories that have developed from ego psychology have considerable importance. They stress: (1) health rather than illness; (2) strengths rather than pathology; (3) present and future coping ability rather than examination of the past; (4) extending the need for change from assisting the client to cope with reality as it is, to responsibility for changing the reality itself.

Innumerable theories have grown out of the formulations of this general approach. Several are sufficiently prominent and widely used at present to deserve detailed consideration. These are crisis theory, reality theory, conjoint family therapy, and transactional analysis.

Crisis theory developed out of work in a public health setting and orientation, with a truly interdisciplinary approach involving medicine, social work, psychology, and psychiatry. In the past few years we have seen "crisis" centers developing across the country, often featuring around-the-clock telephone service in which help is available on an emergency basis. We have seen strong emphasis on short-term service. What is the basis of this effort?

With the acceptance of the idea that a "problem-free" state is unattainable and that life itself poses a series of recurring developmental crises which must be dealt with, workers began to search for ways to deal more knowledgeably with immediate breakdowns and at the same time strengthen the client for the task of coping with breakdowns that inevitably will occur in the future. From this and observation and research on the adaptive processes that people undergo in coping with the hazardous events of life, crisis theory was formulated, with specific goals and specific techniques.

The concept of balance is basic to this theory, for true crisis is an upset in the "steady state" of the reacting individual. Research has defined the duration of the imbalance as limited, as there is an almost immediate effort to recover an operating equilibrium. This period of upset is characterized by a high degree of tension, anxiety, and fear. Three different types of crises have been identified: the normal, developmental ones such as the movement from childhood to adolescence; those related to role change such as first marriage or first parenthood; and the accidental events that occur in all lives such as death, illness, loss of work, and so on. The goal of the worker is to help the client cope with the immediate problem, regain equilibrium, and function anew, hopefully on a higher level than before, for crisis provides significant opportunity for growth. Work is time-limited and focused on the immediate goal of regaining equilibrium. Dealing with underlying conflicts and problems is not the goal of the work.

Practice implications growing out of this approach are:

1. The worker must be immediately available at the time of crisis when the individual is motivated to deal with the problem because of pain and discomfort.

2. Focus should be on the present problem, but because old scars tend to hurt again in such circumstances, opportunity should be given for thinking and talking about past crises.

3. While the worker should provide opportunity for expression of feeling, the rational and adaptive capacities of the client should be supported and strengthened.

4. During the crisis the worker can be more active (and should be) without creating undue dependency. The worker can give advice more freely and be authoritative without fear of undermining the client's capacity to act.

As the crisis is resolved, the worker and the client must decide whether additional help of a different nature is needed through referral to another source, or whether the client will go on alone, hopefully having learned how to deal with crises more effectively.

This theoretical approach can be applied with families, groups, and communities as well as with individuals. A family, group, or community can be stunned and thrown out of equilibrium by a critical event, but soon, almost visibly, begin to pull itself together to start functioning again. The worker who intervenes at this point can count on more openness to change than when an established balance is functioning. A part of dealing with crisis is determining when more extended service is necessary after the current imbalance has been resolved.

Reality therapy as developed by Glasser proposes a model for working with people which is specific and well-organized. While its roots lie in psychoanalytic theory, it also negates the importance of past experience except in understanding the present, emphasizing working in the here and now. Its basis is the belief that the major needs of people are involvement with others and a feeling of personal worth. When these needs are met, the individual is able to assume responsibility for constructive actions. It utilizes both individual and group processes.

1. The client becomes involved with a responsible person (worker) who is concerned with the client's welfare.

2. The client analyzes present behavior and its outcomes.

3. The client makes a value judgment as to whether this behavior is good or bad—whether it leads to fulfillment and happiness.

4. The client and worker plan a "commitment" in which the

former will attempt different behavior for a certain length of time.

5. The client commits himself or herself to this plan.

6. If the commitment fails, there is no excuse, no "punishment" as the failure itself is the punishment. The client and worker simply start over again.

Again, this theory involves many of the basic principles and techniques that are part of the overall model proposed here. It stresses (1) the accepting and meaningful relationship between workers and clients for meeting basic emotional needs; (2) involving clients in considering themselves and their behavior rationally within the safe framework of that relationship; (3) developing motivation for change through responsibility for decision making; (4) learning to accept failure as a basis for renewed effort.

Conjoint treatment, which involves working with two persons, particularly married couples, with emphasis on the interactional problems between them; family therapy, which focuses on the interaction within the family as a unit; and transactional analysis, which emphasizes a specific approach to dealing with breakdown in interpersonal relationships, are all basically concerned with problems of faulty communication. They deal with these problems in terms of current reality, with the goal of promoting health and growth of individuals and families and strengthening their ability to make effective use of the opportunities for a good life. The role of the worker involves acceptance, support, interpretation, and education. While family therapy may use differing approaches and techniques, transactional analysis presents a specific working model with simplified terminology and methodology that can be learned and used effectively with clients. While at present its use is confined largely to small groups, its originators see its eventual extension to larger segments of society.

Clinical Psychology

Contingent with the developments of psychiatry and psychoanalysis, another movement was under way which took a somewhat different turn. Clinical psychology began with work by both psychologists and physicians in the classification of abnormal mental conditions and the study of individual differences. The work focused on devising individual mental tests to be used in diagnosis. A natural outgrowth of this approach to human problems was a strong emphasis on laboratory experimentation and research which has endured to the present. Prior to World War I, clinical psychologists worked primarily in hospitals and clinics for the mentally disturbed and in child guidance programs. In the 1930s, however, there was a change in emphasis. While psychologists continued to work with children, they also began to recognize what the entire child guidance movement had made apparent by this time: effective work with children must include their parents. They began to work with adult as well as childhood adjustment. There was also a shift in focus to developing tests to define personality patterns and adjustment, and these, along with other tests which have been developed and standardized, are invaluable assessment tools for workers. The third change followed logically: the extension of the psychologist's function to that of working directly with clients. To do so, clinical psychologists utilized extensively the practice theory developed by Freud and the early analysts. The education of the modern psychologist involves extensive academic work, usually on a Ph.D. level, with emphasis on laboratory and clinical experience.

Clinical and social psychologists currently have become instrumental in developing a way of working with people that proceeds from a frame of reference differing from that of the psychoanalyst. The present trend toward using what is called behavior modification based on learning theory is one of the most significant in the whole area of working with people. It is being widely used (and misused) and has generated a controversy in which workers have become polarized for or against without evaluating objectively the potentials and utility of this approach. It is damned as being mechanistic, manipulative, unethical, and applicable only in controlled situations not suited to a free society.

Actually, the basic theory has been known and used by workers ever since someone tumbled to the fact that the carrot can be effective in getting desired behavior from the donkey. People expect that their behavior will lead to meaningful, satisfactory outcomes, and when the behavior does so, expected and desired reward reinforces the particular way of behaving. It is possible to condition people to give up or retain and develop certain behaviors through use of reward and punishment without placing the burden of responsibility for change on the client. Presently, workers are attempting to understand and develop specific ways of utilizing this basic principle to change behavior that is destructive and to reinforce that which is constructive.

That this way of working can lend itself to manipulative and mechanistic uses is obvious. However, we deceive ourselves if we do not realize that the worker-client situation is one in which considerable power rests with the worker, regardless of the theory of change favored. With the development of new biological, psychological, physical, and social tools for bringing about change, the importance of the personal philosophic base upon which the worker operates has become apparent. Depending on how it is used, behavior modification can be a growth experience for individual clients, or it can be destructive, even when the desired behavioral changes take place.

Modern workers who opt to use behavior modification techniques are operating directly with individuals concerned, while also attempting to teach other persons significant in the client's life experience, such as parents and teachers, to utilize this knowledge. It is a method that can be incorporated effectively into a generalist's pattern of working as one approach, as it uses some of the same basic principles that the generalist approach does. For example:

1. The techniques used must be suited to the particular client; rewards and punishments are different for different people, as is behavior which needs modification.
2. The orientation is toward solving a problem—the way of behaving that is contrary to both the good of the individual and that of the society.
3. The worker's role is an active one: to interpret, to reward, to punish.
4. The relationship between worker and client is based on acceptance of worth and expectation of capacity for change.
5. Effective work involves the worker's insight into the client's past and future, in that probable behavioral changes can be anticipated.
6. Environmental changes must be made to effect permanent behavioral changes.

Much of the controversy over behavior modification centers on its extension to control and bring about change in the larger society to the detriment of individual freedom and integrity. Life itself is the great "operant conditioner," and when we change and control social situations we obviously change people also. The extent to which human nature can be altered is debatable, however. The self is not nurtured on the bland pap of predetermined decisions and prefabricated solutions. There are vital unanswered questions in using such controls that cause legitimate concern and that will not be easily resolved.

Social Work

Social work originated in the ethical concern of the haves for the have-nots and in the pragmatic view that a healthy society must provide for the welfare of the individuals within it. It represented efforts to deal with poverty and to care for those who could not care for themselves: old people, children, and the handicapped. From its beginnings social work has seen its function as preventive as well as remedial, and the early social workers were dedicated to social change, sometimes by means sufficiently revolutionary in nature to satisfy even the most radical of the current workers who wish to change social institutions by force.

The edge of this early thrust toward social change was blunted by three developments: (1) early growth was largely controlled by representatives of affluent groups who were committed to palliative rather than systemic changes; (2) identification was with a method of working that focused on the role of the individual in change; and (3) recruitment of its practitioners was largely from a middle class that tended to support the status quo.

In an effort to find a way to effect change, social workers developed casework, with its basis of work with individuals and families toward the goal of enabling them to cope with the reality of their existence and to recognize the need to realize their own potential. Peripheral to this was intervention in the community to bring about changes that would make for fuller lives for their clients. In searching for methods and techniques, social workers borrowed heavily from psychoanalytic theory, adopting the medical model of study, diagnosis, and treatment; and utilizing interviewing, gaining of insight, use of relationship and sometimes it seemed, almost incidentally, provision of the material necessities of life—food, clothing, shelter. They also acted as social brokers for their clients. Casework thus combined work with the individual with intervention in the environment in the interests of the individual.

As the nature of social work responsibility encompasses the total social functioning of people, it could not operate effectively from so limited a base. Early social workers had always worked with neighborhoods and communities, but these early beginnings, which were somewhat dormant during the era of emphasis on casework as *the* method, began to develop when social work moved to a more generic approach to practice and incorporated within itself the two growing movements of community organization and group work. These movements stressed creating a healthier environment and maximizing the opportunities for developing individual potential. Both utilized group as well as individual approaches. From the union of this triad has come a new understanding of the need for an all-out approach to human problems through the social work generalist and through interdisciplinary efforts.

Thus the major contributions of social work to the helping services are:

1. Recognition of the essential relationship between social justice, individual fulfillment, and social well-being.

2. Awareness of the wholeness of the individual and efforts to develop a practice theory that encompasses that totality.

3. Development of a mode of supervision that recognizes the basic importance of the worker's self and the necessity of integrating the worker's values, knowledge, and skill in order to perform effectively.

The generalist approach is best illustrated by the social caseworkers and group workers of the late eighteen and early nineteen hundreds. They saw their responsibility as extended: working with people in their total social functioning—as individuals, within a family, as part of many groups, a neighborhood, a community, and a society. Modern social workers operate with differing educational backgrounds, ranging from indigenous workers who, with little formal training, work with those with problems similar to their own; to technicians who, with some training and limited education, perform certain specialized tasks; to those with formal education extending through the doctoral degree. The latter are concerned with planning and implementing direct service with clients—teaching, administration, formulating policy, developing programs and social action designed to implement broader social change.

Presently social work operates on the basic theory of "making the punishment fit the crime." Rather than prescribing particular methods, social work undertakes to design and utilize the particular intervention demanded by the problem itself. This has resulted in emphasis on generalist knowledge and skill resting on the worker's ability to use self effectively as a helping person, to communicate and relate meaningfully with individuals and groups, and to manipulate the environment to produce desired results.

RESEARCH REGARDING GROUPS

An increasingly significant aspect of theoretical knowledge about the individual has come from the study of people in groups.[2] This study has fallen largely within the areas of sociology and social psychology with social work attempting coincidentally to develop practice principles as well as theoretical formulations relating to group life. The impact of group experiences on people and their importance as a medium for effecting individual and social change and growth have been generally recognized and studied for a hundred years. At present research in this area is more widespread than ever and a body of knowledge has been developed that is useful to workers both in understanding the properties and dynamics of groups and in the use of group process to bring about change. Knowledge has been accumulated from testing and from observation and experience over a period of time with many diverse groups.

The basic concepts from small group research have become a part of general knowledge. They are significant for the worker because they provide insights into how groups and the people within them tend to behave under given circumstances and define both the pressures and the freedoms for growth that the group presents. As such they are a vital part of the worker's knowledge base in understanding and dealing with people. Of particular importance are (1) the concepts relating to the position of the individual in the group, such as a social role, with its patterns, expectation and demands, status and the stress that accompanies role change; (2) the concepts relating to the ways in which the group influences its members, such as the impact of the group on self-image, the development of group values and mores, the requirement for conformity, and the rejection of the individual by the group; and (3) the concepts relating to the group itself, the fact that it possesses a gestalt—is greater than the sum of its parts, has a culture of its own, develops subgroups within itself, tends to move toward rigidity, and has a power structure and a capacity for decision making.

Probably the most significant fact about groups for the human

2. For a more detailed look at the worker and the group and community, see Chapter 10.

service worker is that there is a process that takes place within and through them that knowledgeably used can be a tremendously constructive force in the life experience of people. Conversely, groups can also be destructive. The worker who utilizes them, for whatever purpose—education, therapy, recreation, self-realization, social change—should do so only from a base of hard knowledge of their dynamics and potentials. Leadership in a group is a many-faceted role involving knowledge of the way in which it functions, its structure, the impact that it has on its members, and the overall social effects of its existence.

Group work and group therapy, which have developed side by side with small group research, represent efforts to devise a practice theory in which the group and the group process can be used to provide growth experiences for the individual in it, to restore capacities for functioning, and to effect desired social change.

Modern group work evolved from the early settlement house programs which operated on a neighborhood basis to help individuals, families, and groups—particularly new immigrants—adapt to the demands of life in a new country. Strongly democratic in its value system, it stressed self-help and the development of individual and group potential through working together, education, recreation, and equality of opportunity. With the increased understanding of communication, group dynamics, and the meaning of group experience, use of this method has become more widespread. In 1955, the professional organization of group workers voted to ally itself with social work, and this method has become an intrinsic part of social work practice.

The roots of group therapy are sometimes considered traceable as far back as the Greek tragedies. Certainly sharing these early dramatizations of human experience and emotion must have held real meaning for both participants and observers. However, use of the group as a therapeutic tool with conscious awareness of its significance probably originated within the past hundred years, with psychoanalysts and ministers leading the way. At present it is a vital aspect of the entire field of human services, highly experimental, and used to deal with human problems ranging from severe breakdowns in coping ability to enrichment of the life experience of "normal" persons through sensory awakening. In addition to traditional group work and therapy with fairly definite structure and boundaries, new forms and procedures are being tried, all of which strive to achieve some valid and realistic form of human interaction and encounter.

We find psychodrama—the acting out of situations and their emotional components; play therapy—using a play situation to bring out and work through feelings and concerns; marathon encounters—intensive group interaction over an extended period of time; physically oriented groups—in which the body and its physical functioning and the significance of physical contact between people are emphasized; Synanon and similar groups—which employ "attack therapy" to deal with addictions; and other types with special foci, such as the theme groups which concentrate and act on a particular area of human interaction and concern.

Because there are no established rules for these group therapies, structure and operation vary widely. However, some important similarities are emerging. They emphasize (1) total honesty, (2) dealing with the present rather than the past and the future, (3) using both verbal and nonverbal communication, (4) group confrontation, pressure, and support, and (5) personal involvement of the therapist. While none of these is entirely new, all are generally carried to greater extremes than in more traditional therapies.

Community organization, the third area of emphasis in social work practice, shares a growing body of theoretical knowledge with other disciplines such as law, engineering, political science, and so on, as well as the practice theories relating to working with individuals, groups, and social systems. It was late in developing; and as a result, the social problems that called it into being, such as the evils of industrialization and technology, the growth of slums, the development of inadequate and ineffectual social services, and the lack of comprehensive planning, were already well-established. Its origins derived from abandonment of the laissez-faire policy of the pioneer era and development of a philosophical conviction that the society was responsible for the welfare of its members. It involves community development and change through the democratic participation of its members; social planning on a large scale through use of experts skilled in strategies of developing and manipulating social systems; and social action involving organization of disadvantaged segments of the population to bring about changes in both institutions and practices. Work on all three of these levels is based on developing a strategy of action that will bring about change.

In examining these various areas in which workers are striving to create more effective ways of working with people, it is possible to pinpoint trends. These, in part, reflect the natural changes and growth that accompany the accumulation of knowledge with its corresponding development of new insights. In part, the overall social changes that occur dictate the shape and direction that these trends take.

1. It is overwhelmingly obvious that one-dimensional work with many-dimensional people is ineffectual, a waste of time, effort, and resources. This points the way to an interdisciplinary approach to knowledge and to a team approach to practice. It also emphasizes the need for workers to be sufficiently comprehensive in their knowledge and skill to select from a variety of interventive modalities in order to help clients to use both their services and those of other workers who specialize in one particular approach designed to meet a particular need. This realization has come, in part, as an outgrowth of a strongly humanistic trend that has affected the behavioral and social sciences. Theory building that emphasizes the totality of people—the physical, emotional, intellectual, social, and spiritual wholeness—as opposed to a more mechanistic breakdown of people into parts has become increasingly significant.

2. It is also clear that individuals cannot be separated from the social context in which they function, and yet the separateness and uniqueness of each individual cannot be ignored. To be effective, the worker with families and formed groups must be equally aware of what is happening with the individual and what is happening with the group.

3. Although the basic principles of communication and interaction between and among people are only beginning to be understood, their significance is becoming increasingly apparent. Adequate functioning in these areas is essential to a healthy life.

4. The responsibility of clients for their own lives and their own adaptation has never been more apparent, even in a society that seems to be moving toward increasingly mechanistic controls of people. Self-help on the client's part, doing with as well as for on the worker's, are basic to any fundamental change.

5. Changing the environment as a way of enabling the individual to change is being examined from new angles ranging from sophisticated experiments in behavior modification to social action. It is clear that individuals alone can rarely control and change their social situation; the system is much more likely to

perpetuate the maladaptive behavior. We realize that we are "sending a boy to do a man's work" when we help individuals to change and return them to an unchanged social situation.

6. Because of the shortage of professionals in all of the human services, the last few years have seen the development of para-professionals in many fields—law, medicine, nursing, social work, teaching. We are now engaged in the task of defining the roles of the workers on each level and designating the rewards. But in developing these new hierarchies, there is increasing danger that we may lose sight of the client's humanity. The highly skilled professional often does not have time to meet these needs; technicians and aides do not have either the general or the specific knowledge of the current situation and often are not permitted to obtain it. This is particularly true in medicine. Patients complain increasingly of unanswered questions, frightening experiences of tests they do not understand, and technicians, nurses and aides who cannot or will not explain. Somewhere in these definitions of roles, we must make a specific place for the skilled and knowledgeable person who is responsible for meeting this basic human need: the worker who can use self-awareness and involvement in terms of the client's capacity to participate. Otherwise people face the debilitating and destructive experience of being "things" caught in the wheels of a vast inhumane machine.

7. The concept of the role of the helping person—the worker—is changing. "New" workers are freer, less formal, more open in use of self, more direct, more willing to undertake experimental approaches, less inclined to stereotype self and client, and less committed to retaining the status quo of the employing institution. The impact of anti-intellectualism is strongly felt in the worker's role. "Feeling" is often considered more important than "knowing," and workers, under the pretense of "honesty," may use the helping relationship to deal with their own problems rather than those of clients. This tendency to negate the importance of rational processes is unfortunate at a time when the knowledge base of the behavioral sciences is expanding, and sadly, it has happened before. We have long recognized that ignorant emotionalism, good intentions, and operation from a base of intuitive and personal understanding produced little in the way of results. One's

ability to control one's own life will not come from a denial of this aspect of oneself.

RELATED READINGS

(The first six references are basic texts from the various disciplines that have contributed largely to our knowledge of the individual and society. They have been selected, in part, for their readability and general appeal. They are good reference books, and their exposition of basic principles and related bibliographies will point the way for further study.)

Anthropology—Keesing, Roger. *New Perspectives in Cultural Anthropology.* New York: Holt, Rinehart and Winston, 1971.

Biology—Etkin, William; Devlin, Robert and Bouffard, Thomas. *A Biology of Human Concern.* Philadelphia: J. B. Lippincott, 1972.

Psychiatry—Aldrich, Clarence. *An Introduction to Dynamic Psychiatry.* New York: McGraw Hill, 1966.

Psychology—Zimbardo, Philip and Ruch, Floyd. *Psychology and Life.* Glenview, Ill.: Scott, Foresman, 1975.

Social Work—Ferguson, Elizabeth. *Social Work: An Introduction.* Philadelphia: J. B. Lippincott, 1975.

Sociology—DeFleur, Melvin et al. *Sociology: Human Society.* Glenview, Ill.: Scott, Foresman, 1973.

Freud, Anna. *Ego and the Mechanisms of Defense.* New York: International Universities Press, 1946. Interesting and significant link in the development of psychoanalytic theory toward its present social orientation.

Flavell, John. *The Developmental Psychology of Jean Piaget.* Princeton, N.J.: Van Nostrand, 1963. Basic text on the formulations of a key thinker and his way of regarding human development.

Gerwitz, James. *Non-Freudian Personality Theories.* California: Brooks/Cole, 1965. Comprehensive survey of various theories of personality.

Glasser, William. *Reality Therapy.* New York: Harper and Row, 1965. Practical, organized presentation of one way of working with people.

Harris, Thomas. *I'm O.K., You're O.K.—Practical Guide to Transactional Analysis.* New York: Harper and Row, 1967. Good, clear presentation of theory and techniques of one approach.

Kramer, Ralph and Specht, Harry. *Readings in Community Organization Practice.* Englewood Cliffs, N.J.: Prentice Hall, 1969. Comprehensive well-selected collection of readings.

Lowenberg, F. M. *Fundamentals of Social Intervention.* New York: Columbia University Press, 1977. Practical definition of the content and process used in planning and implementing social interventions from a social worker's point of view.

Parad, Howard J., editor. *Crisis Intervention: Selected Readings.* New York: Family Service Association, 1965. Excellent collection of articles on short-term work with people in crisis.

Perlman, Robert and Gurin, Arnold. *Community Organization and Social Planning.* Companion Volume—Ecklein, Jean and Lauffer, Armand. *Com-*

munity Organizers and Social Planners. New York: John Wiley and Sons and the Council on Social Work Education, 1972. Two textbooks—one of theory and practice principles and one of case illustrations for community organizers.

Perls, Frederick et al. *Gestalt Therapy.* New York: Dell, 1951. A study that emphasizes looking at the total person with the potential for self-realization.

Roberts, Robert and Nee, Robert, editors. *Theories of Social Casework.* Chicago: University of Chicago Press, 1970. Collection of articles by leaders in development of social casework.

Rutenbeck, Hendrik. *The New Group Therapies.* New York: Avon Books, 1970. Comprehensive survey of group therapies with analysis of strengths and weaknesses.

Satir, Virginia. *Conjoint Family Therapy.* California: Science and Behavior Books, 1967. One person's definitive model of working with families.

Yates, Aubrey J. *Behavior Therapy.* New York: John Wiley and Sons, 1970. A systematic account of behavior modification, including history, applications in various settings and with various problems, and critical evaluation.

9
Utilizing Skills, Techniques, and Tools

Those who would climb a mountain would do well to sit down first with binoculars and survey the terrain in order to select the best path for reaching their desired goal. They can then pick up ropes, crampons, and ice axes, and start out with direction and purpose. Those who have mastered a valid theory have a pair of strong binoculars. They have the knowledge necessary to consider alternatives and exercise options in both direction and methods of procedure and are able to visualize a goal and probable outcome.

Human service workers who possess a solid base of theory of personality, social interaction, and modes of intervention and who have set an attainable goal must then consider what particular path they will follow and what tools they will need. Their selection and use of tools will be determined by theoretical base, personal style, needs of the client, and what is available. Valid tools and techniques evolve by an orderly procedure from an equally valid theoretical base.

PERSONAL STYLE

It is essential to remember that workers utilize themselves as people. Their weaknesses as well as their capacities and strengths must be considered in selecting methods and techniques of procedure. Because each individual is different, all workers must develop their own style and their own way of handling the tools of the trade. This is the element of artistry that is a vital part of such work.

Complete objectivity is unattainable just as complete negation of personality is undesirable. Only robots or machines are exact duplicates of each other and operate exactly alike. While it is necessary in using certain procedures, particularly certain types of testing and therapy, to minimize as much as possible the factor of the worker's personality, it is always present. One must be oneself, and by knowing and accepting oneself, one can then consciously utilize one's own capacities in working with other people. Maturity, sex, wit, physical condition, warmth, freedom of expression, intelligence, and many other characteristics underpin the individual style of a worker.

Just as our mountain climbers, knowing themselves to be weak in rappel would probably select a terrain that would require as little use of it as possible, so workers, knowing their own capacities, would consider alternate ways of providing necessary help to the client if they have problems with specific techniques.

Thus basic theory and style combine to form a foundation for the helping process from which specific techniques of implementation have been and are being developed. However no list can be complete, because all workers also develop their own methods. We must remember also that there is a difference between a frank and honest assessment of one's strengths and weaknesses—and perhaps even a verbal acknowledgment of this to the client—and a burdening of the client with the worker's own concerns and problems. Again, this is one of those fine lines that workers must tread. How much can they share of their own concerns and still keep the major focus where it belongs—with clients and their problems? There has been a trend in recent years toward more freedom and flexibility in this, but we can err in that direction also. Like all other judgments that workers must make, this will depend on the individual situation and the need of the client.

SKILLS

A technique is no better than the skill with which it is used. The effectiveness of all techniques depends on the worker's mastery and use of the basic skills of (1) differential diagnosis, (2) timing, (3) partialization, (4) focus, (5) establishing partnership, (6) creating structure.

Differential Diagnosis

Differential diagnosis is that capacity of workers to understand the uniqueness of client and situation and to adapt their techniques to this uniqueness. To make valid and realistic adaptation, workers must be aware of the specifics of personality and situation involved, and the diagnosis must be objective. Compassion or anger over pain, social injustice or circumstance, judgmental attitudes or intolerance of behaviors, or feeling for the client must not blind workers to the hard reality of the client's self and situation.

Overidentification with clients because of the worker's personal hang-ups is detrimental to objective vision and clear thinking. This is an area in which good supervision and/or consultation are invaluable, as workers often have blind spots about their own personal needs and problems that can cause inability to be objective about clients' similar problems.

This is particularly important in working with people from varying cultural backgrounds whose ways of thinking, feeling, and behaving may be quite different from the worker's own. A middle-aged foster mother who had raised children of her own might find it quite difficult to accept help from a young, unmarried caseworker, unless she and the worker had very carefully defined the roles of each and recognized the areas in which each had expertise.

Differential diagnosis also, and perhaps most importantly, should involve an assessment of the client's level of functioning. A recent study of printed forms given to clients in a public welfare program revealed that they were largely designed to be understood by people with a college education. Such people are not usually found on the welfare rolls. The forms therefore tended to be meaningless without careful interpretation. The worker's efforts will be equally meaningless unless they are geared to the capacities of the individual client.

Timing

Timing can refer to two different aspects of workers' tasks. The first is the personal tempo by which workers live and operate and the effect that it has on their capacity to relate to people who have different patterns. Do they move too rapidly or too slowly for the people with whom they are working? The client's inability to keep pace with the worker can result in a complete breakdown of the work that both are involved in. We can observe this with both individuals and groups, and workers who are unaware of this difference in life tempo risk losing their clients.

An obvious example is the speed with which people learn. Workers who do not gear their teaching to this—as in giving instructions for completing one of the complicated forms so prevalent in modern life—often fail in their task. Equally, the client whose capacity to see cause-and-effect relationships is quicker than the worker's may be lost to boredom and lack of trust.

The second aspect of timing refers to what Shakespeare called that "tide in the affairs of men" which must be utilized at the strategic point or the momentum is lost. Again the selection of this crucial point is a matter of judgment that the worker must make on the basis of both generalized knowledge of people and specific knowledge of the particular situation. A good example of this is the timing of advice, which should only be given in response to a verbal or non-verbal cue that the client is receptive to it. The man whose anger at authority makes it impossible for him to secure a job may not hear the worker's advice to stay calm until his inability to do so has created a crisis. Then, perhaps, he may be able to begin questioning his own part in causing the crisis.

Partialization

Partialization is necessary because problems rarely occur singly or with only one dimension. They are often of such magnitude that they seem unmanageable. The number, diversity, and complication may be overwhelming and may leave the client temporarily unable to act. The client literally does not know where to begin. The worker's responsibility is to assess the totality, help break it down into manageable units, help the client think about and decide where to begin. For example, a poor, black family may experience a multiplicity of problems including unemployment, poor health, malnutrition, mental retardation, marital difficulties, school dropouts, delinquent behavior. When the factor of racial injustice is added it is clear that some priority must be established, some decisions reached as to where to begin.

Partialization also includes the setting of priorities, the determination of what needs to be done first. A single problem may act as a keystone and when this is dealt with, the others tend to fall into place. Unemployment or underemployment often is that keystone. Better work, more money, better family relationships, better nutrition, better health, etc. may follow in that order. It is essential, therefore, to identify this keystone.

Focus

Focus refers to the worker's skills in concentrating both worker's and client's efforts on the significant aspect of the situation that requires work and retaining that focus until some conclusion has been reached. It involves thoroughness of consideration and may be applied to understanding one aspect of the problem under study, or one alternative for solution. This can be illustrated by looking at the worker's task in dealing with almost any committee which has been formed to study a highly charged social issue about which its members feel strongly—as a committee of students, faculty, and parents created to consider a dress code. The worker must keep the discussion focused on the immediate problem, rather than getting sidetracked on any of the issues that are certain to be raised. With individuals, particularly those under stress or unaccustomed to rational thinking about their concerns, this skill is essential.

Establishing Partnership

Partnership refers to a working association between worker and client in which each understands the role and tasks of the other, and together they form a coherent whole that has purpose and direction. It is based on understanding and acceptance of the differences in these roles and tasks. It is a relationship of complementarity rather than similarity.

The helping services are founded on the belief that both ethically and pragmatically people must be involved in solving their own problems and that effective and lasting change comes from within. Clients must help themselves as much as they are able and make all decisions of which they are capable. The only justification for the worker's existence is an ability to supply what the client lacks. The worker must know how the client's concerns can be effectively dealt with and must be able to help the client use this knowledge. Without this ability, it is a case of the blind leading the blind—a pooling of ignorance.

Although the worker must make the judgment about the type of partnership needed, how it will be developed and used, and where it will go, this can only be done effectively with the maximum participation of the client. One example of this is the partnership that must develop between the worker who is teaching behavior modification techniques to parents of a lively five-year-old who has learned that he can effectively upset them by demanding drinks of water and three bedtime stories every night. In this partnership, the roles of teacher and learner, of enabler and doer, of supporter and dependent are clear.

Structure

Structure refers to the setting and boundaries that are most conducive to the work that needs to be done. Again, the worker is primarily responsible for defining these, but the client should share in the decisions. Physical setting—where, how often, under what circumstances, length of time worker and client should meet; delineation of rules—spoken and unspoken—that will govern these contacts; agreement as to what client systems, what helping systems, what overall social systems need to be involved, must all be decided upon before the work begins. A major part of the structure is the orderly process of helping that the worker utilizes.

Structure must always be flexible if it is to meet dynamic human need, but even the most flexible structure must have a firm foundation, and in this instance it lies in the values, knowledge, and skill of the worker.

TECHNIQUES

The basic skills considered above are implemented through use of various techniques or methods of procedure. We will examine some of the major techniques here.

Small Talk

Frequently, at the beginning of a contact—interview, discussion, conference, or meeting—inconsequential conversation that has no part in the real business of the relationship will be used as an ice breaker or to put client and worker at ease. In a committee, meeting, group or class this could take the form of introductions, a cup of coffee, a speaker's introductory joke, etc. It has utilitarian purpose because it offers clues and affords opportunity for preliminary judgments which are made by all participants about the nature of the persons involved. However, it can create more anxiety than it allays, particularly if carried on too long, or if used to evade the real purpose of the contact. It is a part of the worker's task to assess the utility of this form of communication, use it as needed, and get down to the work at hand at the propitious time.

In a crisis situation when feelings run high or immediate action is essential, use of small talk is usually contraindicated. If used, it should be with sensitivity to the situation and the pressure of anxiety, fear, anger under which the client is laboring. The immediacy of the crisis will have some bearing, as will the client's familiarity with the worker.

Paul and Hobart, two immature sixteen-year-olds who frequently had trouble controlling their own impulses, arrived at the principal's office chaperoned by an angry teacher. Both bore visible signs of combat. The principal resisted the impulse to say, "Again?" (although this might have worked) and asked quite directly, "What's the trouble?" To have used small talk in such a situation would have indicated complete lack of sensitivity to the situation.

Anne, a fifteen-year-old, and her mother came straight to the counseling service from the doctor's office where the suspicion of her pregnancy had been confirmed. Embarrassment, anger, and conflict were evident in the tension and signs of tears as they entered the worker's office, but the needs here were different from those above. To give them a chance to assess the kind of person they were facing in the worker, and the situation that was new to them, the worker opened with, "Did you have any trouble finding the office?" Depending on who answered the question and how it was answered, the worker would then continue in this vein or, picking up on cues given, proceed to the heart of the matter.

How the client defines the worker's role must also be considered. A uniformed policeman appearing at the door usually creates enough anxiety to make immediate identification and explanation of the purpose of the visit desirable. However, small talk and social amenities are frequently initiated by the client and are responded to by the worker who understands the client's need for such communication. When the worker is making a home visit, most clients seem to find it more comfortable to break the ice with inconsequential talk, and in ongoing contacts this can become an almost ritualistic part of interviews that is dealt with and then put aside for the real purpose of the relationship.

The purpose and nature of the relationship itself will determine the extent to which social amenities are a part of the worker's role; the worker should always be aware of how they are being used and what they mean. (In alerting a new worker to the problems inherent in socialization, a rural county welfare department director told the following story: A worker visited an elderly man who lived in an isolated section. As it was lunch time, he urged the worker to share a sandwich and coffee, which she did. On her return to the office, she found an imperative memo to see the director immediately. He had received a call from the old client berating him for sending workers "to eat him out of house and home.")

In socialization, as in all things, a happy medium, knowledgeably arrived at, is the desirable goal. Certainly, from our greater freedom in use of self, comes the ability to combine more socialization with helping relationships. But when we do this we must be prepared to understand all the possible implications and deal with the results.

Ventilation

The term ventilation covers a variety of techniques. It involves bringing to the surface, giving expression to, and opening for consideration those feelings and attitudes which need to be broached. It generally refers to feelings that are profound enough to affect the functioning of the people involved and that are preventing rational consideration of the problem at hand.

Feelings cannot be ignored; they must be dealt with. Positive emotions are accepted and dealt with fairly easily, but negative ones may present more difficulty, particularly in a culture where extreme emotional expressions such as anger, hate, and so on are frowned on. Only as workers are able to create a relationship in which it is safe to express any feeling, regardless of its intensity or nature, will they be able to help clients deal with reality.

Human service workers often find themselves wishing that it were possible to put aside their own and their client's emotions while they utilize their rational capacities to deal with the problems of living. Emotions seem to obscure the real issues and impede solutions. Actually, the feelings themselves often constitute the basic problems that must be dealt with.

> *Mrs. Allen is a case in point. A neighboring university was considering Dr. Allen, a brilliant mathematician and department chairman, for an administrative position. When the team assessing his suitability visited the Allen home, they found considerable tension between the couple and an uncertainty about her hostess role that raised concern about Mrs. Allen's ability to fulfill the social obligations of the new job. Because of his eminent suitability for the position, they arranged for an old professor and close friend of Dr. Allen's to raise this question with him. As a result, the couple went for help to a family counselor, who, after interviewing them together, talked with Mrs. Allen alone. Here her initial anger was quickly dropped and she talked at length about feeling inadequate to handle the demands that her husband's increasing importance made on her.*

After securing her bachelor's degree she had worked for many years as a secretary to put her husband through his graduate work. Her identifications were with the "girls" in the secretarial department rather than with the professionals with whom she socialized. Behind this lay her childhood in an ambitious middle-class family in which the parents were never totally satisfied with the achievements of their children, leaving her with a feeling of basic inadequacy and inability to be comfortable with other people who, she felt, were always critical of her.

In this instance, ventilation of these feelings was far from sufficient; it was only the first step, for reversing a lifetime pattern is not done overnight. But it was an essential step in helping Mrs. Allen to accept and start learning to deal differently with her problem.

Mr. Zeigler, on the other hand, had to deal with a transitory emotion that, once expressed, left him free to proceed with the practical details of straightening out his tangled financial situation. He was obviously laboring under great feeling when he came into the credit counselor's office, and it required only the seemingly casual comment, "You really are shook up today," to release an explosion of anger toward the loan company and the small print, not understood, in the time payment contract that had been his Waterloo.

It is not difficult to get people to express feeling; the problem is knowing how much to encourage and how to deal with what is expressed. The worker must be aware of the fact that mere expression of feeling, too long continued, tends to feed upon itself and assume unreasonable proportions. To leave the client wallowing in anger, self-pity, remembered pain, fear, is to do a disservice. In a sense, expressing feeling is clearing out the underbrush that prevents forward movement, and the worker must be prepared to help the client move into the here and now situation, deal with the problems that occasion or are occasioned by these feelings, and concentrate energies on working toward change.

Human service workers have been predominantly white, middle-class people who frequently enjoy a high degree of affluence and social prestige. We are beginning to recognize and attempt to deal with the anger that this may arouse in clients who lack these attributes. These feelings are exacerbated when insensitive or inadequate workers disregard the reality of what it means to be black, Chicano, Indian or poor in our society. In an attempt to achieve honesty in relationships, efforts are being made to develop ways in which these feelings can be ventilated. Workers who do this have the dual responsibility of knowing and facing honestly their own feelings before they aspire to cope with those of their clients.

Support

Support is another term that encompasses many different techniques. In general it means to encourage, to uphold, to sustain. Workers must first know what they are supporting—an internal strength, a way of reacting, a decision, a way of behaving, a relationship. Once they have decided this, they must select a technique that will meet the need and express it in a way the client can understand and use. These may range all the way from listening to the client talk to sharing responsibility and action. Most of what workers do should be supportive; even confrontation and questioning are done with acceptance and concern for the client's need. In supporting, it is important that workers do not make the client's success or failure in the area being supported a matter of workers' "personal" feeling. If a worker does so, clients will have difficulty in sharing and dealing with the failures which are an inevitable part of life, because they will feel that they have failed the worker.

> *The scene was a gestalt therapy session, and the young man in the "hot seat" had just finished describing a dream. The other members had attacked his explanation of its meaning vigorously and had related this to what they saw as the destructive unpleasant aspects of his behavior in the group. When he sat, crushed and weeping, they crowded around him, placing their hands upon him, raising him up, and physically supporting him with their bodies.*
>
> *Mary Williams, sixteen, and long the scapegoat for her family's problems, was supported by the worker in a family counseling session, when he turned rather pointedly to her and asked, "What do you think is the problem in your family?" Here the worker was supporting the girl's right to evaluate and contribute to the discussion and to see things from her own perspective.*

A teacher, an employer, a doctor, faced with the necessity of helping a student, employee, or patient accept and deal with some failure, will often consciously preface statements about the inadequacy by pinpointing and giving credit for some success. Thus the obstetrician who must take issue with his pregnant patient about her weight gain will first indicate the successful results of the other tests. Sustained by this success and support, the patient is better able to accept and work upon the failure.

To be useful, a helping relationship must be supportive, but the element being supported must be realistic. Support on a false basis is more destructive than no support at all, and support alone is not enough. "She always found something good to say," said the mother of a large family with many, many problems in trying to describe what her worker did that was helpful to her; she finished wistfully, "and sometimes she had to look pretty hard because things aren't very good around here."

A helping relationship by its very nature is supportive through the fact that workers are concerned people in and of themselves. Miss Millis, retired after an active and satisfying career, underwent annual examinations because of previous surgery for cancer. Each time she went to get the results of these tests, she called the agency to ask for a worker to accompany her. She wanted an objective person who could support her in her fear and with whose own emotional reaction she would not have to deal if the results indicated a return of the disease.

Reassurance

Although it can be considered a way of supporting, reassurance is important in its own context. It involves assuring clients that the situations with which they are struggling have an attainable solution. Reassurance is a valid tool, in that there is no life situation to which some adaptation cannot be made, even though the fact itself—terminal illness or the destruction of a family home by urban renewal—cannot be changed. It is important that the worker reassure (1) realistically—not using superficial overall comforting that ignores reality; (2) at the proper time, giving the client a chance to express adequately concern and grief; and (3) knowingly, with awareness that both general and specific adaptations are possible in all situations. Wisely used, reassurance can be comforting and enabling. Poorly used, it can create even greater anxiety, as the client will feel that the worker does not fully understand the seriousness of the problem.

Reassurance can also be used with respect to the client's capacities, feelings, and achievements. Clients are often reluctant, particularly when in a situation in which the worker has considerable power to give or withhold the help that is needed, to express negative feelings. Yet the feelings exist and influence the client's ability to use the service. We see patients who meekly agree with doctors although they question the treatment recommended, students who continue with teachers although they feel they are not getting adequate instruction, poor people who do not raise questions or express negative feelings because they are in terror of losing the basic essentials of life. It is the worker's responsibility to reassure clients that they may air their questions and concerns without fear. We can only reassure in this fashion when the relationship is basically honest.

Clients often need reassurance of the significance of their own achievements and of their own capabilities to deal with the problems that face them. This form of reassurance especially must be based on a realistic assessment of clients' capabilities. It is no help to clients to set them up for a failure. But often the factor that enables them to use what they have is the faith of a significant other person such as a teacher or a peer group who feel that they have the capacity to change and grow and who reassure and support them in their efforts to do so.

> *Johnny Webster brought the employment application from the supermarket to his worker and pointed out the question "Have you ever been arrested?" Two years earlier he had been picked up with several other sixteen-year-olds at a pot party and—fortunately—had drawn a suspended sentence. Now he was trying to find a job. "I'll never get one. If I answer 'yes' they won't hire me; if I answer 'no' and I'm found out, then I'm ruined in this community."*
>
> *The worker reassured him that while this would probably make it more difficult in some instances, it certainly wasn't the insurmountable obstacle that he pictured. "It's a reality we have to deal with—so let's talk about ways in which we can handle it."*

Confrontation

Confrontation may be described as laying the cards on the table and looking at them as they are. Workers can confront the client with the reality of the situation, with feelings and behavior patterns that are destructive, with one's responsibility for one's own actions— one's successes and failures. It is an essential technique in that only as client and worker perceive and agree upon the reality can they deal with it. Misuse of confrontation can be devastating, destroying all previous efforts. Workers must assess the amount and quality of confrontation the client is willing or able to use, and must be able to give support if the reality is overwhelming. Workers must not use it to express their own anger and frustration, although these are certainly a part of the reality with which both workers and the client must deal.

The current emphasis on "telling it like it is" makes confrontation the tool of today, because it offers the opportunity to express all the pent-up angers and frustrations of the time. But we are learning by sad experience that it is only a prelude. Unless workers are prepared to follow up with concrete plans for reshaping the reality that they have attacked, their efforts are often more destructive than constructive.

Sometimes confrontation can be used to create sufficient pressure and anxiety to produce motivation for change. This is evident on a large scale when individuals band together to face representatives of a corporation or institution with a situation that is untenable to them and which they wish to change. It is equally true on an individual basis.

Mr. and Mrs. Phillips were parents of one child, Andy, who was becoming a problem in the school and the community with his acting out, semidelinquent behavior. In their eyes he could do no wrong, and they told themselves and everyone else that this was normal growing up behavior. When Andy, in a rage over his girl's going to a teen dance with another boy, smashed the windows of the cars parked on her street and broke the picture window in her house, the juvenile court worker confronted him and his parents in no uncertain terms. Utilizing a series of events of increasingly grave nature, he pointed out the relationship, direction, and probable consequences of this behavior. Along with this confrontation, however, he recognized the parents' affection and concern for Andy and offered resources from which the three of them could obtain help.

To be an effective first step in change, confrontation should be done in terms of specifics rather than generalities. People can understand and accept the need for change if it is related to a specific source of discomfort. Therefore when committees and pressure groups attempt to effect change, an essential first step is to define and agree upon the grievances for which they are seeking redress and the source from which this relief can come; then they may confront the source with the need for change.

In certain kinds of therapy, particularly those in which the client's insight into his or her own feelings and behavior is the immediate goal, confrontation has a particular meaning. It refers to that part of the process in which the client relates incidents in past and present behavior and feelings which tend to follow stereotyped patterns. When the client is unable to perceive these patterns, the worker may confront the client with them in order to increase the client's awareness of this dysfunctional aspect of a way of living and to help the client utilize this insight to modify feelings and behavior.

Conflict

Although not necessarily a technique, conflict is a situation which requires the use of techniques, and the one used most often is confrontation. Conflict itself—disagreement, opposition, and collision—is a valid, necessary, and inevitable part of life. Individuals need to know how to fight, for when differences occur, feelings tend to run high. While the expression of the emotion is a part of the process, the actual business which results in resolving the disagreement depends on rational considerations. The worker must recognize the factor of emotion, allow for its expression, and use power, compromise, and agreement in the resolution.

"How do you fight?" the marriage counselor asks the couple in front of her, thereby facing them with the inevitability and normality of difference, disagreement and conflict, and the necessity of understanding and utilizing the process involved. "You must learn how to fight in this arena," the public relations director tells the group interested in pushing changes in laws through the legislative body. "Everybody has a right to a different opinion," the teacher tells her third-grade class embroiled in an argument over where to go on the May outing, "but now we must reach an agreement as a group that we can all abide by."

It is interesting that in a country whose whole ideology is based on the right of people to differ and to resolve the differences by a democratic process, we have developed a strong pattern that says fighting is not acceptable, particularly in our personal lives, and that a bland surface serenity must be maintained regardless of what turmoil lies beneath. That we must fight to survive is axiomatic and that workers must know how to use the techniques involved, be able to teach them to their clients, and help them become free enough to use them is equally clear. Conflict is an indication of vitality, and its successful resolution, in spite of possible angers, hurt feelings, and grudges, strengthens any system.

Mrs. Marryett had to be taught how to fight in her marriage. The submissive youngest child in a large family, the lowest one in the pecking order, she transferred her pattern of never complaining to her own home. However, resentment over her husband's highhandedness was there beneath the surface, and when their daughter evidenced trouble in school, the guidance counselor picked this up in their discussions. It was only with considerable support and help from the counselor that she was able to face her husband in a joint conference with the statement that things were not really as perfect in their family as he insisted, and to go on to participate in pointing out the problems and deciding what to do about them.

The new expressway out of the city cut across a neighborhood of old, run-down homes in which families had lived for many years. Their value was too little for the owners to buy elsewhere and in their fear and ignorance, they were a natural prey for unscrupulous real estate developers. The outcry of the residents and concerned citizens resulted in the formation of a housing authority, and Seth Thomas was hired to represent the homeowners. His first step was to bring them together to form an organization, define their objectives, and select a strategy. Together they possessed a strength that as individuals they did not, and they were able to confront the city with reasonable demands which resulted in the provision of low-cost housing.

Manipulation

Because of its connotations of changing others "by unfair and insidious means to serve one's own purposes," manipulation is a "loaded" word. In reality, manipulation also means skillful management and as such is a technique that workers utilize constantly. The process itself is a legitimate one and only becomes questionable when it is used destructively. Because we use it, we must face and assess it honestly. The teacher may manipulate a situation to give an insecure student a success upon which he can build; a worker may arrange a "chance" meeting between two amputees or persons with the same illness. Thus manipulating is acceptable when used as a tool to provide a constructive experience, or to achieve a desirable goal. For example, we are manipulating when we select a particular setting for a conference. The evils of manipulation, as with so many other aspects of working with people, arise when we manipulate to achieve our own personal ends, or to push people around without regard for their need and right to participate.

Manipulation of the environment is an essential concomitant of working with people. As they increasingly recognize not only the significance of the environment, but also the frequent impotence of the lone individual in coping with it, workers are taking greater responsibility in this area. However they must always consider (1) the client's right and need to be involved in both deciding and doing, (2) the client's ability to participate, and (3) the distinction between those activities which are appropriate for the worker and those which are appropriate for the client. When the activity calls for special knowledge and skill which the client does not possess, such as reading a chart, making a diagnosis, searching out laws, participation will be different. Thus the worker as the advocate or representative of the client works in the client's interest and, when possible, teaches the client to use these resources.

> *An articulate teenager, Phyllis, commented that there were certain times when everyone needed an adult to help deal with the system. Therefore when she and several other young people were picked up in a local tavern because two members of the group had falsified ID cards to prove age, they secured a worker, in this instance a lawyer, who knew and understood the operation of the legal system to help them work out their contretemps.*
>
> *The Magays lived in a tenement whose plumbing facilities had long since ceased to work properly, and they had exhausted their own resources to deal with the landlord and the city inspector. The worker who became involved not only used his knowledge of how to deal with bureaucracies, but also through the Magays helped develop an organization of tenants who could bargain more effectively with the landlord and his representatives.*

It is particularly important to be able to recognize when destructive manipulation is being used and to know how to combat it. Frequently in meetings, subgroups will subvert the democratic process in order to control.

> *The State International Women's Year Conference met for three days to elect delegates to the national meeting and take a stand on issues. A militant prolife group elected the total slate of delegates from their own members by stacking the conference on the final day. Because of a technicality which allowed all registrants to vote and made no requirement of participation in deciding issues, they were able to elect a slate of delegates who were personally committed to work against the stand of the conference on every issue. This situation could have been controlled by foreseeing the possible result of the lack of proper registration procedures.*

A large part of the activity of any human service worker is manipulation—or skillful management—of resources and persons. This manipulation is most effectively done from positions of power and authority which are derived from knowledge, status, or strength. Because of the dangers of abuse implicit in this fact, it is imperative that the worker's values be soundly based on the integrity and rights of the individual and of the society.

Universalization

Universalization is utilization of the commonality of human experience and the strengths of others to cope with situations similar to those which are troubling the specific client. It can be used (1) to soften the overwhelming impact of a situation with the realization that others have faced and dealt with similar problems; (2) to share and compare knowledge about ways of dealing with them; and (3) to lend the strength of others to the individual with the problem. The worker who utilizes this technique must be sensitive to the particular situation and the needs of the particular client. Each of us not only is but feels unique, and overreliance on this technique may brand the worker as insensitive and lacking in understanding of the client's particular needs.

> *Timing is of particular significance in use of universalization. When young Alice Brown, on her first job as a statistician in a large insurance office, sought out her supervisor to say that she felt she could never learn to do the work, the supervisor sympa-*

thized with the feelings, helped mop the tears, encouraged her to pinpoint the specific incidents that had caused the feelings, and only then remarked comfortingly that most of the new employees felt that way at some time or other, and generally it was a passing thing.

A group of young mothers, meeting at the well baby clinic to talk about their concerns and problems with their first child, found it particularly encouraging when the worker produced tables on behaviors expected at certain ages, emphasizing the flexibility of these norms and the individual timetable of each child. As one mother said, "you knew what to expect and how other parents had dealt with these concerns, and you could answer your sister-in-law when she bragged about her baby having four teeth when yours at that age had none."

The support that can be secured from an individual or group with similar experiences derives in part from elements of universalization. This is most evident in groups whose membership is based on a common handicap, illness, or concern.

Edward Milton, a vigorous active man of fifty-seven, underwent surgery during which a colostomy was performed. Adaptation to this handicap was particularly difficult for him because of its impact on his self-image, and because it demanded such radical changes in his whole style of life. His immediate reaction was severe depression. After helping him overcome his feeling that he "didn't want to run around with a bunch of cripples," the worker introduced him to the members of the Ostomy Club who were well-equipped to help him face and cope with the problems that his physical condition imposed.

Advice Giving and Counseling

Advice giving and counseling are two of the most frequently misused techniques of workers. The dictionary, with unexpected humor, pinpoints the problem by saying that they are based on "real, or pretended, knowledge or experience and wisdom." Actually they are activities which are used much too freely, with very poor timing, without valid assessment of the client's capacity to hear or use them, and to meet workers' own needs to be experts. They become too personally involved in the success or failure of the advice given and frequently tend to base it on a value system that is personal and incongruent with the client's life style.

Despite these problems, advice giving and counseling are valid techniques, and, wisely used, can be effective. Workers must be sensitive to the clues that clients give which indicate that they are asking for or need advice and direct suggestion. To be most effective, they should be based on knowledge, objective analysis of the situation, and judgment of the client's capacity to accept counsel.

The authority of knowledge as a basis for these activities implies that workers who use them know more about how to deal with clients' concerns than clients know themselves. They should be based on objective and realistic evaluation of all of the factors involved, including the actual wishes and desires of clients!

It was reported recently that a physician teaching a course on human sexuality was attacked for lecturing about homosexuality when he himself was not "gay." He responded that he had never been pregnant either, but he could teach about pregnancy. It is true that experience may provide unique learning, but unless accompanied by other knowledge, it rarely affords the wide range of wisdom essential for this authority. Unfortunately, there is a trend toward thinking that experience per se provides all essential knowledge to deal with a particular situation. While its importance cannot be negated, it does not represent the totality and may actually lead to a narrowing rather than a broadening of insight.

Workers frequently have the frustrating experience of proposing solutions and giving advice which the client either agrees with verbally and does not follow, or carries out in such a way that it fails and then says in essence, "See, I knew it wouldn't work." It is a moot question whether workers should give advice based on personal experience, labeling it as such. In general, it is probably not a good idea to say, as one worker who had raised a family of children did, "With my oldest son, I always set midnight and insisted that he be in then." This lends a personal element to the situation that can lead to trouble. Certainly workers use what they learn in their personal experiences, but when logical discussion of solutions is underway, it is better not to personalize the situation.

In the final analysis, the success or failure of this technique depends on the client's capacity to use it and the worker's ability to make valid assessment of this capacity. Clients are most frequently able to use advice and counseling successfully:

1. In crisis situations when their own ability to deal with the problem is inadequate, and they are suffering anxiety, pain, fear, and so on.

2. When they have a well-founded confidence in and respect for the giver of the advice, either as a person or as a representative of a particularly responsible group, such as ministers, doctors, lawyers, supervisors, and so on.

3. When their cultural conditioning or life situation is such that they tend to depend on others rather than themselves for direction and solution.

4. When the advice is given in such a way that their integrity and right to be self-determining are respected, and it jibes with their needs and wants.

5. When circumstances are such that they have no alternative.

Advice is most helpful when it deals with means to achieve ends rather than the ends themselves. Generations of social workers have recorded with great self-satisfaction, "I advised Mrs. Brown to clean up the house" (this may be recorded fifty times in one file) instead of confining their advice to ways in which this could be achieved, if indeed, Mrs. Brown wanted to achieve it, and if it was really necessary and desirable. As one client put it, "I don't need her to tell me what's wrong—I know things are wrong—what I want her to tell me is how to go about setting it right."

> When Mr. and Mrs. Masterson had reached an impasse in their battle even though they were determined to preserve the marriage, they turned to the worker asking for specific advice as to what to do. At this point he was able to suggest specific action—finding a different home for Mrs. Masterson's mother, budgeting, talking over and making joint decisions as to how to deal with the children.
>
> Elizabeth Smelser asked for help from a telephone crisis service when she was depressed, drinking, and had taken several sleeping pills. The worker not only instructed her quite directly to waken her landlady, but also offered and arranged to get emergency care to her.
>
> With her group of nine-year-old Camp Fire Girls, Thelma Campbell used advice to point out that an overnight in the city park was not a good idea, basing it on the danger in this poorly patrolled section. She combined it with suggestions of alternate places they could consider. She also introduced a discussion of behavior appropriate on such an occasion, rather than telling them directly what they should and should not do.

Activities and Programs

In trying to establish communication, create a working atmosphere, and resolve problems and create opportunities for developing the many different kinds of potential for growth inherent in individuals, workers may opt to use adjunctive activities and programs. These can be used to meet needs that are difficult to deal with through other media, and extend the reach of the worker. They permit expression of feelings that are difficult to express and deal with directly on a nonverbal level or in a game situation.

The list of activities is limited only by the ingenuity and resourcefulness of the worker in adapting them to the needs of particular clients. Music, dancing, games, drama, handicraft, naturecraft—all provide additional resources. The worker who uses these techniques must develop knowledge and skill that will help in selecting the medium best adapted to the needs of the situation. This requires knowledge not only of the client and the situation, but also of how well the medium selected meets the needs of the particular situation. When involved with therapeutic and growth producing groups of all ages and conditions, workers tend to turn naturally to programming and activities which can serve many different purposes. To the greatest extent possible the group itself should participate in selecting the activities, and when well-chosen and planned they tend to further the goals of the members and worker.

> *Brad Sills was a probation worker who numbered among his boys a group of seven between the ages of ten and twelve who could be defined as more neglected and predelinquent than delinquent in behavior. They tended to be underachievers and to lack confidence in themselves. Although they were loners, the group gave them protection and support among their peers. They chose to call themselves The Rejects because of their common trouble in being part of any official group endeavor in the school. Reflecting the current trend, the boys chose hiking and camping as their main interest and with Brad's help planned and carried out an eight-day back pack trip into a wilderness area. This common experience with its shared triumphs and demands welded the boys into a group which carried status and gave them an experience in following through on a project successfully, and in the meaning of interdependent relationships.*

When involved with individuals, workers also use such activities to good purpose. Play with children is a widely used and respected technique. Nonverbal adults can sometimes respond to overtures when there is a common activity through which they can express themselves. In a group living situation such as a home or hospital, the withdrawn, nonverbal person who feels lost as an individual can often begin to relate to another person through the medium of activity.

> Old Mr. Wharton, whose paralysis following a stroke made it necessary for him to live in a nursing home, was angry, depressed, and withdrawn from the overtures of his fellow patients. Mr. Felton, a volunteer with many years experience, made this isolated, lonely, bitter man a special focus of his efforts and, in time, capitalizing on the latter's skill as a bridge player, was able to inveigle him into playing cards. At first this was solitaire; then he agreed to make it a doubles game with Mr. Felton, and from there they progressed to cribbage and eventually to a bridge foursome that involved other patients. In this instance, the activity provided the medium through which the client was able to begin relating to people again.
>
> The new executive of the stenographic service, Jane Phillips, came into an office rife with dissatisfaction, suspicion, and alliances among small conflicting groups. A direct, comfortable person, she chose to start her first staff meeting with the seventy odd employees with a game called "gossip," in which a chosen statement is whispered from one person to another with the final hearer repeating it aloud. The physical closeness, the informality, the laughter, and the discrepancies in the final product of this exchange paved the way for an open discussion of channels of communication, sources of dissatisfaction, and suggested changes.

Logical Discussion

Logical discussion is a technique in which the ability to think and reason, to perceive and appraise reality factors, to see possible alternatives and to anticipate and evaluate consequences is utilized. It is most effective when the feeling elements in the situation are under control and the cognitive strengths of the client and worker can be brought to bear on the concern at hand. However, it cannot be successful if the feeling aspects of the problem are ignored. Time and again planners face programs and solutions to problems that founder on the rock of feelings, and this is particularly true when plans are being made for other people without their participation. The competent worker—administrator, therapist, or aide—will allow for expression of feeling reactions along with logical discussion, but such expression should not become the major focus.

> *Mr. and Mrs. Braeburn opposed the necessity of placing his senile mother in a nursing home but, having weighed the effects of her presence on the family, reluctantly concluded that it was essential. Discussion and realistic evaluation of both the situation and possible alternatives for solution were facilitated when opportunity was given first for recognition and ventilation of these feelings.*
> *Andy Roberts ran a small machine shop with ten employees. It was an informal business with considerable intimacy and friendship among the workers. When young Paul Jones, the newest employee, was arrested for child abuse, feelings ran high among the men, but Andy, after talking with the probation worker, felt that nothing would be gained by firing him. Over lunch he sat down with the men and raised the question of keeping Paul on—some had threatened to quit if this were done. After considerable expression of strong feeling, they were able to discuss rationally the probable results of his being fired and to agree, at best grudgingly, to keep him.*

Reward and Punishment

Reward and punishment, or positive and negative reinforcement, are techniques that workers have been theoretically reluctant to use (1) because of questions about whether they were a valid part of the worker's responsibility; (2) because of the judgments involved; (3) because of a philosophical belief that they were a result of the event and need not be externally imposed; and (4) because they often so meet the emotional needs of workers that they are afraid to use them. Actually they have been used extensively on a more or less intuitive basis. Hopefully with the development of the theoretical knowledge underlying use of behavior modification techniques, they can be employed more definitively with greater understanding of the causes and greater ability to anticipate and control the consequences.

Behavior modification poses a specific model, and the worker who opts to use it needs specific learning, particularly regarding the behavior to be reinforced and the methods of reinforcement. However, as theoretical knowledge of behavior and causation grows, as diagnostic tools become more accurate, as methods of working are tested and their correlation with causation and change and their validity established, we will be better prepared to develop classifications in which causation and symptoms point to definitive methods of such treatment.

Thus the principles of reinforcement are being more widely used with greater understanding than has been involved in the past. As with all techniques, this awareness of what we are doing and why is imperative. Without it, we often succeed in reinforcing that which we would prefer to extinguish.

For example, Sarah, at five, has a well-established pattern of screaming and tantrums whenever she is denied anything she wants. Initially when she used this behavior, her parents, delighted with their first girl after four boys, thought it was "cute," gave in to it, and unknowingly reinforced it to the extent that they now have a serious behavior problem on their hands with a child who has learned to manipulate in a destructive manner.

Justin was an unhappy, withdrawn patient on the men's ward in the state hospital. When the behavior modification approach was adopted by the staff, efforts were directed to reinforce those scraps of behavior he exhibited that expressed his need and capacity for relationship with others. These were rewarded with tokens that in turn he could exchange for cigarettes or candy at the canteen, and in time he was able to use himself more effectively with others. Essential to these efforts was agreement as to the behavior to be reinforced, the method of reinforcement, and the presence of knowledgeable workers, ward aides as well as others, to judge and act when this behavior was exhibited.

Role Rehearsal and Demonstration

In the complexity of modern life, individuals and institutions are called upon to make many changes in the roles they fill. Often these are unfamiliar roles, whose demands, as well as the anxiety occasioned by the change, may create difficulties. The worker, whose view should encompass the general aspect of the situation as well as the part the client plays, can enhance functioning by rehearsing role performance either through discussion or actual role play. The parents participating in the unfamiliar juvenile court hearing, the patient who cannot talk with the doctor, the group wanting to make a presentation to the city council, the committee testifying at the legislature or working out a labor conflict—all can benefit by use of this technique. The worker may choose to demonstrate how these actions can be carried out without using role play. In this instance learning takes place through identification and using the model the worker creates. This is a useful technique for lessening anxiety in approaching an unfamiliar or stress situation, for opening new aspects of it for consideration, for developing new insights into its meaning.

Living in an increasingly complicated society is particularly difficult for people of limited intelligence, and yet current studies in care of the retarded indicate that in many instances the most successful and satisfying placements are within the community itself and not in an institution.

At eighteen Allen faced the problem of having to return to the community after ten years in a school for the mentally retarded. He was fortunate in that he was educable and his studies had been focused on practical living problems. The worker who was assigned to prepare him for discharge utilized extensive role rehearsal of buying, making change, using a telephone directory and bus schedule, following simple instructions, and performing the many other tasks of daily living that are automatic for most people. As part of a group of five boys and girls, Allen went into the community, either alone or with the group, to try out his skills and then returned to discuss his experiences with the others.

Role rehearsal can be used extensively when learning is required, either by discussion or actual setting up of role play situations or by demonstration. By participating in the simulated situation, the client has the advantage of assuming and developing some of the feelings that the actual event will call into play, which can then be identified and discussed. For the retarded, such as Allen, who often carry visible physical evidence of their retardation, the reactions of other people can be a problem. Feelings about this reaction can be brought out in role play and dealt with there.

Studies of Head Start children and of their parents several years ago indicated that these families often have no concept or awareness of how to use the facilities that are the joint property of all the members of society.

> *Conchita Valdez, the five-year-old child of migrant laborers,*
> *faced with her parents the additional disadvantage of seldom*
> *being long enough in any community to become familiar with*
> *it. During the six weeks' picking season, the Head Start worker*
> *who drove Conchita and the other migrant children to school*
> *took them on frequent field trips to see and use community*
> *facilities. In the classes, they learned to relate to each other and*
> *to work with people in a group, to use books and games, and*
> *to create for themselves. The worker also got to know the*
> *Valdez family well, and capitalizing on their desire for a good*
> *life for themselves and their children, helped them to develop*
> *the social skills that would enable them to deal more effectively*
> *with the larger society.*

The use of simulated or actual experiences or demonstrations has the advantage of not being heavily dependent on concepts or use of words to communicate ideas. People with little skill in using language can often benefit from this type of learning where a more verbal approach would be meaningless. With a group of foster mothers whose common problem was children who tested their acceptance with severe misbehavior, the worker arranged demonstrations behind a two-way mirror. They observed child-care workers dealing with these behaviors in a small group, then discussed and role played their own methods of handling similar situations.

Audiovisual Devices

Various audiovisual devices such as tape recorders, television recording, films, two-way mirrors can be extremely useful in particular situations such as work with families or groups in which interaction is a problem. The family can view itself in operation and become cognizant of patterns of functioning. Workers in children's clinics can demonstrate to parents various ways of relating to children which can supplement verbal discussion.

In any of the teaching responsibilities inherent in work with people, audiovisual aids are invaluable. They can extend the reach of the teacher and open new ways of learning. However, there are three principal factors that the worker must keep in mind in preparing to use these aids. In general, it is almost axiomatic that discussion should accompany their use, during which the client has an opportunity to question, react to, and supplement this learning. Otherwise much of their potential is lost.

Second, the worker should master the mechanical details of operation in advance. The malevolence of inanimate objects is a well-documented observation and is particularly evident when their operator is on display as in teaching, interviewing, leading a discussion, and so on. With the perfection of these devices, chances of mechanical failure are lessened, but this is one more instance in which advance preparation will pay dividends.

Finally, these devices should never be used without the client's knowledge or consent. To do so is not only an invasion of privacy but also self-defeating when the client learns of their unauthorized use.

TOOLS

There are other major tools that workers utilize including innumerable ones that are uniquely their own. They may encompass many of the above techniques. All are dependent on three overall skills: interviewing, discussion, and referral.

Interviewing and discussion are unique in themselves but also contain elements of similarity as follows:

1. Each involves two or more people.
2. Both are dynamic processes involving a give and take between and among the participants.
3. Communication within them is both verbal and nonverbal.
4. Both have as their purpose the reaching of some kind of understanding or decision.
5. Both may be formal or informal, planned or spontaneous.
6. Goals of both are both immediate and/or long term.

The differences lie in structure and process.

Interviewing

Interviewing is usually considered a face-to-face meeting between two or more people, although purists would argue that when there are more than two people present, it automatically becomes a discussion. The purposes of an interview are many and varied—information getting or giving, therapy, resolution of a disagreement, consideration of a joint undertaking, and so on. As usual the roles of the worker and client differ, with the worker carrying major responsibility for establishing communication and seeing, hearing, and being sensitive to the client and the client's need. The worker's activity or passivity will be dictated by the practice theory adopted and by the needs of the client.

Although maximum privacy, comfort and lack of interruption are eminently desirable elements in some situations, significant interviews can be conducted in a crowded hospital ward, in a kitchen overrun with children and dogs, and even in a noisy subway. The interruptions of television, demanding children, other workers, phone calls, and so on, can be more disturbing for the worker than the client, whose natural life style may include them. Utilizing the criteria of what both participants can be comfortable with, where there can be the most open and honest thinking and communication, and what is necessary to achieve the purpose of the interview, the worker can be free to capitalize on both informal and formal opportunities.

Interviews that occur within the framework of a purposeful helping relationship are a part of the process of realizing the purpose, and obviously there should be both a general and a specific goal for each. In evaluating the interview, the worker must consider how it moved the relationship toward the ultimate goal, as well as how it met the immediate one.

An interview should have its own structure—a beginning, a middle, and an end. It should begin with the establishment of common understanding and, in an ongoing contact, be related to what has happened before; it should continue through the work of weighing and considering feelings, behavior and events, and conclude with a summing up of what has taken place with agreement of what the subsequent activity will be. In a series of interviews, this helps to provide continuity.

In talking with people, there are ways of putting words together that tend to bring about desired results. In general, the worker will find that judgmental attitudes will inhibit honest communication. The worker's role is not to impute blame but rather to observe the nonverbal cues, listen to the verbal ones, and relate speech and action to what is being seen, heard, and sensed.

WORKERS CAN QUESTION AND RESPOND IN WAYS THAT HELP CLIENTS TO EXPRESS AND UNDERSTAND FEELINGS AND ATTITUDES.

1. By seeing and putting into words both sides of an ambivalent reaction. ("You are both pleased and displeased with your boy's independence?")

2. By taking the client's own words and phrasing a question around them. ("You say you feel funny about adopting a child?")

3. By identifying the attitude or emotion and then taking time to talk about it. ("It sounds to me as if you are frightened. Why does this behavior scare you?")

4. By commenting about what the client is saying and something that has been said or done before. ("And you felt the same way about your first husband?")

5. By accepting silence, encouraging gesture, movement, or murmur.

WORKERS CAN QUESTION AND RESPOND IN WAYS THAT ENCOURAGE THE CLIENT TO THINK ABOUT AND TRY TO UNDERSTAND THE SITUATION.

1. By repeating the client's words in the form of a question. ("You never did get along with any teacher?")

2. By asking for further clarification of a statement. ("Did you mean——?" or, "I don't quite understand what you mean.")

3. By restating the main point the client is making. ("You think that the work of the committee is a failure?")

4. By directly inviting the client to express an opinion or a feeling about the subject under discussion. ("What do you think is causing the increase in drug use among the young people around here?")

WORKERS CAN QUESTION, COMMENT, AND RESPOND IN SUCH A WAY THAT THE INTERVIEW BECOMES A STRUC-TURED LEARNING SITUATION ON WAYS TO LOOK AT AND DEAL WITH PROBLEMS.

1. By selecting and commenting on the area of greatest concern to encourage the client to focus on it. ("You're most uncomfort-able right now about Rick's being so unhappy in school.")

2. By questioning and commenting on ways in which the client has attempted to deal with the situation and the results of these efforts. ("You mentioned that your talk with Rick's teacher wasn't very successful—what actually happened?")

3. By picking up alternatives that the client has suggested or sug-gesting new ones. ("You had considered asking for a conference with both the teacher and the guidance counselor?")

4. By involving the client in future planning and assigning homework. ("Before we talk on the twentieth, would you like to try
setting a regular time for working with Rick, and we can then
see how it worked?")

DIRECT QUESTIONS WHICH CALL FOR SPECIFIC ANSWERS
ARE USEFUL AS A KIND OF SHORTHAND, ALTHOUGH
THEY DO NOT TEND GENERALLY TO LEAD TO MAXIMUM
PARTICIPATION.

If the relationship is good, clients will usually answer truthfully to
the best of their ability, if they are certain that it is safe to do so,
and that the question is relevant and appropriate.[1]

Discussion

Discussion is a type of verbal interaction, of "informed" conversation among a group of people. Ideally it is a democratic pattern of
communication in which each contributes thinking and participates
in the decision making which is arrived at through consensus. Increasingly, life in modern society demands group membership and
group participation, although valid concern is being voiced that in
the process the individual may become lost. Groups come in almost
every combination and size, are formal and informal, and exist for
almost every purpose—learning, therapy, socialization, problem
solving, recreation. They are characterized by a developmental process from formation to maturity to discontinuation which can be
conceptualized as proceeding by stages, much as does individual
development.

Group discussion has the advantages of providing opportunity for
contributions from differing points of view, for participating in
decision making and hence greater motivation for accepting and
translating decisions into action, for developing creative potential
of group members, for learning, and for growth and change. Its disadvantages arise from the fact that groups tend to repeat the social
conditions in which they exist and to develop norms for behavior,
power constellations, and pressures toward conformity that can be
destructive. They can be and often are nondemocratic, and the
isolate outside the group is often the isolate within.

1. See Appendix C for example of interview.

Purpose, Leadership, and Dynamics

Workers who opt to use groups and group discussion in working with people will need to keep both these aspects of group membership in mind. They will also need to be concerned about purpose, leadership, and dynamics. Purpose, or the reason for the group's formation, will determine composition, size, structure, and function—how it is organized, how it can achieve the purpose for which it was formed, as well as the method by which it operates. By virtue of their position, workers will almost automatically exert leadership in the discussions even if theirs is not the titular role. While their function may vary in the discussion and activities of the group, it will be their responsibility to see that (1) the interpersonal relationships in the group are constructive rather than destructive by creating a climate of acceptance of difference, encouraging universal participation, and helping to resolve conflict; (2) the process of discussion is facilitated through setting initial direction, seeing that there is clear understanding of the thinking that is taking place, summarizing and emphasizing concerns and agreements; (3) workers contribute new ideas and thinking, encourage others to do so, and facilitate critical evaluation of all contributions.

The dynamics of a group are those operating in any system: (1) the internal relationships among the members, and (2) the external relationship to the environment and task of the group. These relationships fluctuate with the changes within the individuals, with the alignment, realignment, and function of subgroups, and with the process that goes on in the group, both internally and externally as it matures. They are expressed in the development of bond and contract, conflict and resolution, achievement and growth.

In discussion, channels of communication are multiplied in direct proportion to the amount of interchange taking place among the discussants as well as the number of discussants. For example, a classroom situation where the channels are limited to those between the teacher and students could hardly be called a discussion in the true sense of the word. If, however, the discussion is enlarged and communication channels opened back and forth among the students and the teacher, it can become a true discussion with each contributing thinking and analyzing the contributions of others.

What starts as an interview between a worker and two people often ends as a discussion among three people, particularly if the worker is skillful. The basic patterns of communication will alter to encompass all the persons present. The larger the group, the greater the number of possible communication channels, both verbal and non-verbal, and the lesser the chances of total participation, with the possibility of apathy, of formation of subgroups, and use of concealed agenda which enables one individual or subgroup to manipulate the total body in accordance with a preconceived plan. The most significant interchange usually takes place within small groups.[2]

Referral

Referral is the process which helps a client to move on to use another resource for service.

Just as an individual worker cannot be all things to all people, so there is no one social institution that will serve all the needs of a complex individual in a complex society. One of the major problems is that while people may feel strongly that help is needed to effect change, they do not know where or how to get it. They find themselves either at the wrong place, or because of the essential specialization of programs and services and the multifaceted aspect of need, faced with the necessity of going elsewhere, sometimes two or three times. Regardless of whether the need is one occasioned by breakdown in some life area, or by efforts to enlist support for an idea that can afford new opportunities for people, the process is basically the same. The person who advocates an idea usually has an emotional investment in it that is as personal as the one of the person needing help.

Being referred often carries with it elements of rejection, anger, hope, and expectation. The rejection arises when clients are unable to get help needed and wanted from the original worker and must make themselves known and understood elsewhere. An additional step is involved when the impetus for the referral arises with the worker rather than with the client. The worker is faced with the necessity of convincing the client that help is needed and available and encouraging and supporting the client in developing the motivation to seek and use it.

For the client, the following steps are necessary in making use of outside resources:

1. Awareness and acceptance of the need to look outside oneself and one's own resources for help. Development of motivation to act.

2. See Appendix C for example of discussion.

2. Search for appropriate sources through other individuals or institutions, or channels available to public.

3. Selection of a specific source of help, initial approach with statement and clarification of need.

4. Referral made by this particular resource to another division, area, social institution, clinic, and so on.

Sometimes, in the course of an illness, in solving a social problem, in working for the desired social change, it may be necessary to repeat the fourth step several times. The process may be so demanding of both physical and emotional energy and so frustrating that the client may give up before reaching the desired goal and relapse into angry or apathetic indifference.

A competent worker with good knowledge of and skill in the use of referral procedures can so facilitate the process that the client can make maximum use of those aids which are available. Primarily the worker must know what is available to the client and how to help the client use it.

The "what," people and social institutions, are grist for the mill of referring workers, whose initial task is to become familiar with what is available in the particular community. But they will be handicapping themselves unnecessarily if they confine themselves to organized institutions and services. There is a wide range of people, with varying knowledge and strengths, who can be useful as volunteers and as consultants. In some communities they are available through organized volunteer services; in others there are no such groups. In a small community or neighborhood, skills and strengths that can be called upon are often widely known. For example, "everyone" knows that the druggist and his wife will welcome the chance to extend a personal hand to a child in need. As systems grow larger and more complicated, it is often difficult to know not only what is available, but also how to use it. Whenever possible workers should be personally conversant with the persons or institutions to whom they make referrals. There is no substitute for this.

Having located what they consider the appropriate referral resource, workers must decide on the best way to proceed. Their referral is the first step in the client's using the resource and sets the stage for what is to follow. To make the necessary decisions, workers must have answers to the following questions:

1. How much can the clients do for themselves? Is it necessary to

precede an initial visit with a phone call, a report, or to accompany them? Whenever possible, it is desirable for clients to make their own arrangements but, again, people exist on a continuum from being able to manage alone to requiring a great deal of help. It has been found that when workers do more than merely direct in the referral process, clients are much more likely to reach and use the other resource.

2. What is the role of the referring worker with the individual or agency which is becoming involved? This will be determined in part by the nature of the information to be shared (specialized legal, medical, social information which the client either does not have or does not understand will require special activity) and in part by whether the referring worker will continue to participate and work cooperatively with the new resource.

3. What task is necessary to help the client use this resource? Enlisting the help of another person (and technology to the contrary, institutions always operate through people—receptionists, regular staff, and so on) means presenting oneself in an asking role without prior knowledge of what the reception will be or what is in store for the petitioner as a result of this effort. It means risking oneself again with another person, and there is always some attendant anxiety, greater or lesser in degree according to the individual's capacity to deal with it. Thus the worker's initial decision, after gathering enough data to determine where referral should be made and the degree of the client's capacity to accept it, is to decide how the client can best be enabled to use the service. The worker may:

a. Opt to suggest several sources of help, explain each, and encourage the client to evaluate them and choose among them. This is often done with older people who are selecting a nursing home, or with older children in foster placement.

b. Direct the client to go down the hall, or across the city, or to a neighboring community to see a particular person or service. Physicians do this with patients who need evaluation or care from other specialists.

c. Give specific and concrete help on a graduated scale from a preliminary telephone call or letter, provide transportation, arrange for accompaniment, or actually accompany the client on the initial visit and on subsequent visits as necessary.

d. Provide opportunity, as needed, for the client to ventilate feelings of anxiety or frustration and realistic support. By "realistic" we mean interpreting the service in such a way that the client does not see it as a total and easy solution, but as a resource to be used in working toward this solution.[3]

In summary, discussion of skills, techniques and tools can be unending, and as we develop and test them we become more definitive in prescribing their use in particular situations. However, we must always keep in mind the uniqueness of the individual. There will always be the person whose reaction differs from the general one. It is this that calls for the element of artistry and lends much of the challenge to work with people.

RELATED READINGS

Benjamin, Alfred. *The Helping Interview.* Boston: Houghton Mifflin, 1969. Excellent, down-to-earth book on how to talk with people. One of the best.

Barnlund, Dean and Haiman, Franklyn. *The Dynamics of Discussion.* Boston: Houghton Mifflin, 1960. A look at what actually occurs when people are talking together.

Berne, Eric. *Transactional Analysis in Psychotherapy.* New York: Grove Press, 1961. Formulation of a specific way of understanding and working with people.

Branmer, Lawrence and Shostrom, Everett. *Therapeutic Psychology—Fundamentals of Counseling and Psychotherapy.* New Jersey: Prentice Hall, 1960. Basics of counseling theory and technique.

Brilhart, John. *Effective Group Discussion.* Dubuque, Iowa: William C. Brown, 1974. Good, practical fundamentals of discussion.

Cumming, John and Cumming, Elaine. *Ego and Milieu: Theory and Practice of Environmental Therapy.* New York: Aldine, 1966. An effort to correlate theory about the relationship of the individual and society with practice.

DeSchweinitz, Elizabeth and DeSchweinitz, Karl. *Interviewing in Social Security.* Washington, D.C.: U.S. Government Printing Office, 1961. Basics of interviewing as applied in a particular setting.

Fenlason, Ann, Ferguson, Grace and Abrahamson, Arthur. *Essentials in Interviewing.* New York: Harper and Row, 1962. Interviewing skills and techniques with particular emphasis on the effect of cultural differences on the process. Good basic material.

Field, Minna. *Patients Are People.* New York: Columbia University Press, 1967. Fundamentals of working with people who are ill.

Garrett, Annette. *Interviewing: Its Principles and Methods.* New York: Family Service Association, 1942. Good, simple, clear explanation of fundamentals.

Gordon, Raymond L. *Interviewing—Strategy, Techniques and Tactics.* Home-

3. See Appendix C for example of referral.

wood, Illinois: The Dorsey Press, 1969. Sound and useful analysis of the process of interviewing. Extensive bibliography.

Kadushin, Alfred. *The Social Work Interview*. New York: Columbia University Press, 1972. Detailed and comprehensive study of dynamics of interviewing with excellent practical examples and exercises.

Klenk, R. W. and Ryan, R. H., editors. *The Practice of Social Work*. Belmont, California: Wadsworth, 1970. Collection of timely articles on methods of social work practice.

Mahoney, Stanley. *The Art of Helping People Effectively*. New York: Association Press, 1967. Simple and straightforward discussion of the process of working with people.

Middleman, Ruth. *The Non-Verbal Method of Working with Groups*. New York: Association Press, 1969. Excellent discussion of use of adjunctive techniques.

Reed, William and Shyne, Ann. *Brief and Extended Casework*. New York: Columbia University Press, 1969. A look at the advantages and disadvantages of short- and long-term work with people.

Rich, John. *Interviewing Children and Adolescents*. New York: Macmillan, St. Martin's Press, 1968. Useful and stimulating book, the concepts of which can be extended to all interviewing.

Spergel, Irving. *Street Gang Work: Theory and Practice*. Reading, Mass.: Addison-Wesley, 1966. Ways of approaching work with gangs.

————. *Community Problem Solving—The Delinquency Example*. Chicago: University of Chicago Press, 1969. Working with community resources to deal with the problem of delinquency.

10

Working with People in Groups–Families, Small Formed Groups, Communities

During the course of a lifetime, people share in many different group experiences, some constructive, some destructive, often without occasion for ever being concerned about what a group is and what is actually happening within it. Workers in the human services need to be aware of the potential that groups, when skillfully used, hold for improving social functioning and bringing about social change. They need to have the basic concept of the group as a system made up of interrelated parts and they must be knowledgeable about the dynamic relationships that exist between and among these parts that do so much to determine the effectiveness of the total group and the impact that it has on the individuals within it.

For purposes of this discussion, groups, as used as a mode of working with people, will be classified into four categories.

1. The family or family surrogate.
2. Task groups—committees, teams, boards, councils, panels, etc.
3. Developmental groups—education, recreation, personal growth such as encounter, assertiveness, sensitivity and T groups.
4. Treatment groups—these are of infinite variety and make use of a wide range of theoretical frameworks, such as gestalt and transactional analysis.

While any one of these classifications will contain elements of all—

for instance, a good educational group will certainly be developmental by definition and even therapeutic in the broadest sense of the word—it is important to be able to designate specific purpose. This understood commonness of purpose is the glue that holds a diverse group of people together. It dictates the group's size, structure, composition, goals, tasks and roles, process and life span. It may grow out of a common experience, such as alcoholism or heart disease; it may be a felt need, such as the ability to relate better with other people; it may be a desire to develop a community betterment project; whatever it is, it is an interest shared by the members of the group which motivates them to operate together as a group.

Because people have a basic need to relate to others, *natural* groups form in the normal order of things. Outstanding among these, of course, are the family and friendship groups to which people belong. People who work together will also fall into a natural group which meets many of the social needs of its members. There are also *formed* groups which are consciously created in order to deal with a specific circumstance that is of interest and/or concern to many people. In no group does the unity and cohesion that is essential for "groupness" or gestalt (that characteristic of the group that means it is more than the mere sum total of its members) occur simultaneously with the bringing of several people together. In no group does an individual become a group member by merely being present in the group.

THE FAMILY AS A GROUP

While the family is in many ways a unique group, the dynamics involved in any group formation are applicable to it and it partakes of the characteristics of all groups. It is important, however, to be aware of its special elements which lie in:

Purpose—The family is a social institution sanctioned by society and charged with responsibility for (a) nurturing the young; (b) meeting the basic survival and emotional needs of all its members; (c) acting as the first level of socialization and social control. Regardless of the form the family takes, which may vary greatly in different cultures and with changing social conditions, these basic purposes seem to be universal.

Nature of relationships—The family provides a kind and degree of intimacy that is rarely present in other groups. The level of emotional involvement is high and intensity of feelings tends to be great.

Duration—In contrast to most groups, which are time limited, the family evolves with the expectation that it will be a lifetime grouping. In spite of the fact that the rate of family breakdown is higher than ever before, this expectation remains the norm and is often the reality.

Range of differences in members—The family takes in people at all stages of development from infancy to old age. At present the trend seems to be for the generations to not live in the same household, but they are still encompassed in the family group.

TASK GROUPS

Task groups are those which are organized in order to solve a particular problem. They are working groups in the sense that the work done is considered more important than the changes that may or may not be taking place within the members as a result of the group experience. They are generally, but not always, time limited and are disbanded when the work is complete. The variations in life span may be very great. The task force developed to plan orientation for new workers in a plant may have only one of two meetings and then disband; the State Committee on Children and Youth may be ongoing for many years with changes in membership that are staggered in order to give continuity. Task groups are almost infinite in their variation. They may include committees, councils, boards, clubs, and they deal with a great variety of problems. The major criterion for their formation is that the task at hand is one that can be better handled by a group rather than by an individual. Overuse and improper use of groups—particularly, it seems, committees in organizations—is counterproductive and is one of the reasons that they have fallen into ill repute, leading to the development of definitions such as a "committee is a group of the unprepared assigned by the unwilling to do the unnecessary," or "a camel is a horse created by a committee." Task groups have many advantages but must be appropriately and knowledgeably used.

One form of task group that is being extensively used in human service agencies is that of the interdisciplinary team. The complexity of people and services and the need for specialization have made this development essential, beginning with the delivery of health services and extending throughout the entire area. By definition a human service team is a "a group of people, each of whom has individual expertise and each of whom is responsible for making individual decisions, who meet together to collaborate, communicate and consolidate knowledge from which decisions are made, actions taken, and future plans made."[1] As with all forms of practice in the human services, teamwork is a composite process of values, knowledge, and skill, and often team efforts fail because workers either do not espouse the basic values of collaboration, do not possess the requisite knowledge of small group process to understand the dynamics of the team, or do not have skill in conscious use of self in a team relationship—or all three! With the increasing importance of this model, however, it is essential that workers develop the values and master the knowledge and skills necessary for effective collaboration.

DEVELOPMENTAL GROUPS

Developmental groups are those which are designed to enhance the ability of individuals to realize their potential for a meaningful life—to "actualize" themselves to the fullest degree possible. They, too, are infinite in their variety, including the many and various forms of educational groups ranging from those designed to make use of and develop conceptual thinking to training groups designed to impart skills and techniques such as sewing and cooking. They can be highly structured or very fluid. They include all kinds of recreational groups, the more recently developed personal growth groups such as encounter, sensitivity, assertiveness and T groups. In contrast to task groups, they are geared to bring about some change within the individual's self, but they are not based on the assumption that the individual is sick or unable to function.

TREATMENT GROUPS

Treatment groups are those which are designed to serve the person who has an impairment in functioning. Various theoretical approaches such as gestalt, transactional analysis or theory of small group process variously provide a base for what takes place in the group. Usually the commonness in the group is a problem such as mental illness, handicap, addiction, breakdown in social functioning. The worker here usually works as a therapist.

1. Naomi Brill, *Teamwork: Working Together in the Human Services* (Philadelphia: J.B. Lippincott, 1976).

FORMING GROUPS

Bringing individuals into a group is not always easy, particularly when the rationale and impetus for the group rests with the worker or the society through its social institutions rather than with the potential group members. The first, and often the most difficult, task is to get people involved. It is important that these potential members be homogeneous to a degree—that they share a commonness of interest, problem, circumstance, etc. that will serve as a potentially cohesive force in getting and holding them together. One of the strengths of the group, however, lies in the *heterogeneous* character of the individual members, each of whom brings different perspectives and different strengths to the common undertaking. The worker will need to consciously strive for a balance of these two characteristics among the prospective group members. It is this heterogeneity/ homogeneity balance that makes democracy so essential to maximum group functioning. Members must be able to use their differences to advantage and must be made to feel free, safe, and undefensive in order to do so. The climate of the group which ensures this freedom for everyone is a significant factor in attainment of this maximum.

Group formation should be planned on the basis of established need and with input from potential users or consumers so that the service will be relevant to their concerns. This input can be either in the form of personal involvement of consumers in the initial stages of planning or in the accumulation of data to determine need and interest. The success of the effort to get a group off the ground will depend, to a large degree, on the manner in which the worker deals with both this type of information and with the necessary logistics of time, place, transportation, opening up of communication channels, etc. Although people in general are much more knowledgeable about group participation, it is often necessary to do a selling job. Use of the media for communication, notices, letters, and invitations can be effective, particularly with motivated consumers, but for individuals who are not knowledgeable about group experience, there is no substitute for personal contact with opportunity for a give-and-take discussion about the planned group and its relevance to the individual. Beginning commitment can develop here.

The first meeting is of vital importance in determining whether and how the group will actually materialize. This is true of both voluntary groups such as educational ones for which people have registered and paid and for involuntary ones such as a planned group of problem boys from a juvenile court. In the first meeting, individuals involved look at themselves and each other and at the worker in light of personal needs and expectations. The transactions that take place here will determine whether people return, whether they can begin to commit themselves, whether they can risk themselves with each other and with the worker. The second meeting is equally crucial because the initial euphoria that accompanies a new experience is diminished and members are faced with the vision of the work ahead and the realization that nothing comes quickly and easily.

Good planning is essential in successful group formation and the following guide attempts to stress the essentials.

GUIDE FOR FORMATION OF GROUPS

I. *Preplanning*
   A. *This is the stage in which the individual or the "initiating set" of two or more people decides that there is a problem about which something needs to be done and that the group may be the way to do it.* Need is established by brainstorming, a survey, observation, all of which should include input from potential consumers. The basic questions to be decided here are:
      1. Is there a problem?
      2. Is the problem one that can best be dealt with by a group?
      3. What is the purpose of the group?
   B. *Kind of group in terms of size and composition that will best suit the purpose and need.* Although fifteen is generally considered the maximum number that can be included and still have fairly intensive interaction, an educational group could be larger and many groups will be smaller. Consideration should be given as to whether the group is to be voluntary or compulsory and whether it will be a closed group or will be open to new members after the initial meetings.
   C. *Preliminary decisions as to structure.* This again is related to need and purpose. A formal group might have prescribed roles such as officers, a constitution, specific meeting dates and places and a ritual that is mandatory. Certain needs and purposes would demand a less structured group which provides maximum freedom for members to interact spontaneously. At this point some thought should be given to the worker's posi-

tion in the group structure—will the worker lead directly or be an enabler for the leader?

D. *Relationship of group to the host or sponsoring institution (if applicable).* Such institutions constitute the group's immediate environment and may be the source of its funding and make provision for its staffing. Linkages with the sponsoring institution must be established and maintained. Frequently they provide sanction for the group's existence and purpose.

E. *Location and commitment of the necessary resources to establish and maintain the group.* This includes provision for the essential equipment as needed, space, special needs such as baby sitting, special facilities such as audiovisual equipment, etc., and provisions for paying for them.

F. *Reaching potential members.* This initial contact serves the dual ends of (1) interpreting the purpose of the group and its probable activity and membership and (2) informing potential members of the time and location of the first meeting and inviting attendance. As previously stressed, personal contact by the worker or coworker is the best way in which to answer questions, develop interest and secure beginning commitment. In cases where group members are children, it is usually important to talk also with parents or parent surrogates. Not all groups require this kind of reaching out in the initial stage. Letters, the telephone, public announcements such as posters, flyers, and radio and TV spots can be used. Again, the purpose and composition of the group are the deciding factors in selection of the technique for reaching the potential members.

G. *Planning the initial session.* Almost inevitably, except in compulsory groups, not all potential members will become members. The rate of attrition will be lessened, however, if the worker plans this important first session with two things clearly in mind.

1. Why is this group being established? What is its purpose? Do special activities need to be designed to serve the members? What is the anticipated number of sessions? What are the goals of the group?

2. What is known about the prospective members? Special personal characteristics such as age, sex, family composition are important. It is also important to know what it is that qualifies them for membership in this particular group and

whether they have had prior group experiences, good or bad. Occupation and/or school attendance are significant and, depending on the kind of group and its purpose, the worker may need to know the nature of the individual's capacity for social functioning.

II. *The first meeting.* In some types of developmental groups, members are left very much on their own in the initial stages and evolve their own group. However, the worker should be clear as to how this first meeting should move and whether or not to be obviously active. It is helpful to visualize five steps in this process:

A. *Arrival of members.* This will involve direction to facilities such as meeting room, baby sitting, etc., introduction to worker and/or others if desired, name tags if desired, refreshments if desired (maybe here or later).

B. *First total group activity.* What is it to be, how is it to be started, how is participation to be encouraged?

C. *Transition to working on major tasks.* How will the group move from the initial introductory activity into the major work of the meeting? How will the purpose, roles and tasks and goals within the group be defined and responsibilities designated? How will the contract with the worker be defined? How will conflicts be resolved and decisions made?

D. *Future plans.* Will there be a second and subsequent meeting? When, where, how often? Will other members be solicited? What resources are needed to facilitate work of group and how are they to be secured?

E. *Ending.* How will the session end? At a predetermined time? If cleanup is required, who will do it? Is there homework to be assigned? Is the worker responsible for providing transportation for members?

III. *Flexibility and readiness to change plans if necessary.* Because groups are unique and dynamic entities, the best laid plans of the worker might not be appropriate to the situation. Therefore the worker must be prepared to "read" the group and be adaptable enough to change if necessary.

THE WORKER AND THE GROUP

The worker approaches the group with the same problem-solving stance used with individuals but with the added dimension and complexity of the group process itself. The worker needs to be aware of and able to deal with this, not always by controlling it but by knowing what is taking place and when and how to intervene. There are various developmental stages involved in the process by which a congregation of individuals becomes a group. Theorists have visualized them in many ways, but in general they consist of:

1. *Orientation* during which individuals become acquainted with others in the group and begin to understand and to relate to the group.

2. *Accommodation* during which communication channels are opened, values agreed upon and norms established.

3. *Negotiation* during which roles and working arrangements are developed, as individuals have begun to find themselves in the group pattern.

4. *Operation* during which the group moves to perform the task for which it was developed.

5. *Evaluation and, if appropriate, dissolution* when the purpose of the group has been achieved and some assessment is taking place of what has transpired.

These stages are not definitive or absolute and may have to be re-worked if new individuals enter the group or if the group breaks down. Development is continuous and ongoing during the lifetime of the group just as it is with individuals. The strength of the group and the real determinant of its ability to achieve its purpose lie in the re-lationships that exist between the individuals and the manner in which they can work together. Such relationships are dynamic, and, as they change and develop, need to be understood by the worker.

One of the most useful tools workers have developed in thinking about such relationships is some form of the sociogram, which is a chart by which to designate, at any one moment in time, the patterns of communication and the closeness in them.

Marker Junior High School asked the local YMCA to provide a worker to plan a group experience for five seventh-grade boys who seemed to be particularly friendless in the larger school to which they had transferred from various neighborhood ele-mentary schools. By talking with them, their parents, and their teachers, John, the group worker was able to involve them and get the group going. The boys selected Nature Study as a pro-

gram and immediately planned an overnight at a local lake for their fourth meeting. John was concerned by what appeared as a tendency on the part of the boys to scapegoat Mike, a large, obese boy with markedly feminine characteristics. Observing them around the campfire, he developed a chart of their communication patterns as indicative of their closeness of relationship and on the basis of it, moved to tackle the problem of relationships that threatened the life of their group.

Many workers dealing with the family as a group use charts and diagrams extensively not only to develop understanding and insight in the worker but also directly with family members who need to understand what is happening that affects their functioning as a family. As long ago as 1955 workers began to use genograms, which are charts of the relationships that exist in multigenerational levels of families. As family members develop these, they can gain in understanding of the factors affecting current relationships (see Figure 12). Such designs and charts, by making concrete what has been merely a thought, can not only enhance understanding, but also lead to ideas of ways in which changes can be facilitated.

Worker Role and Position
Group workers will find it necessary to occupy different roles and positions in the group, depending, again, on its purpose and the kinds of interaction desired. The three major roles are:

1. Teacher—who imparts knowledge and develops interests and learning skills in a variety of ways.
2. Therapist—whose purpose is to heal or cure and who uses the group process to facilitate this.
3. Enabler—whose job is to make it possible for the group to function and get its work done.

In addition, the workers have to decide what position they will hold in relation to group leadership. They can either be the actual leader or a facilitator for the designated leader who may or may not be elected by the group. In addition to the designated leader, natural leaders will doubtless emerge, and one of the worker's tasks may be to assure compatibility between the two.

In filling the demands of the various roles required of them, group

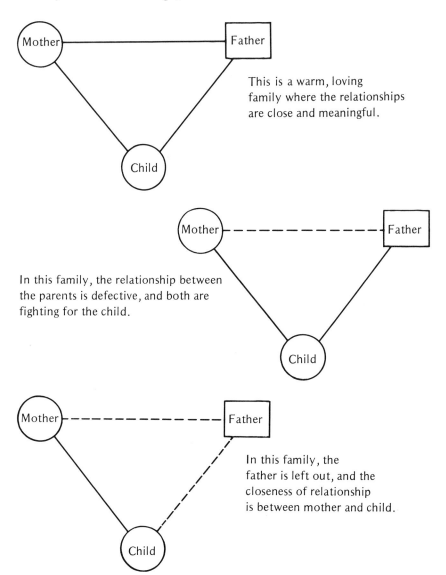

This is a warm, loving family where the relationships are close and meaningful.

In this family, the relationship between the parents is defective, and both are fighting for the child.

In this family, the father is left out, and the closeness of relationship is between mother and child.

Figure 12 The Use of Triangles to Clarify Parent-Child Relationships. Dotted Lines Signify a Defective Relationship and Little Closeness. Straight Lines Signify a Healthy, Close Relationship. (Adapted from theories of family therapy. See Murray Bowen, "Theory in the practice of psychotherapy." In Philip Guerin (ed.), *Family Therapy: Theory and Practice*. New York: Halsted Press, 1976.)

workers will consciously behave in a variety of ways, using their knowledge and skill in understanding of human behavior and group dynamics, as well as concrete knowhow about the availability of resources and the ways in which to use them to meet group and individual needs. To be effective in performance of these roles, workers will need considerable self-awareness, because as people they will be representing a set of values and norms and affecting the other group members by conscious and unconscious modes of behavior as well as by use of the authority they represent.

> *Mary Evans teaches socialization and work skills to a group of retarded adults in a sheltered workshop. These three men and two women are classified as trainable and have all been institutionalized for a period of years. She is a warm, accepting teacher, using demonstration and support on an individual basis. She limits, mediates, confronts and guides. She uses the group strengths to support the efforts of the individuals and is a part of the group but with a very specialized position and status.*

> *Robert Phillips is a therapist working with a group of professed alcoholics in a community Chemical Dependency program. He is in a definite leadership role in which he confronts and interprets aggressively on a basis of acceptance and concern. The group assists him in these behaviors as well as in support of the individual members. In addition, his role is an enabling one in that he opens the way to use of resources for necessary physical care and family and employment counseling.*

> *Ellen Breck is a community organizer employed by a neighborhood association. As such she forms committees and task groups to deal with community concerns. She acts as a planner, enabler, teacher and adviser. Her leadership role is peripheral as her purpose is to free and develop the groups and the community for self-leadership. She is the professional staff person who provides knowledge and skill that enables the committees to plan and to act.*

In addition to workers role in the group, each individual member has a role to fill and these roles must be complementary in order to achieve the desired wholeness that is the group's strength. One of the major internal organizational tasks of the group is to decide who does what, when, where, why, and how in relationship with all the other members of the group. Roles and the behavioral norms that they carry are subject to negotiation both early in the life of the group and, when necessary, throughout its existence. This negotiation takes into consideration not only the personal qualities of the individuals that affect their relationship with the other individuals and with the group as a whole but also their specialized knowledge and skill. Roles can be considered as *structural*—those which are mainly concerned with internal life of the group such as chairperson, leader, secretary, etc.; *task*—those concerned with getting the necessary work done; and *personal*—those which arise out of personal characteristics of members such as specialized knowledge, humor, personal warmth, which affect the life of the group.

Conflict resolution and decision making are equally important to group life. The healthy group provides opportunity for the existence of differences, for open expression of ideas and discussion of issues and for decision making based on maximum participation possible in light of the purpose and structure of the group. One of the major tasks of the leader is to get closure—to move the group to a decision and to action to implement that decision, whether it is when and where to go on a picnic, how to change community attitudes toward adolescent behavior, what a family will do about its faulty communication patterns. Edgar Schein's six ways of reaching group decisions constitute a reminder of the fact that the decision-making pattern of a group can be both constructive and destructive to realization of the group's fullest potential.[2] He cites decision making (1) by lack of response; (2) by authority; (3) by a minority; (4) by the majority; (5) by consensus; and (6) by unanimous consent. Obviously this table represents an ascending scale of desirability, although the purpose and nature of the group will determine to a large degree how much authority the leader has and how it is used.

As a result of its internal organization and its external relationships, the group reaches a *contract* both among its members and with its environment. Usually this contract is unwritten, except in institutional organization plans, and often unspoken, but it represents an understood agreement among the members, between the members and the worker, and between the group and its host setting as to the manner in which the group will work and the purpose for which it is constituted. It is also well to remember that groups do not exist in a vacuum and that some sort of larger social sanction is essential if the group is to survive. This is as true when groups are used by

2. Edgar Schein. *Process Consultation* (Reading, Mass.: Addison-Wesley, 1969), p. 58.

private practitioners as when they are part of a constituted social institution.

Finally, the extensive use of group methods in working with people is not without its problems, one of which is overuse itself—group work is not a panacea. Groups have power, and this power can be used for destructive as well as constructive purposes. Power can be destructive to individuals within the group and can perpetuate or exacerbate personal problems. The tendency of a group to push its members toward conformity with group values and norms can be destructive to creative thinking and behaving. The tendency to isolate or punish nonconforming members can be dangerous. The tendency of all groups, as social systems, to move toward rigidity and closure can be stifling and can only be combated by awareness and provision for new input and use of opportunity for self-actualization of the group.

Responsibility lies with the worker to see that the group experience is a good one for all of the members involved, that the purpose is constructive, and that the group is changed or disbanded if it becomes ineffectual or destructive. The initial composition of the group should be given serious consideration and the vulnerability of the potential members assessed. Creation of a climate that is nonpunitive, that can accept and adapt to individual differences, that provides support for the individual even though the ideas or behavior might be unacceptable, that is flexible enough to work toward change and self-actualization of the group, is paramount.

In the final analysis, the key words in use of groups in human service are "differences," "similarities," "participation," "collaboration," and "wholeness." Group strength grows out of the ability of the group to achieve cohesiveness around a common purpose, to make use of the differences of the people involved through development of a pattern of interaction that allows for maximum participation and working together as a totality.

RELATED READINGS

Brill, Naomi. *Teamwork: Working Together in the Human Services.* Philadelphia: J. B. Lippincott, 1976. Concise practical text using basic small group theory to understand and use the team model.

Guerin, Philip, editor. *Family Therapy: Theory and Practice.* New York: Halsted Press, 1976. Excellent collection of articles on theory and practice of work with families. See particularly Murray Bowen's, "Theory in the Practice of Psychotherapy" for charting to understanding family dynamics.

Hartford, Margaret. *Groups in Social Work.* New York: Columbia University Press, 1972. Survey of theory and practice related to the various uses of groups by social workers.

Horwitz, John. *Team Practice and the Specialist.* Springfield, Mass.: Charles C. Thomas, 1970. Clearly written, useful, complete little book about the dynamics of collaboration on teams.

Klein, Alan. *Social Work Through Group Practice.* Albany: State University of New York, 1970. *Effective Groupwork.* New York: Association Press, 1972. Two well-written generic texts on using groups in human service that give the reader a well-rounded view of the basics.

Lewin, Kurt. *Field Theory in Social Science.* New York: Harper and Brothers, 1951. Old but good. Represents a breakthrough in thinking about group dynamics.

Miles, Matthew. *Learning to Work in Groups.* New York: Teachers College Press, 1959. Practical and ageless, this small book looks at the problems of educating people to use groups.

Wise, Harold et al. *Making Health Teams Work.* Cambridge, Mass.: Ballinger, 1974. Analysis of the practical application of the team model of service delivery in a difficult multidisciplinary community health setting.

11

Reaching
the Vulnerable People

To be poor in an affluent society; to be old and slow in a world
that values youth and speed; to be a child when the family tends to
be weak and when proliferating no-fault divorces are mainly concerned with the rights of adults; to be a member of a minority group
that is by definition considered of less worth—to be any of these is to
be isolated, stereotyped and dehumanized. It is to know that within
the society there are institutionalized supports that tend to maintain
the prejudice and discrimination and close the doors of opportunity.
It is to know the frustration of powerlessness, the bitterness of
knowledge that these conditions tend to be self-perpetuating, the
loneliness of being the outsider, the deadening defeat of unfulfilled
potential.

People caught in such a situation tend to develop one of three patterns of behavior in coping with it. They can (1) mobilize personal
and social resources to deal with the situation and, insofar as possible,
change it; (2) become helpless and dependent (although rarely consciously) and force the society to care for them; (3) strike out in
fear and rage against the forces that they often do not fully understand and cannot control. Human service workers in all areas—the
doctor in the emergency room; the social worker in the welfare department; the teacher in the ghetto school classroom; the public
health nurse visiting the old person in a lonely tenement room; the
foster care worker facing the thirteen-year-old whom nobody wants—
are in immediate and personal contact with the victims of this sys-

178

tem, who are "lonely and afraid in a world they never made," to paraphrase Housman.

In preparing themselves to face this challenge, workers need to be equipped with special knowledge and skill soundly based in a personal value system that assures commitment to understanding these problems in all their magnitude, and motivation to work for their alleviation. Prevention and remediation need to go hand in hand in approaching the needs of the vulnerable people. It is important to know who these people are and where they are found in our present social organization.[1]

The *aged,* by definition people over 65 years of age, constitute about 10 percent of the population or close to 25 million people.[2] They live in urban areas, in rural settings, in special institutions or community developments, in their own or family homes. Their major problems are unemployment, poverty, health problems, legal problems, housing and, increasingly in later years, inability to care for themselves. While the life span has not increased markedly, more people are living to be older, thus increasing the size and seriousness of the problems. In addition, the aged suffer from changing social values in which the old person is no longer considered a desirable member of the family with a useful role to fill, but is a care and an economic liability. Family supports are many times either non-existent or not provided, and the old become objects of economic exploitation by unscrupulous people out to make money from their need.

Children, in large numbers, are at risk in modern American society in part because of the changes that are taking place and affecting the family, which has as one of its basic functions nurturance of the young. These major changes include (1) the increasingly large number of families in which both parents work outside the home; (2) the growing number of children living in single-parent homes; (3) the expansion of urbanization and suburbanization with their attendant problems; (4) the developing trend toward abdication of responsibility by parents for difficult adolescents. In addition, unemploy-

1. Those mentioned above are not the only people who, as groups, suffer from the ignorance and prejudice of the larger society. The handicapped, homosexuals, and, to some extent, women face the same problems.
2. It must be remembered that statistics change constantly and a specific figure describes only a moment in time. Check current material. The statistics in this chapter except as otherwise designated are from the 1976 Statistical Abstract, Bureau of Census, U.S. Department of Commerce.

ment and poverty and the everpresent discrimination based on race and ethnicity affect children profoundly.

These changes are reflected in the following statistics:[3]

In 1974 there were 970,000 divorces or reported annulments involving roughly 1.2 million children.

In 1975 one in every six children under eighteen was living in a single-parent family.

Seven million children presently live in families in which the mother works.

More than 1 million school-age children have no formal care at all between the hours of school closing and parental return from work.

Between 250,000 and 300,000 children live in public and private residential institutions for the mentally retarded, emotionally disturbed, delinquent, physically handicapped, dependent and neglected, and physically ill.

Twenty million children do not receive adequate health care including primary care, immunizations or treatment of disease.

Fifteen and a half percent of children live in families with incomes below the government-defined poverty line.

It is estimated that 284,000 children live in foster family homes, a significant number of adolescents live independently, and 70,000 children are in the final stages of adoption.

The increasing evidence of child abuse is only one indicator of the family under stress, which tends to turn on the most vulnerable member.

The *poor* constitute over 12 percent of the total population or over 25 million people. This figure is based on the governmentally defined poverty line, which designates an income of $2,700 per year for an individual and $5,500 for a family of four. Below these figures, a family is considered as living in poverty. These do not include those marginal people, the underemployed who do not earn enough and the old whose savings are shrinking, who are statistically above the poverty line but cannot live adequate lives on their incomes. Poverty is a fundamental problem for a high percentage of the old and the minorities and profoundly affects children and families. The economic situation, with inflation and its mandatory high percentage of unemployment and underemployment, tends to ensure a poverty class that

---

3. These statistics are from *Toward a National Policy for Children and Families,* published by the National Academy of Sciences, Washington, D.C., 1976.

is self-perpetuating. Critics of the welfare system see it as a way of keeping the poor sufficiently satisfied so they will not resort to violence but providing no real out for them. Contrary to general opinion, however, most of the poor are not on welfare, just as most of the poor work. People are poor for a variety of reasons. Many do not possess the education, skills or power to compete equally. The impact of the ancient belief that equates poverty with lack of morality is still strong and is a handicap in developing adequate programs to alleviate poverty. The poor live in large concentrations in the inner cities as well as in the rural areas where they are often forgotten because of their isolation.

Minority groups generally recognized in current American society include Asian Americans, Black Americans, Mexican Americans, Native Americans and Spanish Americans. They constitute roughly 13 percent of the total population and are found in disproportionately large numbers among the poor. They live in both urban and rural settings, with major concentrations in ghetto areas of large cities, on reservations, and in certain rural settings where migratory labor is extensively used.

Historically the United States has been committed to the melting pot concept as far as white peoples from differing ethnic groups were concerned. This meant that cultural differences were minimized and all people were blended into one uniform group. This solution to the problems created by differing peoples living together was successfully applied to the immigrant groups of Czechs, Irish, Jews, Russians, etc, but was not applicable to nonwhite people. Laws relating to intermarriage, ownership of property, enfranchisement were not uncommon, and only limited integration of nonwhites was permitted. As the minority peoples pushed to become a total part of the society, American racism became increasingly apparent—racism based on color with black being at the lower end of the continuum, white at the higher end, and brown and yellow somewhere in between. This racism rests upon a value system relating to the greater worth of whiteness and is supported by various social institutions which are designed to perpetuate it. Such institutionalized racism is evidenced in education, in the legal system, in economic life, in political and social institutions and—to our everlasting shame—in the human services.

With the realization that the doors to participation and integration of minorities will remain closed without major changes in the dominant white society and with the awareness that people need tremendous supports to develop and maintain healthy self-images in the face of constant prejudice and discrimination, a movement for development of a so-called pluralistic society has grown up in which each minority group would retain its own integrity, develop its own culture and institutions and deal with the opportunities and restraints of the larger society with its group strengths. Obviously such a social system has both advantages and disadvantages, but the tenacity of institutionalized racism in white society has made it attractive to many people.

One aspect of this movement has been the demand for the provision of workers who are members of a particular minority—racial, religious, sexual (such as women or gay people)—to work with members of that group. Proponents of this idea believe that only such workers can truly understand the perspective and culture of the clients involved and only such people are committed to equal service. This concept has been used in the human services in employment of the so-called indigenous workers, but research tends to indicate that it is not the race or religion or personal characteristics of the worker and client that determine success but the worker's competence. The challenge to workers, regardless of background and origin, is to develop the ability to work with people who differ in language, customs and behavior from themselves.

The four specific groups of people postulated in this presentation have two major characteristics in common: (1) they tend to be stereotyped, segregated, and discriminated against and (2) they find themselves personally powerless to deal with the social forces operating to maintain them in this position. Leon Chestang, writing of the black experience, has studied character development in a hostile environment, one characterized by social injustice, societal inconsistency and personal impotence.[4] This environment tends to place responsibility for the problem situation on the individual rather than on the society. It poses a massive personal task of integration in making a healthy adaptation to the demands of a society that denigrates both the individual and the group. In order to survive in the larger society, members of these groups are forced to come to terms with a potent force that constantly and in many ways says they are no good. This is truly an impossible dilemma, and it is not surprising that people react with rage and fear, turning inward against them-

---

4. Leon Chestang, *Character Development in a Hostile Environment* (Occasional Paper No. 3, November, 1972, University of Chicago).

selves or outward against others. It is surprising that so many of the victims of this situation retain the ability to function adequately and to mobilize themselves and others in a constructive way to try to change the society in which they must live. It is understandable that social pluralism becomes increasingly attractive as a way of changing a destructive system.

One of the less constructive ways that clients may use to cope with this situation is learned helplessness which may consciously or unconsciously be adopted as a mechanism of defense. Recently psychology has come up with some interesting laboratory experiments dealing with the effect of learned helplessness on motivation and capacity to survive in animals. Rats, when physically restrained for periods of time, will struggle frantically for a while and then lapse into passivity. When dropped into containers of water they give up and drown much more quickly than those in the control group who have not been restrained and who make much greater efforts to survive. The feeling of helplessness appears to involve physical changes as well as changes in motivation, cognition and emotion.

Although there is some danger in applying the findings of laboratory research on animals to human beings in a "free" setting, it is obviously possible to observe the same dynamics operating with people who have never developed (or who have lost) the sense of being able to control their inescapable situations. Generally, they too will fight until they learn that their efforts to control outcomes are ineffectual. When the sense of ineffectualness becomes overwhelming, passivity, dependency, depression cannot be far behind.

The major goal of workers in such situations must be to help clients develop and maintain feelings of personal adequacy that will help them mobilize themselves and others to change the destructive environment. However, workers will have to deal first with the feelings involved and must expect that these feelings will be dumped on them as representatives of the destructive society with which these vulnerable people must cope. These feelings were well expressed by the skinny ten-year-old foster child who turned on her worker shouting, "Don't you come around here bringing me a Coke and telling me you love me when next week you'll be gone." Increasingly workers report their own frustration and concern about the apathy, anger and possible violence that they must face. The answer does not lie in teaching workers karate or other means of self-defense as has been done in some welfare programs, although there might be situations in which they could be useful. The answer lies in recognizing the normality and predictability of such reactions and in being prepared to cope with them in a more constructive manner while at the same time, often, being required to administer programs which are in themselves reflective of the destructive forces in the society that created them. While workers cannot totally defuse a situation with a client who is using a worker as a whipping boy for personal frustrations and the ills of the system, it is possible to be forewarned and prepared to deal more effectively with the situation.

Workers must see clearly what is happening; be prepared by knowing how they as individuals fit into what is happening; be able to maintain within themselves "an oasis of sanity" in a schizophrenic situation. They need to be equipped with five major tools in working with the vulnerable people:

1. Self-awareness—workers must know how they stand in relation to these people who are considered of lesser worth by the total society.
2. Awareness of the impact of the worker's self on others and the manner in which worker and situation are perceived by clients.
3. Motivation and ability to deal with the special problems of communication brought on by differences in language and culture.
4. Possession of concrete data regarding the group and the client as a member of that group. As no group is monolithic, individualization is of tremendous importance; stereotyping is not only stupid but ineffectual and often dangerous, as evidenced by the recent movement to disenfranchise gay people.
5. Understanding of the social situation that contributes so largely to developing and perpetuating problems, and knowledge and skill in working to change both society and its institutions.

On the basis of these values, this knowledge and these skills, the worker attempts to remedy the destructive effects of the social situation and prevent their continuance. A major role in serving these people (which, it must be remembered, is also serving the total society) is that of advocacy in both the legal context of "one who pleads the cause of another" and the political definition of "one who argues for, defends, maintains or recommends a cause or proposal."

As an advocate:

on an individual level, the worker might, as a guidance counselor in the school system, go to bat for a troublesome teenage boy who had been excluded from the school because he got into a fight. The appeal would be based on his legal right to an education.

on a citywide level, the worker might, as a health service planner, spearhead a community effort to develop a maternal and child health clinic in the inner city which is poorly served by hospitals. The clients in this instance would be the people of the neighborhood, and the advocacy would be based on the right of all people to adequate health care.

on a state level, the worker might, as a social worker in the Commission on Aging, work to ensure adequate inspection of nursing homes, enforcement of standards of care and improvement of those standards. The clients in this instance would be old people and their families, and the advocacy would be based on the right of all people to safe and adequate living situations.

on a national level, workers from many different specializations in the human services might work to ensure the passage of legislation to put teeth into the housing laws that permit people to live wherever they wish regardless of race, creed or color. The clients in this instance would be primarily members of racial and religious minorities and the poor, and the advocacy would be based on the right under the law of all people to live where they wish.

As is obvious from the examples cited here, workers cannot be effective advocates without considerable knowledge of the rights to which people are entitled—both inherent rights and those guaranteed under the Constitution and the laws of the country.[5] One of the major problems of human service workers in this area is that they tend to champion people and causes on the basis of ideals and emotions rather than on the basis of hard knowledge.

Rights are those things to which people or society have a just claim and cannot, in American society, be denied to them without due process of law. Both individual and societal rights are relative and exist within a state of balance that may fluctuate as relationships are perceived differently, as technology develops, as conditions change. For example, individuals owning land have the right of private property, but when coal is discovered under that land in this day of energy shortages, the society has a right to use that coal for

---

5. I am indebted for much of this formulation of the material on rights to an unpublished paper, "What Social Workers Don't Know About Rights," and conversations with the author, Dr. James Garrett, School of Social Work, University of Nebraska.

the "greatest good for the greatest number," particularly if that land happens to be an Indian reservation! The teenager in our first example has the legal right to an education, but the other students have equal rights in this area, and the school system has administrative rights to operate an effective educational program. A current question among human service workers is whether, in light of what we know about the nature of human development and the demands of parenthood, young adolescents twelve to fifteen years of age have the right to have children. Statistics being gathered seem to indicate a correlation between dependency on public support and adolescent parenthood, as well as between child abuse and adolescent parenthood. Public welfare and family counseling agencies express increasing concern over the numbers of young people, still children themselves in many ways, who are taking on the demands of parenthood with no real awareness of what is involved. If the pressures become great enough, society will be forced to decide if this is an inherent or legal right.

This relativity, expressed by Rousseau in *The Social Contract* as far back as 1762, is even more meaningful in our present complex society with its many different people and demands. Rousseau said that "social order is a right—a sacred right that serves as a basis for all other rights; it does not . . . flow from force. Yet it does not flow from nature either. It therefore rests upon agreements."[6] Such agreements are in a constant process of being reworked, and we are presently taking a hard look at those relating to the rights of individuals and those of groups.

It is easy to see that there are built-in conflicts in the concept of rights, and workers who aspire to be effective in this area must be prepared to understand and deal with them. In order to be effective, they must either be personally knowledgeable regarding the laws on all governmental levels that codify and establish most of the rights that we have, or have access to resources that will provide the necessary knowhow. Increasingly law schools are emphasizing humanistic aspects of the law; the American Civil Liberties Union is an invaluable resource, and educational programs for human service workers in all areas are including knowledge of the legal system and ways to use it in their curricula.

In addition to knowledge of the legal system, knowledge of the

6. Jean Jacques Rousseau, *The Social Contract,* Willmoore Kendall, tr. (Chicago: Henry Regnery, 1960), p. 2.

legislative process is of paramount importance. Not only must workers know how to develop, introduce and support legislation effectively, they must also know how to be pragmatic lobbyists. One of the major current trends in human service systems is what is known as their "politicization"—their entry into politics in an effort to affect the system in which we live, not only in their own interests but in the interests of their clients. Workers who will operate here effectively will do so on the basis of knowledge of communication of innovation, ability to form and work with coalitions, and ability to compromise, all of which must rest on a realistic assessment of social situations.

The role of advocate and that of social changer go hand in hand. Changes involve three different levels:

1. The society as a whole when conditions exist that are destructive to people. The society gives final and overall sanction to change and therefore must be involved.

2. The large social systems such as political parties and professional disciplines, which may, either unknowingly or because of self-interest, perpetuate destructive patterns. These are, in a sense, the gatekeepers of change, which is passed on to the society through adoption and enforcement of laws and policies and education of practitioners.

3. Organizations which, for many reasons, may not be responsive to changes in their environment such as population shifts, changes in public policy, practice method, social values and organizational styles.

Because societal change is generally a long-term process and comes in response to a multitude of variables, workers will need to be able to mobilize a variety of people and interests in their efforts to facilitate such change. One of the most useful and effective tools is the mobilization of the vulnerable people into self-help groups. This is one of the great strengths of a pluralistic society, providing, through numbers and organization, power to the powerless. When a number of such groups exist, coalitions among them to work on common interests can provide even greater strength and bargaining power. Such groups are seen presently in the Gray Panthers and other organizations of old people; in the various racial caucuses and groups such as the National Association for the Advancement of Colored

People; in the organizations of the poor. Only the vulnerable children cannot use this tool themselves and need people to use it in their interest, such as the parents of retarded children.

As with individual rights, group rights are a matter of balance between those of the total society and those of the subgroup and between the subgroups. When one group benefits at the expense of others it can lead to a polarization that is potentially destructive to the whole. In developing such groups, workers need to keep this reality in mind. In staffing such efforts, the worker's role is an enabling one—enabling people to use their own strength, so that the worker bows out and people take over for themselves—which is as it should be.

Organizational change is often equally difficult, as workers may be faced with the need to make changes in organizations of which they are a part, and there is an element of personal risk involved. While it is a generally accepted concept that systems (an organization is defined as a social system created for a specific purpose—see Chapter 13) tend to move toward closure and self-maintenance rather than toward dynamic productivity, we tend to forget that there is an equal tendency toward survival, development, and realization of potential for growth and change. No organization is impermeable to the changes that take place in its environment, and environments are dynamic and always changing. Organizations may accept or reject pressures but they cannot ignore them. For example, the adoption of an affirmative action policy on a national level and the attachment of this to the allocation of federal funds has constituted an environmental change for organizations such as hospitals and universities that has mandated internal change.

A good organization has built-in provisions for self-appraisal and established channels for input from its environment, the consumer, and its own personnel. Changes in policy and personnel that reflect the environmental changes going on around the organization can often be initiated by concerned people within the organization.

The role of the human service worker in serving the vulnerable people cannot be limited to work designed to enable individuals to adapt to the status quo. This merely perpetuates the destructive nature of the situation and the problems inherent in it. There is certainly a place for work with individuals and families struggling to deal with their environment in a constructive way, but along with this must go an all-out effort to make the environment a healthier one.

There is an old story of a social psychiatrist and a psychoanalyst walking together along a river. They came to a drowning man, jumped in and rescued him. A little farther along they saw another and rescued him. When they came to the third, the social psychiatrist said to the analyst, "You jump in and pull him out. I'll run ahead and see who's pushing them in."

It's time we ran ahead.

RELATED READINGS

The related readings for this chapter are endless and those cited here are the ones that I used in preparation. Readers are urged to look for the writings of people who live or have lived these lives and to supplement them with experiential learning—talking, working, living with the vulnerable people.

Alinsky, Saul. *Reveille for Radicals.* New York: Random House, 1969. *Rules for Radicals.* New York: Random House, 1971. Still the best practical primers for workers aspiring to make social change. Erudite but pragmatic.

American Civil Liberties Union Handbooks on the *Rights of Americans.* New York: Avon Books, current. These invaluable little paperbacks, which are constantly revised to keep them up to date, deal with the rights of groups of people—Women, Students, Teachers, Suspects, Poor, Gay, etc., etc.

Barry, John R. and Wingrove, C. Roy. *Let's Learn About Aging.* New York: John Wiley and Sons, 1977. Excellent and up-to-date compilation of articles dealing with all aspects of aging—good for understanding and practice.

Chestang, Leon. *Character Development in a Hostile Environment.* Occasional Paper No. 3, November, 1972, School of Social Service Administration, University of Chicago. Profound analysis of what happens to people, in this instance blacks, who live in a destructive environment. Excellent for basic understanding.

Daniels, Roger and Kitano, Harry. *American Racism: Exploration of the Nature of Prejudice.* Englewood Cliffs, N.J.: Prentice Hall, 1969. Clear and understandable analysis of racism in America.

Knowles, Louis and Prewitt, Kenneth. *Institutional Racism in America.* Englewood Cliffs, N.J.: Prentice Hall, 1969. Collection of well-edited articles relating to the origin of racism and the institutionalized factors that tend to perpetuate it.

National Academy of Sciences Advisory Committee on Child Development. *Toward a National Policy for Children and Families.* Washington, D.C.: National Academy of Sciences, 1976. Useful, clearly written and brief report on a study of the major current problems of families and children with pragmatic recommendations for dealing with them.

Rousseau, Jean Jacques. *The Social Contract* (1762), translated by Willmoore Kendall. Chicago: Henry Regnery, 1960. Fascinating, amazingly current little book that all students of the human condition should be familiar with if only for the statement, "Man was born free but is everywhere in bondage."

Satir, Virginia. *Peoplemaking*. Palo Alto: Science and Behavior Books, 1972. Good, simple, easily readable and usable book by one of the real pros in work with families.

Seligman, Martin E. *Helplessness: On Depression, Development, and Death*. San Francisco: W. H. Freeman, 1975. Report on the findings of the psychological studies dealing with learned helplessness.

12

Dealing with Dependency

In winter, the plains of Nebraska are often characterized by snow and ice storms and severe cold. Life for both humans and animals can be difficult. The friend who sat beside my desk was a child of the pioneers who, a short hundred years ago, learned to live with this land. She was six months pregnant with her first child, her husband was out of town, and her tears were occasioned by the fact that the pump on the windmill was frozen, the cattle were without water, and the truck she drove to do the morning chores was stuck in the frozen ice and mud in the barnyard.

"Surely there's someone in your family who can help you with this work," I suggested.

This occasioned fresh tears. "I want to do it myself!" she sputtered angrily.

From a people within a culture at a particular time in history had developed this resolute, determined young woman who found it so difficult to say, "I need help," "I need to depend on someone else."

So strongly is the ethic that lauds independence as the great virtue inculcated in our society, so difficult is it to admit and voice the need for help, so great is the fear and loathing of "dependency," that often only a tragedy makes it possible for people to request necessary assistance. There is something shameful in admitting that one is incapable of dealing alone with the demands of living. Human service workers—physicians, teachers, social workers, police officers, ministers—are all too familiar with the people who come for help too late and then only when a crisis occurs that permits no other solution.

Why do we protest so greatly against what is a natural and necessary state? Why do we deny this part of ourselves and worship the myth of an isolated and independent soul riding alone into the sunset? Like Shakespeare's lady who "doth protest too much," is the extremity of our denial an expression of our very need to be dependent upon each other?

The whole question of dependence is fraught with emotion and characterized by cloudy thinking and inconsistent behavior. Our society sets no clear guidelines for its members. By creating absolutes of the two states, dependence and independence, we have lost sight of their relative nature and their essential coexistence. By glorifying the kind of competitiveness that must inevitably end in a winner and a loser we have created a system that does not allow people to relate naturally in a supportive way to each other.

No one is ever totally dependent or totally independent. We are interdependent both as individuals and as societies, and interdependence is made up of both dependence and independence in a state of balance. In themselves, these two characteristics are neither good nor bad; rather it is the totality, the weaving together, the balance in which they occur that makes them desirable or undesirable, constructive or destructive.

Humans as a species are characterized by the need of a longer period of nurturing than any other life form. Despite this, there is a drive toward self-determination within the infant, whose dependence is only a matter of degree appropriate to its particular stage of development. If one tries to confine the seemingly haphazard movements of an infant's arms or legs, its face will redden with rage as it opens its mouth to scream. The infant wants to do what it wants to do when and how it wants to do it. The extent and manner in which these early strivings develop will depend on the way they are dealt with. A child can be given total freedom of movement, thought, and feeling or can be wrapped in intellectually, emotionally, physically, socially, and spiritually confining swaddling clothes. The need to free oneself for development in all life areas is built-in and scheduled to unfold in accordance with one's own individual timetable. In no sense, however, does one develop from one absolute state to another— from absolute dependence to absolute independence. Rather one exists in a state of relative dependence/independence according to one's need at a particular time in the life cycle. Given a perfectly healthy individual, in a perfectly healthy milieu, a perfectly healthy balance of these two needs would result. But in specifying a healthy milieu, it must be emphasized that we do not mean one without stress which ultimately is essential for development, but one in which there is a good balance of challenge and support.

THE FLEXIBLE CONTINUUM
OF INTERDEPENDENCE

Using the concepts from systems theory provides an effective way of looking at interdependence. When we define a system as a whole made up of interrelated parts, we are also defining interdependence. Each part supplements and complements the others, and the system that attempts to function without this give-and-take relationship gradually moves toward ineffectualness and eventual calcification through its own rigidity and isolation. So it is with the individual's balance of dependence/independence needs. However, perfect balance is a static concept and can scarcely be applicable to anything as dynamic as life. When we look at individuals, groups, and societies, we see a constant shifting and changing as they adapt to changes in each other. The healthy system possesses a flexibility that enables it to make these adaptations to both internal and external changes. This adaptability, this capacity for adjustment and readjustment is the essence of healthy interdependence.

The individual who requires hospitalization is a case in point. One of the secrets of a successful hospital stay is the capacity to be dependent, but it is equally important that upon recovery the patient be capable of giving up this dependence and moving again toward independently making the decisions and performing the activities that were done by others during the illness. Diverse problems arise when the patient needs and wants to remain a patient.

Thus we could say that every system—and the individual is as much a system as are groups—possesses a range of capacity for interdependence, involving a continuum from extreme dependence to extreme independence. Adaptations to the demands of living require the ability to move back and forth freely along the scale, and inability to function except on one extreme or the other tends to be pathological. The person who needs and wants to be totally free of commitments, of give-and-take relationships with others, constitutes as great a problem to self and society as the person who can never walk alone.

TWO ASPECTS OF INTERDEPENDENCE

Our interdependent society might be viewed from two different frames of reference: (1) that which revolves around the essential give and take that is required to provide material needs and services; and (2) that which relates to self-determination, capacity for decision making, and relationships with others.

Given the myth of the independent individual, which is fostered from earliest infancy in this society, one who finds oneself in a position of requiring outside help in either of these two areas frequently faces a situation that is destructive to morale. The stigma attached to admitting need and seeking help often creates as much trouble as the actual difficulty itself. The very nature of human services requires that practitioners deal constantly with the problems caused by these attitudes, with those created by individuals who are on either extreme of the continuum of interdependence, and with those which arise from the nature of the helping relationship itself, which contains within it elements of dependence and authority.

THE ROLE OF THE WORKER

Workers themselves are products of this society and culture, which have created an unrealistic monolith and made a fetish of independence. They cannot avoid being affected by these attitudes. In addition, they have within themselves the same dependence/independence strivings which are a part of individual identity. They may have selected their jobs because of their own needs to control others and have others dependent upon them. Consequently they sometimes approach their work as a divided person, as did the student who wrote in his analysis of the impact of his own cultural conditioning, "I will always have to watch my own attitudes in working with men who do not support their families. In my home town, that man was the lowest of the low."

As always, the worker's first task is to look at the reality of the situation, consider if it should and how it can be changed. The problem created by society's attitudes is a frustrating one because it not only creates difficulties for individuals in need, it also prevents the enactment of laws and development of programs that would create the conditions leading to the growth of capacity for healthy interdependence. Fortunately, however, we seem to be maturing in our capacity to accept not only our own personal needs for outside help, but also the similar needs of other people. Society in general seems to be accepting the reality of human need and assuming greater responsibility for those who are unable to provide for themselves. When the causes of dependency can be visibly demonstrated, as with children, old people, and the physically handicapped, recognition of the need for social responsibility comes more easily than, for example, with the healthy appearing adult who cannot work.

Despite these attitudes, recognition of the interdependence of all people seems more pervasive than ever before. The very existence of wide-range planning to enable people to realize their maximum potential—regardless of how limited it may be—bears witness to this. The ecological movement extends this philosophy, and we are beginning to recognize the interrelationship of all life forms. A major problem seems to hinge on developing the knowledge necessary to enable us to create a good society, but if the dynamic developments in the behavioral sciences have any validity, we should find ourselves possessed of increasingly effective tools for this purpose.

However, workers' tasks go beyond developing new knowledge. They must use what we at present know: (1) to attempt to create the social conditions that lead to the development of the individual's maximum capacity for interdependence and (2) to utilize sound practice methods that tend to lessen the client's need to function on either extreme of this continuum.

What must the society provide so that its members may develop maximum capacity for healthy functioning? It must provide the basic human needs:

1. Insurance of access to adequate material resources—food, clothing, shelter.
2. Provision of opportunity for growth in all areas, according to the potential of the individual.
3. Provision of a climate that does not overprotect and ask too little, or demand so much that it cannot be achieved, but one that involves a balance of opportunity and responsibility.
4. Provision of reward for risk and supports in failure.
5. Provision for increasing self-determination and involvement in decision making according to the capacities of the individual.
6. Provision of opportunity for satisfaction of emotional needs, and the development of a value system that gives meaning to life.

The reader will note that not only should these six conditions be a part of the entire social order, they are also an essential part of family life. The developing child who has these advantages within the smaller family unit has a good chance of developing into a healthy adult who possesses a flexible balance of dependence/independence.

SOCIAL CHANGE

It is obvious in looking at this list that there are many people in our society who do not have even some of these advantages. As a society we pay dearly in human suffering, in loss of the potential strength that these people represent, and in actual financial cost of caring for them. It is to the advantage of the total group that its members develop a healthy capacity for interdependence. It is equally clear that the individual worker cannot effect the massive social changes necessary to make this possible. Collective planning and action on the part of clients, workers, and representatives of the general public are essential, for all of us have a stake in this necessary change. The unique contribution of the worker to this undertaking should be knowledge of how to proceed that is not derived from any one discipline or approach. So simple yet fundamental a change as safeguarding small children from nibbling at lead paint in slum dwellings requires varied knowledge of: (1) drafting and putting through ordinances that will require this protection such as those in some cities which require covering the painted walls with plasterboard; (2) knowing and utilizing the power structure and bureaucracies in the city to see that the laws are enforced; (3) developing and using channels of communication to enable the people involved—landlords, tenants, and homeowners—to know their rights and responsibilities and how to discharge them; (4) knowing how to work with people to help them to secure and use necessary legislation and develop the motivation to act. All this, for one small aspect, and we have not even touched the basic problem—the absence of decent housing that our people can afford.

In our anger, our moral indignation, and our frustration, and under the misnomer of social action, some of us have advocated burning the house down. Workers without adequate knowledge and preparation have rushed forth "to bring about change" without knowing what they need to change, how they will make the changes, what they will replace the present systems with. They forget that confrontation is only a technique within a strategy and to be effective must be followed by action to replace and build. Too often they succeed merely in polarizing the various factions involved, and because they do not have the vision to anticipate the possible reactions to their action, leave the situation worse than it was before they started.

Social change can and has been achieved, but it can only be constructive when it involves use of a disciplined, knowledgeable action based on assessment of the reality factors involved and development of a strategy to deal with them. Perhaps this is what we have learned as, in the 1970s and 1980s, we settle down to struggle with the social problems that the violence of the 1960s brought inescapably to our attention. Without sophisticated knowledge, we can never understand and deal adequately with sophisticated human beings and their increasingly sophisticated society.

RELATIONSHIP ROLE

In practice, workers will have to deal with the end result of the overall social system in its effect on people, as well as the limitations inherent in personal endowment. They will work with those who are so severely damaged that they possess little or no capacity for directing their own lives, or of relating effectively to other people. A part of the initial assessment will involve looking at where the client is on the continuum of dependence/independence and meeting the client on the basis of this reality. The helping relationship should provide a firm floor at the level of clients' needs, upon which they can stand for support as they move toward increasing ability to exercise their own capacities to a greater degree.

It is extremely difficult to establish this firm footing for people when there is no way of assuring them freedom from want of the material and spiritual necessities of life, and when there seems little realistic hope that circumstances will change for them in their lifetime. Nevertheless, this is the task that workers are faced with, and the kind of relationship that is established must be based on recognition of this hard reality. It must be characterized by acceptance of people as they are, of expectation of what they can be, and based on a mutuality of understanding and interest in dealing with the personal and social reality which they are facing.

The worker's initial assessment should establish the client's capacity for self-determination and for decision making which leads to action, as well as for give-and-take relationships based on flexible interdependence. The dependence that causes the greatest possible concern is a matter of attitudes and feelings that make it difficult for clients to take responsibility for themselves and their own actions and to be overly dependent on someone else in these areas. This has little relationship to economic status—although the poor are most frequently accused of "dependency." Once the level of this capacity has been established, the knowledgeable worker relates to it in terms of expectations of what the client can and will do and gears the opportunities presented and demands made to this level.

The client's involvement in the total process supports and extends the capacity for self-determination. The self-help groups which have developed so widely in the past few years among many different kinds of people with common interests and concerns are a good example of this. The worker's emphasis is "we will work with you to solve your problems" rather than "we will solve them for you."

Much of the so-called dependency of clients is not a true dependency at all but a paralysis caused by lack of opportunity or lack of knowledge of existing opportunities. The worker must differentiate between true psychological dependency—incapacity to be self-determining—and that which is only situational.

There are some people who have never developed their capacity for independent thought and action for a variety of reasons. Overprotective parents on all social levels often help to produce this condition in their children. In instances where the traumatizing experiences have been too great, some individuals will never be able to stand on their own feet. Clearly all these people do not fall into the groups of those whose dependency society is able to accept—children, the aged, the handicapped. Some of them are healthy appearing adults, who unfortunately are emotional children. With them, the worker's task is often to provide the kind of decision making for them which they cannot provide for themselves.

It seems axiomatic that the more monolithic and undifferentiated we become in our attitudes and thinking, the less real understanding we possess. Life is infinitely complex, and uniformity rarely exists within the whole. Nowhere is this more true than within individuals and their societies; nowhere is it more true than in our understanding of interdependence. To deal with the problem realistically we must dispel the obscurity of distorted values and emotions and recognize the clear voice of reality that testifies to our essential and unending need to rely on each other.

RELATED READINGS

The reports of the various President's Commissions include timely and pertinent material about the social problems that contribute to dependency. Some of the more useful are:

"The People Left Behind." U.S. Advisory Commission on Rural Poverty. Washington, D.C.: U.S. Government Printing Office, 1967.

"A Time to Listen—A Time to Act—Voices from the Ghettos of the Nation's Cities." Washington, D.C.: U.S. Government Printing Office, 1967.

"The Challenge of Crime in a Free Society." Report of the Commission on Law Enforcement and Justice. New York: Avon Books, 1968.

"Kerner Commission Report." National Advisory Commission. New York: Bantam Books, 1968.

Carter, Genevieve. *Growing Up Poor*. Washington, D.C.: Welfare Administration Publication No. 13, 1966. An assessment of the impact of poverty on families and children.

Harrington, Michael. *The Other America*. Baltimore: Penguin Books, 1963. A classic that deals with the extent and meaning of poverty in this country.

Irelan, Lela. *Low Income Life Styles*. Washington, D.C.: Welfare Administration Publication No. 14, 1966. Assessment of research on how poverty affects the life style of people.

O'Neill, Robert. *The Price of Dependency*. New York: E. P. Dutton, 1970. A lawyer describes what happens to the civil liberties of the poor.

Pearl, Arthur and Reissman, Frank. *New Careers for the Poor*. New York: Free Press, 1965. A proposal to "hire the poor to serve the poor."

Reissman, Frank et al. *Mental Health of the Poor*. New York: Free Press, 1964. An assessment of what happens to the mental health of people who live in poverty.

Will, Robert and Vatter, Harold. *Poverty in Affluence*. New York: Harcourt Brace Jovanovich, 1970. The meaning of being poor in an affluent society.

In addition to these readings, which deal mainly with the dependency induced by lack of social justice, see those appended to Chapter 5 which relate to the meaning of dependence/independence in helping relationships, those of Chapters 7, 8 and 9 which are concerned with considerations of theory and practice, and particularly Chapter 11 on the vulnerable people in our society.

13
Being Accountable for What We Do

The human services have come a long way since the initial efforts of the Good Samaritan, who undoubtedly existed in every developing human culture. They have become institutionalized, increasingly large and complex, utilizers of a sophisticated technology and of a growing proportion of the national income.

The total gamut of social services designed to promote the highest possible functioning of individuals and society and to remedy individual and social breakdown is so great that it is difficult to comprehend. Included are those services designed to provide prevention and remediation of problems and opportunity for maximization of potential in all of the five life areas—the physical, social, emotional, spiritual and intellectual. In a sense we presently consider the major business of society to be ensuring the "good life" for its members, as both a moral obligation and a pragmatic way of providing for the health and survival of the society itself.

The period of the late 1800s and early 1900s when such services began to be institutionalized could be considered the "honeymoon period." Tremendous leaps were being made in knowledge about the nature of the human condition, and with their usual incurable optimism, people believed that we needed only to study, understand and control in order to eradicate human problems. The medical concept of cure as following automatically from study, diagnosis and treatment, and the misunderstood promise of the early psychoanalytic theorists of new, pristine inner selves contributed to this miscon-

200

ception, which, unfortunately, is reinforced presently through the news media in order to secure support for both politicians and programs.

Within the last decade, however, particularly since public funds began to replace private contributions as the major source of financing for services, there has been an increasing and healthy emphasis placed on both ensuring the quality of the services provided and evaluating their effectiveness. With sober second thought has come the realization that the best intentions in the world and increasingly large amounts of money do not ensure permanent solution of human problems which are more realistically perceived as a normal part of life.

Within this framework has come a demand for "accountability," so much so that the word has become almost a cliché and is often used without real understanding of its significance or of who is accountable for what and to whom.

The word *accountable* is defined as meaning "liable to be called to account or capable of being accounted for or explained." Implicit in these definitions is the significance of the concept for human services. Accountability in human services involves being responsible not only for what is actually being done but also for improving the quality of what is being done. Implementation of this need for accountability requires constant evaluation and reevaluation of structure, program and policy of the various social institutions planning and delivering service; of the practice of the workers delivering the service; and of the results, both short- and long-term, of the service. It requires the development of forms, instruments and procedures used in collection and evaluation of data; it involves critical analysis of the forms, procedures and instruments themselves; it requires a flexibility of workers and institutions that enables them to both know and use new ideas and procedures that are being developed.

Accountability in human service exists on three levels: (1) to the clients, users or consumers of the service; (2) to colleagues and to organization or agency; (3) to the society that sanctions the entire operation. Sanction by clients is expressed by their use of the services; sanction by society is expressed by financial support, by laws, by participation of laypeople on boards and committees, by work as volunteers in the programs. The interests of the clients on the one hand and the representatives of society on the other may be in conflict, and the worker and/or the agency may be caught in the middle, particularly when one is demanding changes that the other does not support.

For many years Bethesda Hospital had been an essential and well-used part of the downtown area of the city. With the movement of most of its medical staff and clientele into the suburbs, the Board of Directors voted to close the facility in the inner city and rebuild farther out of town. The people in the area, predominantly black and Puerto Rican, who made heavy use of the hospital's emergency room facilities, would have been left without a hospital. As consumers they organized to retain the care that they needed. The conflict was between them as the consumers and the social sanctioners as represented by the Board of Directors. The staff was in between.

Sanction is also expressed through licensing, certification and membership in professional organizations which are designed to ensure competence of workers and responsibility of institutions and to protect both the consumer and the public at large. Here, again, there is a possibility of conflict of interests, particularly if professional standards and agency practices do not jibe. For example, in some of our large public welfare programs workers may be called upon to use procedures that they perceive as detrimental to the welfare of the client. A consultant at a local Social Security office, called in to deal with the low morale of the staff, learned that when a computer error on a national level caused delay in mailing of checks, workers were instructed to make calls for clients to Regional Offices with full knowledge that such calls were ineffectual. Such procedures, born, perhaps, out of desperation and efforts to bring pressure for change, were directly contrary to the ethics of the workers and of no help to the clients. Equally, referring clients for mandatory job training programs to develop skills in areas where there were no jobs would be considered unprofessional and poor practice.

Accountability to colleagues, the employing agency, and total service system of which the worker is a part involves responsibility for cooperative endeavor within the system itself. It cannot be emphasized too strongly that this overall concept of accountability involves not only responsibility for things as they are, but also for improving the quality of what exists and what is being done. This means that data must be collected that can be used in research to enable better understanding of the human condition and more effective practice methods. The individual worker is responsible for maintaining a record of the basic data needed to evaluate what is being done and what needs are unmet. Such data can be secured by

(1) observation; (2) interviewing or discussion; (3) use of questionnaires or some other devices for securing valid information. For many workers, except those actively engaged in research, the day-to-day recording of information is the bête noire of practice. The whole question of how best to secure and store data so that they are not only valid but also usable is a yet unanswered one. In order to serve their purpose, data must be brief (the cost of maintaining records is a large proportion of any budget); be accurate (although allowances must always be made for the fact that data are filtered through the recorder); be available without too much effort or the consumption of too much time; possess a degree of uniformity that allows for comparison and statistical accounting. The development of audio and video tapes held promise, but these have proved too time-consuming for extensive use except in teaching and supervision of practice and in storing data.

A major concern in the collection of data and the keeping of records about people is that of the individual's right to privacy and the whole question of confidentiality, of which people are properly assured when they are involved with one of the human services. The legal right to see personal files is now assured. There is increasing openness about the fact that information is recorded and shared knowledge of the manner in which it is to be used. Clients are entitled to this knowledge and the assurance that such information will not be used in an irresponsible manner, without their knowledge and consent, or for purposes other than those agreed upon either tacitly or by written contract.

It is important to remember, however, that confidentiality is not an absolute, and that particularly in this day of specialization where many different helping persons and services may need to be involved and where review committees are an increasing part of the effort to assure quality of service, information must be shared widely. While there is currently much greater openness in discussing personal problems, most people still have a need to keep certain information private. This again is one of those issues in which individualization of the client, in which the client is helped to understand and accept the need to give certain information, how it will be collected, and how it will be used, is a basic essential of good practice.

Involvement of the client in the collection of data is important for another reason—the factor of the meaning of data to the client, which is often just as important as the bare facts themselves. The extent to which it will be necessary for the worker to know this meaning will depend, to a large degree, on the nature of the problem and the kind of service needed. Feeling is fact, but the amount of feeling that must be shared varies greatly. For example, the fact of a divorce shared with a lawyer will be quite different from the fact shared with a marriage counselor. This again is an area where we can say that the client has the right and need to be involved to the extent that is necessary in the individual instance.

Another major factor in the recording of data is the increasing use of computers, by both researchers and review boards in quality assessment and assurance, to work with the raw data. This means that recording must possess a degree of uniformity and the ability to be classified to a much greater extent than previously. It means that present workers must acquire new skills in using forms and tables and new workers must be trained in them as a part of learning to work with people. Each agency tends to develop its own forms and procedures for the recording and classification of data, and their use is a part of inservice training for new workers. We are in the process of learning to use this new technology, and procedures and forms are being developed on national levels (as the Professional Standards Review Organization designated by the federal government to carry out a program designed to promote the effective, efficient and economical delivery of quality health care); on state levels (as the tracking systems being used in various states to determine the situation and location of children in foster placement) and on local levels (as the local Community Fund survey of needs as a basis for allocation of funds).

A major problem for human service workers in attaining the specificity of recording needed by technological devices is the number and kind of individual variables that affect the functioning of human beings and the fact that, by inclination and by education, such workers see their major responsibility as dealing with the unique needs of individuals. The rank and file worker is in the position of having to "tailor" the requirements of programs so that they are usable by many different kinds of people, which makes uniformity and specificity of recording different. Nevertheless, if we are to make use of the advantages of such systems, workers need to learn their use.

In addition, the worker must learn to differentiate between "observation" and "inference" in gathering and recording data. One definition of observation is "scientific scrutiny," also, "the record of such examination and the data connected with it." Inference, on the other hand, is defined as a "deduction," a "conclusion," a "conjecture."

Too often, workers record inferences based on observation rather than the actual observation itself. At this stage in the development of our knowledge regarding the human condition, inferences can be little more than "scientific guesses." Whether the material recorded is being used for evaluation, for diagnosis, for research, it needs to be an accurate observation rather than an inference of the meaning of that observation.

In order to attain the maximum degree of efficiency in use of self in working with people, workers will usually need to record on two levels: (1) for personal use and (2) for use by the employing agency and through it by the overall social system. One of the major uses of recording is for personal improvement, for education, and for supervision of workers. For this purpose, the worker may choose to use what is known as *process recording*, in which the actual content of the interview, discussion, meeting is recorded either on tape or by dictation so that it can be scrutinized and evaluated to improve both understanding and practice methods. While the form of process recording may vary, content should generally include:

1. Identifying data;
2. Purpose;
3. Observation;
4. Interaction;
5. Evaluation;
6. Worker's role;
7. Future plan.

Obviously, process recording tends to be lengthy and expensive, and except for teaching agencies it is rarely used either for a total case load or for permanent files. It is extremely useful, however, for both beginning and experienced workers, particularly if they have good consultation available as a way of looking at the reality of what is happening between worker and client—whether that client be an individual, a family or a group.

In the management of the job, workers usually opt to keep a *day sheet* or *log*. This is mandatory in some agencies. Sometimes printed forms are developed for this purpose; sometimes the individual worker devises a personal form. These can be used to plan work, as a basis for preparation of permanent records, as a source of agency statistics and reports that serve to justify programs and expenditures, and as a basis for research. This is an extremely important and too often neglected dimension of the people-oriented worker's job performance. Trusting to memory is a poor way to keep records, and workers should plan time to make immediate notes on what has been done.

Permanent agency records usually take the form of a *summary,* which is prepared at the close of a contact with a client, at the end of a definite time period, or at the end of a phase of work. The advantage of a summary, in addition to its brevity, is that its preparation involves thinking about and evaluating work over a time period when trends, patterns, and changes can more readily be observed than in an isolated interview, discussion or meeting. The disadvantage is that specificity of detail may be lost.

Recording of group interaction poses a special problem for workers, particularly if they wish to have some record of the dynamics of the group—the process that takes place in contrast to the actual content of the meeting. The worker might opt to use one of the various forms of sociometric diagrams or charts that have been developed (see Chapter 10 on working with groups). Again, the kind of recording needed will depend upon the purpose of the group; the committee or board meeting might well do with factual minutes unless the worker was very concerned about the interactions taking place among the members and wanted to analyze them, perhaps with consultation. The therapy group or family counseling session, on the other hand, might benefit from detailed recording or taping of what took place.

One of the major recording tasks of human service workers is preparation of *histories* to be used in diagnosis, in planning interventions, and by interdisciplinary teams. The focus of the history will be determined by the purpose of the working relationship as well as by the specialization of the worker. Medical histories are prepared by doctors and nurses; educational histories by guidance counselors and teachers; family histories by therapists; social histories by social workers, etc. Almost all agencies that use histories have a form for this purpose, but it is important to remember again that the feelings around the historical facts and the relationships between them are as important as the facts themselves. Skill is required in the use of a form in order to avoid its becoming a mere question-and-answer process that produces bones with no meat.

Two frequently neglected aspects of recording are (1) recording for publicity and (2) recording for research. Accountability to the society involves not only being responsible for what is being done and for improving the quality of work but also for keeping people informed of what is being done. The human services are dependent on public support and such support can only be secured and maintained if the public is accurately informed in a way that they can understand and appreciate. The worker supplies the raw material from which such interpretation is made as well as that from which studies are planned and carried out. Workers need not only to record their material accurately and usably but also to be sufficiently aware of these two programmatic needs to be constantly alert to trends, problems and possibilities that can be used for either of these purposes.

Accountability for the individual worker not only involves the provision of the basic material by which accountability to the consumer and to the community is established. It also requires extensive knowledge of the agency and the community in which the worker operates. Good recording and good practice are inseparable. Equally, good management and good practice are inseparable. With the increasing size and complexity of the systems providing the human services, demands of management have been compounded. Even the individual rank and file workers who have no managerial responsibility in the agency find it necessary to know something of the principles of good management in order not only to manage their own individual assignment, but also to be able to use the system of which they are a part. While not all workers will be able or need to become specialists in management, all need to be aware of the basic principles involved.

Social agencies are organizations which are established to achieve a definite purpose in the area of providing human services. As such they are subject to all of the major principles characteristic of social systems. They must relate to their environment, maintain their internal structure, and work effectively toward achievement of the purpose for which they were created. They generally possess all of the following characteristics:[1]

1. *Every organization has an identity of its own* with its own supporters and antagonists; it has its own territory program, schedule, table of organization, rules and procedures, division of labor, status and rewards, history and vocabulary.

2. *Almost all organizations, except for the very small ones, have suborganizations or subsystems,* whose interests are not completely

---

1. I am indebted for the following material to an excellent little "nitty-gritty" book, *How to Run Any Organization* by Theodore Caplow (New York: Holt, Rinehart and Winston, 1976).

compatible with those of the larger system. Their major concern is maintaining themselves; the major concern of the parent organization is maintaining itself and achieving its purpose, and there may be conflict between these two divergent interests.

3. *At any point in the history of an organization, it will be growing, stable, or declining* and this will affect all parts of the organization and the workers therein.

4. *Organizations, like people, frequently develop crises* and, as with people, can grow from these crises if they are well managed. However, too frequent crises can destroy organizations as effectively as they do individuals and families.

5. *Organizations as a part of internal management* are concerned with appropriate use of authority on different levels; with establishment and maintenance of effective channels of communication; with the best use and the maintenance of morale of workers; with productivity and with facilitating changes necessary to keep the system relevant to the needs of the society. This internal management directly affects individual workers who are the vital part of it, and to be effective they must be aware of this and conscious of how what they do affects the total.

The first thing that new workers need to do in order to operate effectively is to learn their agency. A sample outline to guide in securing the data follows:

1. Name of agency.
2. Address.
3. What are the functions of the agency?
4. Under what auspices does the agency operate? Governmental? _____ Voluntary? _____ Note if under sectarian or other special auspices.
5. On what geographical level does the agency operate? Local _____ State _____ National _____ Other _____
6. What geographical territory does the agency serve?
7. In what year was the agency established?
8. How did the agency originate? (e.g., established by statute; by voluntary association of interested persons; by some other organization; by bequest, merger, federation, etc.)
9. Prepare an organization chart of the agency. Attach to this report.

10. In relation to the organization of the agency:
    a. What is the "group of ultimate control"?
    b. Is there a membership? What are the qualifications for membership?
    c. Is there a board?
       (1) What is it called?
       (2) Is it directive (policy-determining) or advisory?
       (3) By whom is it elected or appointed?
    d. Who appoints the executive?
    e. What major departments are there, if any?
    f. What districts or branches are there, if any?

11. What is the basic document which is the source of administrative authority for the agency?

12. What is the nature of this document—law, executive order (of whom?), charter, constitution, by-laws, etc.?

13. By whom was this document adopted or promulgated?

14. What topics does this document cover?

15. How could this document be amended or revised?

16. Is the agency:
    a. a branch of any other state, local, or national agency? If so, what agency?
    b. a member of a united fund or community chest? Name of fund or chest?
    c. A member of a community welfare council or council of social agencies? Name of council?

17. What is the major source of funds of this agency?

18. If possible, give approximate figures for the following:
    a. Current budget or
    b. Total expenditures for last fiscal year.
    c. Number of staff personnel: authorized, filled, total.
    d. Administrative and professional.
    e. Clerical and other.

In addition to knowing their specific organization, workers need to know their community. This includes not only the service community—the other social agencies that go to make up the network of services—but also the community at large.

When the service community is of any size, there is usually an overall planning agency responsible for seeing that it is an effectively functioning system. A major and ongoing concern is that in spite of efforts, services are still fragmented and people tend to "fall between the cracks" with their needs remaining unmet. The worker is a vital link in this overall system and should work both as an individual and as part of an agency to develop and strengthen good working arrangements between different agencies. Overall community and regional planning councils, centralized intake centers, and multiservice centers have developed in an effort to meet the needs of the total person.

In studying a "community," it can be thought of as *geographic* (people living and interacting in a particular territorial area); as *functional* (people who share specific interests and characteristics such as an ethic or a religious group); or as *problem oriented* (people with certain characteristics in common such as poverty, mental illness or retardation, delinquency). There is some overlapping in these classifications; probably the most significant common factor is that a community is made up of a group of people who share a common interest or concern. An urban area is usually made up of a whole series of communities, and workers need to be able to define that community in which they are working at a particular point in time. They also need to be aware of the relationships between the particular communities in their territory. A sample *Framework for Analyzing Communities* follows:[2]

I. *Background Information*
  A. History and traditions of community
  B. Size, territory, and boundaries of community
  C. Major institutions, organizations, and characteristics
  D. Stable vs. growing or declining community
II. *Specific Components of Community*
  A. *Demographic Characteristics*
    1. Make-up of population (number, age, sex, marital status, etc.)
    2. Ethnic-racial-nationality groupings
    3. Economic and social structure
    4. Occupational and income profile
    5. Education attainment levels
    6. Mobility and residential characteristics
    7. Other variables: religious, political, housing, crime rates, welfare, etc.

2. I am indebted for this material to the Faculty of the Graduate School of Social Work, University of Nebraska, who developed and use this form in teaching.

B. *Value System of Community*
Identify major predominant values shared by majority of community, reflecting the objectives or purposes of the system. Most problems involve value dilemma—values not being realized. Usually values are implicit, not explicit.

C. *Leadership Structure* (Power)
Substructure. Who influences decisions and where lodged? Often related to organizational involvement.

D. *Economic Structure*
Free enterprise system? Local or related to region or national? Single or diversified?

E. *Governmental Service System* (Health, Education, Welfare, Recreation)
What is structure and nature? Great or small? Local or state or national?

F. *Private Welfare System* (Health, Education, Welfare, Recreation)
Voluntary health, welfare, and recreational services. How many, what services, who served, where located, how funded, who controls, etc.?

G. *Associational System*
Reflects the common interests and values of people. Fraternal organizations, religious groups, service clubs, cultural groups, etc.

H. *Communications Subsystems*
Formal communications systems—newspapers (local and area-wide), TV stations, radio stations, organizational newsletters (e.g., PTA, churches, business and industry).

I. *Religious Subsystem*
Council of Churches, Ministerial Associations, denominational groups, etc.

J. *Legal Subsystem*
Bar Association, Legal Aid Projects, etc.

K. *Informal Support Systems*
Unorganized individuals or small groups known for offering help, advice, support, or material aid to others.

L. *Feasibility of Change in Various Areas of Concern*

With the expansion of greatly needed services into isolated sections of the country, the question of how best to operate within a rural setting has assumed a new importance. Increased urbanization and the fact that most educational programs are carried out in urban settings have resulted in human service workers who are not competent to deal with the demands of rural practice either from personal experience in living or from education. Medicine, in particular, is struggling with this situation in its effort to provide care for people in isolated areas. Workers, accustomed to the supports of a network of agencies, unable to adapt personally to the values and culture of a rural community, lacking in sufficient personal and professional flexibility to adapt procedures to the local situation, often find themselves unable to operate in such settings.

The key to effective practice in all settings lies in the abilities (1) to use resources imaginatively, (2) to "read" the situation realistically (not expect farmers during the haying season to have time for conferences, or harassed mothers with too little money to feed their families or maintain a decent home in a crowded ghetto to be too concerned about supervising adolescent children), and finally (3) to adapt personal knowledge and skills to the needs and characteristics of the individuals and groups being served.

An essential part of good practice is going through the procedures that enable individuals and organizations to be accountable in the largest sense of the word for what they are doing. The pressure of human need is so great that such procedures often seem merely time-consuming and onerous, but it is the only way that we can start "seeing the woods instead of just the trees" and, as such, is well worth the time and effort.

RELATED READINGS

Caplow, Theodore. *How to Run Any Organization.* New York: Holt, Rinehart and Winston, 1976. Practical, down to earth, small book that will help readers not only to understand their organization better, but also enable them to work in it and even to manage it.

Fulmer, Robert M. *Supervision—Principles of Professional Management.* Beverly Hills: Glencoe Press, 1976. Excellent text on managing yourself, using supervision, using administration. Detailed and practical.

Ginsberg, Leon, editor. *Social Work in Rural Communities—A Book of Readings.* New York: Council on Social Work Education, 1975. Good collection of readings on practice in rural settings.

Siporin, Max. *Introduction to Social Work Practice.* New York: Macmillan, 1975. Good practice text with practical emphasis on planning and evaluation. Also sample forms of recording in appendix.

Spergel, Irving. *Community Problem Solving—The Delinquency Example.* Chicago: University of Chicago Press, 1969. Simple, direct discussion of work on a community level.

Turabian, Kate. *A Manual for Writers of Term Papers, Theses, and Dissertations.* Chicago: University of Chicago Press, 1973. Classic manual for writers of academic and scientific papers.

Weissman, Harold. *Overcoming Mismanagement in the Human Service Professions.* San Francisco: Jossey-Bass, 1973. Good discussion of work to change a single system.

14

Integrating the Personal and Professional Self

Never before in human history have human service workers been so significant a part of the total social order. There is every indication that their importance will increase and spread if we continue in our present course.

With the rapid growth in population, problems of interrelationships and social planning and control become greater. It is one thing to enact legislation and develop programs to deal with these problems, and another to ensure their acceptance and use. Communication, motivation, interpretation, and the enabling of people to utilize what is available to them are essential, and the role of the worker as a social broker is becoming increasingly important.

Along with the population growth, an increasingly complicated society has developed, in which rapid change is taking place and the social systems are becoming more and more highly sophisticated. Although these drastic changes are uneven across the face of the society, their effects are all pervasive. While certain groups within the society are capable of dealing with them, others who still exist within the dying social order of the past century are ill-prepared to deal with the technology that we have developed.

This technology places people in a classic double bind. On the one hand, it demands greater options for variety in living. On the other, it demands greater conformity in order to use these options. It is a matter of giving up certain freedoms to obtain others, and in the process an increasing impersonality develops. Examples of this are the mushrooming day care centers for children and institutions for old people, where the physical care—health, nutrition, housing—are often superior to the home setting, but where the impersonality can be, literally, a killing factor.

These rapid changes have caused changes in values and the development of anomie or valuelessness. The old values are attacked and no longer serve as guidelines, and new ones develop slowly. Adolescents, part of whose life task is challenging existent values, are particularly vulnerable to this kind of social condition. The whole sexual revolution with its related disturbing increase in venereal disease is an example of this lag in the development of an effective value system.

With these social changes has come a breakdown in the social controls once exerted by the family, the neighborhood, and the small community which frequently served almost as an extended family. Each member of these groups felt and exercised a responsibility for the other members that was rarely inoperable because they hesitated to become involved. Assuming this kind of responsibility was a part of their role.

The functions of the neighborhood and indeed of the family itself have been taken over by various social institutions—the school, the religious group, the court, the social welfare programs, recreation departments—the list is endless. Sometimes it would seem that this formalization and bureaucratization tend to exacerbate rather than correct the problems. The intense emphasis on competition and the artificial breakdown of children into rigid age groups in recreation programs are examples, as is the definition of delinquency that often accompanies fairly mild developmental problems of youth simply because there is no one else to deal with them except institutionalized correctional programs.

Despite these factors and the frightening implications of ideas such as those implicit in the work of the extreme behaviorists and the ever-present totalitarian thinkers, the essential humanity of people remains unchanged. It has been said that human beings are capable of adapting to any conditions, but that the social changes we are facing now will demand adaptations that will run counter to this humanity. This prediction does not seem to be borne out either by history or by individual reactions to present dehumanizing experiences.

Nothing is more dehumanizing than slavery, and over the centuries, people have been enslaved repeatedly. But unless they are physically destroyed, in time they will be free and their humanity—their concern for each other—will exert itself anew.

Nothing is more dehumanizing than the great cities of the world which have gotten out of control and are struggling with overwhelming problems of dirt, noise, congestion, and poverty, and yet the visitor to any one of them will find experiences in common humanity that run counter to all the gloomy predictions of modern writers and thinkers. Nothing is more dehumanizing than racism, prejudice and discrimination on any basis and yet, even when faced with this, people are able to remain concerned for each other and to continue to attain a better world for all.

The vast bureaucratized systems of society such as the military services and penal complexes tend to dehumanize those within them—yet people retain their essential humanity while a part of them.

Anyone who has tried to interpret social programs to an exasperated public, overwhelmed with the demands of their own lives, can bear witness to the phenomenon that occurs when one stops talking about programs as a totality and talks about individual people, or, better yet, lets individual people talk about themselves. The need for identification and relationship with other individuals is inherent in humans. Between individuals, the paranoid "they" does not operate.

For human service workers, the demands of this common humanity are both an asset and a problem. They provide motivation to "do good"—to strive for conditions that allow for the maximum development of each individual and to derive satisfaction from improvements in both individual lives and social conditions. These satisfactions represent the great unearned increment of service work, the basic satisfaction that comes from another's achievement and fulfillment, and the conviction, reinforced anew, that people can in truth work out their own problems.

On the debit side, workers are pushed toward overidentification with their clients. When they become overinvolved personally, they can find themselves saddling clients with the necessity for dealing with the workers' feelings as well as their own. There is a fine line between objective acceptance of, concern for, and satisfaction in successful outcome on the one hand and overidentification and personal involvement on the other. The teacher who can sit beside the unhappy, frustrated boy who cannot read and teach him the word "hug" by suiting the action to the letters must be able to do so and yet retain her own ability to see him as he really is and not as she would like him to be.

THE PROFESSIONAL SELF

The development of what we may call the "professional self" which is part of the personal self and yet not identical with it is an ongoing process throughout the lifetime of the worker. It is compounded of increasing self-awareness, knowledge of people and society, and skill in use of both self and learning. In no other area has the knowledge explosion been greater or come more swiftly, but mastering it on an intellectual level is one thing, integrating it into the personality of the worker another. Only with time and experience does this knowledge become translated into a functional portion of the tools of trade of the worker, and the personal self will often get in the way and create a myopia that blinds the worker to reality (see Figure 13).

The knowledge explosion as well as the increasing complication of the social order faces workers with the need for specialization. Although conditions under which they work—physical isolation and lack of communication—may necessitate a generalist approach, they can probably operate most effectively if they choose to focus on one

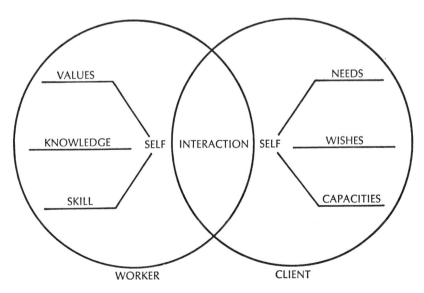

Figure 13 The Overall Task of the Worker

particular area of service and master the growing body of knowledge available within it. One of the problems inherent in this approach is that while we possess the necessary tools of communication and the knowledge of how to deal with social and individual concerns, we have not yet learned how to make them available to people, either in congested urban areas or isolated rural ones. One need only look at the great cities of the world to realize that urban dwellers are as lacking in essential services as are their rural counterparts and that as cities grow, this is one of the first areas of breakdown. Workers operating in either area may find themselves faced with the necessity of both delivering the baby on the kitchen table and working for legislation to ensure a safe and adequate water supply; of dealing with a psychotic patient and working to create conditions in a community that will contribute to mental health; of distributing money and goods to alleviate the effects of poverty and working to create a social system that provides more equitable distribution of the wealth.

It is clear that these extremes call for different knowledges and skills and can frustrate the worker who attempts to encompass the demands of both, and yet they are so interrelated that it is impossible to deal adequately with one without at the same time dealing with the other. Of necessity, workers will continue to struggle with these problems for some time. Until we face and do something about the need to limit the size of urban areas or to plan them better, problems will continue to exist in these oversize cities. Until we work out plans for providing more comprehensive coverage for rural areas, problems will continue to exist there.

As awareness of the need for such a comprehensive approach is accepted, we are increasingly able to pinpoint the areas of generalist knowledge and skill that all human service workers need. Such things as ability to use self flexibly, to recognize and overcome barriers to communication, to observe clearly and make inferences from these observations on the basis of sound knowledge, to understand the dynamics of personal and social systems, to make valid judgments and to act responsibly and effectively—all are essential for such work. Specialization develops "on top" of these.

Use of Resources

Workers who must deal with these conditions must concentrate on developing extensive, imaginative, and flexible use of resources and of volunteer services. To do this they must know that they do not necessarily need to be the primary persons in providing service.

Indeed they are often less effective in this task than others who exist within the daily life experience of the client. We have learned this lesson well through the opportunities offered in the various poverty programs; through the work of organizations such as Alcoholics Anonymous; through the innumerable hours of effective service contributed by volunteers or lay workers in all walks of life. In developing these resources, workers are limited only by their own limitations in imagination and resourcefulness.

Frequently workers will say they do not have the time for this kind of development. Although it is time-consuming and requires endless patience and flexibility, in the long run it pays in improvement of services offered, in interpretation of needs, and in provision of opportunity for exercise of common humanity, the need for which exists in all people.

The example below illustrates how the use of this approach can benefit both individuals and the community.

> *Over the past fifty years, the small towns of this nation have been dying. Young people have left the rural areas and often only the older people are left.*
>
> *Old Mrs. Weller lived alone in a dilapidated frame house in such a town. The furnace needed a part no longer manufactured, and the toilet had never been connected to the new sewer system. Winter was coming, but she wanted to remain in her home despite the drawbacks of lack of heat and the fact that she couldn't use the outdoor privy as she was partly crippled with rheumatism.*
>
> *There were no services in the technical sense in the community, but the Old Age Assistance worker went to the village bar, which, in this Bohemian culture, was the social center for the whole family. There he found and talked with the unofficial mayor of the town. The man who ran the filling station across from Mrs. Weller's house was handy at fixing things—and someone came up with a part for the furnace. Four men spent a Saturday morning digging a ditch and connecting the sewer. While they were there, they braced the steps and fixed some cracks in the old walls. People became interested and promised to "keep an eye on Mrs. Weller" when the weather got bad.*

No money was involved—there wasn't any—but a town mobilized itself, became conscious of the needs of its people, of its capacity to do something about them, and of the satisfaction that could be derived from its acts.

The Worker as a Team Member

In addition to a capacity to utilize the unorthodox and try the unfamiliar, the modern human service worker faces the overwhelming necessity of learning to work effectively as a member of a team. Human problems are too large and too complex to be dealt with by one discipline. Between the professions in this field—medicine, law, psychiatry, psychology, education, social work, nursing, nutrition, home economics—there is a sad history of jealousy, lack of adequate cooperation, a feeling that each has "the answer," that each must guard its own little empire, that each must be the dominant representative in any joint undertaking. There is a delightful but sad story told of a conference between representatives of various professions in which the physician present referred to the others as "paramedical" personnel. When an enraged colleague in return spoke of the "parasocial work" personnel, it was only with great difficulty that the meeting was continued.

A certain amount of this kind of feeling and thinking is natural and inevitable. Indeed a part of professional education itself is the indoctrination of a "professional" culture that carries status implications and an arrogance that runs counter to effective communication across disciplinary lines. The old, established professions have a deeply ingrained tradition of their own uniqueness and importance. Eventually, these attitudes are destructive to the interests that all serve. There are strong indications in the present emphasis on interdisciplinary research, teaching, and practice that perhaps the old barriers may begin to crumble and inherited old controversies may not be as strong as they once were.

Workers who must deal with this kind of situation can do so much more effectively if they strive for development of four conditions: (1) that they like and be comfortable with themselves; (2) that they develop the maximum knowledge and skill in their own area of which they are capable—and this requires constant education and reeducation; (3) that they learn to respect the other person's knowledge and skill equally with their own; (4) that they learn how to fight. Healthy differences and controversy can act as stimuli for development—personal feuding and back biting, often sparked by feelings of inadequacy, lead nowhere.

Seeing the Totality

People who work with other people must develop broad vision. The consequences of our lack of sufficient capacity to see the whole and to envisage the results of our interventions on a sufficiently broad scale are devastating. The basic physical principle that for every action there is an equal and opposite reaction holds true in human relations, and the concept of total balance is a vital one. While it is impossible to know or foresee all of the consequences of an action, it is inexcusable to find oneself surprised by major reactions that one did not anticipate. Only as we use a broad base of knowledge and understanding in looking at human problems can we avoid the pitfalls that await the worker whose field of vision is too limited.

Finally, human service workers are just that—they serve human beings. Years ago, when social institutions first began to replace personal charity, a bitterly prophetic, anonymous couplet was written:

"Organized charity, measured and iced,
In the name of a cautious, statistical Christ."

This early fear that institutionalization could lessen the orientation toward the essential uniqueness and humanity of people has been well borne out as we see the person increasingly lost in the system. The worker's highest responsibility is ensuring the client's opportunity for retention of that humanity from which the meaning of life is derived and without which physical survival is relatively insignificant and often time-limited. Somehow we must manage our social systems so that they and the workers within them possess built-in provisions for meeting this most basic of human needs.

Somehow we must manage ourselves, our learning and our personal experiences, so we can use the ability for creative thinking about the human condition and the problems of people. The mythology about the limitations on creativity is gradually disappearing in light of scientific research, which is "uncovering the various components and revealing their potential for development in all of us."[1] As long ago as 1920 a model for the creative process was developed that is still considered valid. It was visualized as consisting of four steps:

1. Preparation—the acquiring of the essential tools of knowledge and skill through education and research.

1. John Douglas, "The Genius of Everyman." *Science News,* April 23, 1977.

2. Incubation—the thinking about, during which the thinker "steps back" from the assumptions previously made and looks at the totality with new eyes.

3. Illumination—the insight or realization of a new possibility to answer old problems.

4. Verification—the elaboration of the new insight in which there is critical thinking about, testing, and developing a solution.

It is this kind of thinking, flexible and rigorous, that we need in approaching human problems combined with the courage to try new ideas and new solutions.

The millennium is not imminent. The human condition ensures that we will never attain a problem-free existence but in the struggle itself lies the opportunity for growth and development. There are no greater challenges or greater satisfactions than those derived from work with people, and we possess a sizable and developing body of theoretical knowledge upon which to base methods, skills, and techniques. Workers who continue to study, to learn, and to use the insights that they gain will enjoy the "greater freedom" in use of self that is the most fulfilling reward of education.

RELATED READINGS

Abbott, Edith. *Some American Pioneers in Social Welfare.* Chicago: University of Chicago Press, 1937. An early pioneer in social welfare writes about the leaders in working for social change.

Addams, Jane. *Twenty Years at Hull House.* New York: Signet Books, 1969. Fascinating collection of material about the early years in a social settlement in Chicago.

Billingsly, Andrew. *Black Families in White America.* Englewood Cliffs, N.J.: Prentice Hall, 1968. Study of what happens to black families in the United States.

Brown, Dee. *Bury My Heart at Wounded Knee.* New York: Holt, Rinehart and Winston, 1970. History of the American Indians written in a manner that makes it impossible for the reader to avoid personal involvement.

Caudill, Harry. *Night Comes to the Cumberlands.* Boston: Little, Brown, 1963. A native of Appalachia writes about the abuses of his land and people.

Lindeman, Edward. *Social Discovery.* New York: Republic Publishing Company, 1924. The most significant book of an "experimental idealist who refused to accept the status quo and recommended a pragmatic, nondogmatic approach to problems."

Offenberg, Bernice. *The Angel in Hell's Kitchen.* New York: Bernard Geis Associates, 1962. Experiences of a public welfare worker in New York City.

Reisman, David et al. *The Lonely Crowd.* New Haven: Yale University Press, 1950. A classic study of American society and its impact on the individual.

Romanyshyn, John. *Social Welfare—Charity to Justice.* New York: Random House, 1971. Current text emphasizing the philosophical changes in attitudes toward social welfare.

Slater, Philip. *The Pursuit of Loneliness.* Boston: Beacon Press, 1971. An examination of modern American culture and what it means.

Toffler, Alvin. *Future Shock.* New York: Random House, 1970. Timely and highly readable analysis of the impact of current and future social conditions on people.

Zamera, Julian. *La Raza: Forgotten Americans.* South Bend, Indiana: University of Notre Dame, 1966. Reports on the place and problems of the Spanish-Americans in American society.

Appendices

The illustrative case material included in these appendices consists of composites from many different records in different settings. Names have been changed and situations disguised. If they seem recognizable, it is because of the commonality of the human experience rather than the uniqueness of persons and incidents involved.

A

Using Systems Concepts to Effect Change

The new governor had used as one of the major planks in his platform a promise to do something about Fairbury State Hospital, an institution for the mentally ill which was a recurrent source of scandal in the state. He promptly appointed a new director of institutions from out of the state who brought young Dr. Blaisdell with him and put him in charge of Fairbury.

The hospital itself had been a closed system for years, existing within the community of Fairbury and yet not of it. It consisted of a series of many smaller closed systems each jealously guarding its own position, rights and privileges with very little meaningful input from or outgo to each other. The boundaries of these internal systems could be defined either on the basis of the wards which tended to be autocratically operated entities or on the basis of the various levels of service—physicians, nurses, psychologists, social workers, technicians, attendants, maintenance staff, and on the very lowest level, the patients for whose benefit these services supposedly existed. Each of these levels was so concerned with maintaining its own status in relation to the other systems that the overall task suffered badly. The boundaries were rigidly defined and communication and interaction were based on rules and patterns that tended to be less than constructive.

Dr. Blaisdell's goal of improved services for the patients was based on the creation of a so-called therapeutic milieu—a healthy total life situation for them in which the specialized services would form a

227

coherent whole. To achieve this, he was faced with the need to break down the barriers between the various systems and create new service systems. His first step was creating a series of teams composed of representatives from each of the different services. He recognized the significant and essential contribution that each representative could make and defined status equally. Responsibility for selecting a team leader and definition of roles then lay with the team members.

In addition to the internal reorganization, Dr. Blaisdell moved to include representatives of the community in the new service systems. Many of the patients were old people who could be better and less expensively cared for in nursing homes in their local communities. New therapies made it possible to control extremes in behavior so that patients could be returned to employment and their families relatively quickly, thus avoiding the dangers of institutionalization. The problem of recidivism had been a severe one, partly traceable to lack of adequate communication and cooperation between the community and the institution. Therefore, a planning conference might include not only the team members from the hospital but also potential employers, family, social workers, doctors or other specialists from outside the hospital, and frequently the patients themselves.

Dr. Blaisdell also had to consider the overall system of services within the state, of which his hospital was only one part. As a result of its position within the Department of Institutions, Fairbury existed within a statewide system of other institutions, competed with them for staff, funding and programs, and cooperated with them to form a total service system. As part of a political system, Fairbury and its staff were involved directly and indirectly with the legislature and the electorate.

On an even broader scale the hospital and its staff were participating in the overall problem of providing care for the mentally ill and in the systems that had developed to do so. By virtue of his special professional education, Dr. Blaisdell was equipped with the knowledge and, hopefully, the attitudes that would enable and motivate him to question and evaluate the status quo and at the same time encourage new ideas and practices. It was his responsibility to be open to the entire spectrum of theoretical knowledge and the changes coming from practice, to correlate the two, and to work toward the development of new practice and new knowledge.

While Dr. Blaisdell was thinking and working in systems terms on these four levels, for the benefit of all of the patients, Agnes Threneau was directly responsible for a defined group of patients. An aide on the men's ward, she became an integral part of the new team system with a major responsibility for the patients on her service. Both her status and her salary had always been minuscule, yet she was actually with the patients more than anyone else. Although changing these factors was difficult, for salaries were dependent on legislative action and status was defined by the hospital culture which was resistant to change, the significance of her contribution to the total effort was recognized and defined. Her ideas and observations were a part of the team discussion, she participated in decisions about how the treatment model recommended by the specialists would be carried out, and had an active role in its operation and in the evaluation of its results.

Bob Johnson, from the Family Service Association in Fairbury, worked and thought primarily in terms of individuals and their needs and only secondarily with the total problem of caring for the mentally ill. He was assigned to work with Earl Wilson, a twenty-three-year-old man on Agnes Threneau's ward, whose long and pitiful history included abandonment by his natural parents when he was eight, a series of ineffectual foster homes and eventual hospitalization for depression that involved an abortive suicide attempt. Although he had one sister with whom he had lived prior to going to the hospital, the relationship between them was such that the hospital had recommended he live apart from her.

Bob was brought into the hospital service system while Earl was still an inpatient, to participate in planning conferences and to become engaged with his client. His major task was to facilitate Earl's return to life in the larger community. This involved a job, a place to live, social contacts, and ongoing treatment as needed. Bob defined and, in part, created, a new service system in which the various facilities that met these basic needs existed in interrelationship. Obviously, what happened in one affected what happened in the others.

The job came from a man who, as a member of one of the community service clubs, had been involved with the liaison committee for the hospital, was willing to employ ex-patients, and recognized their possible special needs. Because Earl wanted to live alone, Bob helped him find a small apartment but also encouraged him to get a small puppy to assuage the loneliness that this kind of living can bring. Although Earl had been a loner and knew few people in the community, his sister—at arm's length—and old Mr. Anderson, a former foster father who had been unable to help Earl during his turbulent adolescence but maintained a real fondness for him, provided personal interest. The local chapter of Recovery, an organization of ex-hospital patients, provided social contacts and further group treatment. As Fairbury Hospital had no outpatient clinic, arrangements were made with a local physician to continue drug therapy as needed. Once this new system was operating, Bob's role was to keep the wheels greased and be available to Earl when he needed help, but gradually to free him to learn to stand on his own.

Clearly the kind of change being sought here is not easily or quickly achieved. Changes in policy and organization and opening up systems that have become closed are often accompanied by or dependent upon changes in personnel. Questions of status and rewards are highly significant. The important concept for the worker is understanding interrelationships which can be defeating to an effort that ignores them. The process outlined here should tend to create a dynamic interaction, with a structured provision for input, processing, and output through a series of open or vital systems, and should be applicable across the board in working with individuals, families, groups, communities.

B

Basic Processes

BASIC PROCESS—I

As one illustration of this helping process, let us use a so-called multiproblem family, the Kinkaids. In one sense of the term, every family could be so classified, for certainly life consists of a continuing series of problems for which solutions must be found. However, there are some families for whom the number and severity of the problems often combined with lack of coping ability on the part of the individuals and the unit itself, or a lack of the essential social resources to make solutions possible, cause a breakdown in capacity to function. This breakdown is usually evidenced at the most vulnerable point, which may be a shaky marital relationship or the capacity of children to meet the demands placed on them in their life experience.

In the Kinkaid family, Richie, age eight, the oldest child, was that vulnerable point, and the school nurse was the worker who first perceived his unmet needs. Young Mrs. Hopkins had become aware in her three years experience in an elementary school that the child who came to her office frequently with colds, headaches and minor ailments was often in trouble in other aspects of his life—home, school, community. She became concerned about Richie who rarely missed a week without coming in—with his pallor, his thinness, his frequent sore throats and colds, and his fatigue which caused him to fall asleep on the cot in her office and lie there for hours. Mentioning this to his teacher, she learned that he was one of the faceless children in class, neither good nor bad enough to be outstanding or remembered—just there, doing minimal work and causing no trouble.

ENGAGEMENT: Thus alerted, Mrs. Hopkins was particularly aware of Richie's tests on the upcoming health screening and was not surprised when the examining physician noted swollen tonsils and underweight with a question of malnutrition and recommended follow-up by the family doctor. Before contacting the Kinkaids, Mrs. Hopkins secured as much data as she could about them as a family from the school records. Mr. and Mrs. Kinkaid had both been born in Caney Creek, Kentucky. Mr. Kinkaid (twenty-eight) worked as a clerk in a small variety store. Mrs. Kinkaid (twenty-seven) was a housewife. There were five children, Richie (eight); Linda (five) who was in kindergarten; twins, Robert and Phillip (three); and an infant, Peter.

The classroom teacher reported that Mr. and Mrs. Kinkaid came to Parents' Day faithfully, but were not active in any of the school organizations. Richie tested a little above average in intellectual ability, but with his absences and his passivity earned the all too frequent comment "not achieving up to capacity." Linda's file indicated the same pattern. Both children had all of their desired immunizations.

In considering how to approach the Kinkaids, Mrs. Hopkins decided that instead of sending the usual form reporting on the tests and asking the parents to come to the school, she would offer to visit them. She did this because of the number of young children and the expense of baby sitters, the fact that she wanted to talk with both parents together, and her realization that the problems indicated by the children's symptoms might be very broad indeed. Therefore, with the reports she sent a note asking if she might visit in the evening, on a specific date and time. Richie, pleased to be singled out for special attention, faithfully carried the note home and brought back a verbal reply that it would be "all right for her to come." (If the Kinkaids had rejected her offer and had not visited the school, Mrs. Hopkins could have dropped in one evening, confronted them with the test results, and attempted to involve them in a discussion of what they meant and what could be done about them.)

ASSESSMENT: The Kinkaids lived in a small prefab house, one of a block of six built in an area of much larger and more expensive homes. Theirs was outstanding for its meticulous appearance. Mrs. Hopkins commented on this to Mr. Kinkaid when he met her at the door, and he came outside and showed her around, talking about his yard and garden. He was a slender, wiry, tense man, clearly accustomed to meeting the public and putting his best foot forward.

Inside, the house showed considerable contrast to the neat exterior. Clean but cluttered, it presented an air of confusion and disorder that was aggravated by the noise of the television which Linda and Richie were watching and the sound of the twins who were obviously being put to bed against their will. When Mrs. Kinkaid joined them, she was carrying the baby and a bottle. She was a very attractive young woman, but obviously tired and harassed. She attempted half-heartedly to send the two older children to bed, and when she met with no success, their father arbitrarily switched off the TV and ordered them out. At this point Mrs. Hopkins suggested that if the parents agreed she would be glad to have the children stay to listen as they were going to be talked about. "Remember how you used to feel when the teacher came to visit?" she asked.

It was agreed that they could stay, and Mr. Kinkaid commented that his school had been so different from Cherry Street that it was unbelievable. Both the Kinkaids had lived "up the hollow" and ridden the bus to a consolidated school. Determined to leave the hopelessness of Appalachia behind them, they had married immediately after graduating from high school and gone to Cincinnati where Mr. Kinkaid had gotten a job similar to his present one. He stressed that he had always done white-collar work. They had moved to their present home five years ago because they wanted to live in a smaller town, and to escape the racial tensions and problems in the city where they felt lost. They wanted better schools for the children, and had selected this neighborhood because of Cherry Street School.

Initially Mr. Kinkaid tended to do most of the talking, but as the discussion progressed his wife became more dominant. While he was inclined to pass over problems lightly, Mrs. Kinkaid, in a petulant voice, complained about the unfriendliness of the town and neighbors, their limited income, the fact that she never got out, how hard she had to work. This seemed to embarrass her husband who at first tried to stop her but finally withdrew from the conversation. The two children sat quietly through this as if it were an old story. Richie, sitting next to Mrs. Hopkins who had her arm around him, seemed to have relaxed almost into sleep.

The picture that emerged was of a young family struggling hard to function adequately, but with breakdown in crucial areas that promised severe problems in the future.

DEFINITION OF THE PROBLEM: As Mrs. Hopkins talked with

the parents, she was trying to assess what they were saying, to raise questions when her understanding was not clear, and to empathize with the deep feelings that were obvious, albeit mostly under the surface. It was apparent that these problems were causing a strain on the marital relationship and between the parents and the children, and that what had begun ten years ago as a fairly strong relationship with potential for a full life was fraying around the edges. The problems were numerous and on many different levels.

1. The income was not adequate to meet the needs of the family. Mr. Kinkaid was ashamed of this but the problem lay not in poor management but in the fact that his salary was too low. The burden of indebtedness was climbing, and it seemed that his marketable skills were so minimal that it would be difficult for him to qualify for a better job.

2. While Mr. Kinkaid seemed to be adapting well to the change in setting, Mrs. Kinkaid, perhaps because of her early cultural experiences (and this is often true of housewives confined to the home by the demands of their job) had been unable to establish an effective and satisfying pattern of living in her new community. Her values, attitudes, and ways of living remained those of the mountain town where she had grown up.

3. The family had too many children too soon. Each family unit has the capacity to deal, financially, physically, and emotionally, with a certain level of demands, but when the demands become too great, the family breaks down. This was evidenced in part by the fact that the first two children had had good medical and dental care, but the twins and the baby had only the minimum.

4. Each of the family members was adapting to these problems in an individual way, but all in ways that were destructive. Mr. Kinkaid tried to shut his eyes to their seriousness and drove himself harder and harder as he became more desperate. Mrs. Kinkaid adapted by giving up. Meals had become sporadic and inadequately planned. The children were not given the care they needed, or the opportunity for stimulation so vital in these early years. In her fear she had become passive, only taking action when forced to, and complaining in a whining way that was destructive to the morale of her husband and children. The two older children had followed her pattern of passivity and evidenced signs of intellectual, emotional, and physical starvation.

5. Adequate social resources to meet their need did not exist. Social planners have never dealt adequately with the situation in Appalachia in which the roots of the problem lay. It has become a

sore spot and a testimony to inadequate planning and lack of protection for people and resources. In their present setting, the Kinkaids fell into the category of low-income families for whom medical and dental care often become nonexistent and for whom the only flexible budget item is the money they spend for food. They did not qualify for public welfare programs. Mr. Kinkaid was most reluctant to use what free services did exist because he did not want to be "dependent," and Mrs. Kinkaid's hopelessness presented a strong barrier to learning to deal with the demands of a hard reality.

The immediate problem was where to start. It would be easy to turn away from such a situation, particularly in light of all the other problems involving severe antisocial behavior that demand attention, and yet the results of this kind of situation can be great not only in terms of human suffering but also in financial cost to the overall society. Although realizing all of this Mrs. Hopkins could not at this point share all of her understanding with her clients. They saw the problem as the children needing health care which they could not afford, and it was here that all efforts had to start. Because they saw this need as "respectable" and divorced from welfare, they could probably accept help with it.

SETTING OF GOALS: The overall goal of both Mrs. Hopkins and the Kinkaids coincided and this was a strength that the worker could use. Also there was basic affection and trust between them, and they wanted a good life for themselves and their children.

The immediate goal, securing further examination and medical care for Richie and Linda and preventive care for the younger children, was one on which, again, everyone agreed, and when they had talked about the school examination, Mr. Kinkaid said they would call their own doctor.

SELECTION OF ALTERNATIVE METHODS AND AN INITIAL MODE OF INTERVENTION: Mrs. Hopkins replied that of course they could do this, and in the final analysis, they might decide to do so, but she wanted them to know what else was available. They had told her and she knew how hard it was to spread a salary over all of the young family's needs. The town was fortunate in that the Health Department had a good Well Child Clinic where examinations were free and shots could be gotten at a minimum cost. Many of the parents of Cherry School District used it and found it helpful. She had brought a couple of brochures on the clinic which she gave to them.

(Mrs. Hopkins did not add that this clinic afforded a broad range of services including a mothers' group to discuss nutrition and how to feed a family well and inexpensively, specialists who worked on both an individual and group basis in helping parents meet the emotional needs of children, and family planning clinics. She saw the mothers' group as possibly providing the entree that Mrs. Kinkaid needed to begin developing a social experience similar to that her husband found with his fellow employees at work. She did not want the Kinkaids to feel that she was taking over their lives as this would quickly alienate the independent Mr. Kinkaid.)

ESTABLISHMENT OF A CONTRACT: After considerable discussion and many questions about the nature and financing of the service (Mr. Kinkaid talked about his horror of welfare as he had known it during his childhood in their little mountain town) the parents decided that they would try it. It was agreed that Mrs. Hopkins would make known the results of the school tests to the clinic worker. Unfortunately, the clinic hours coincided with Mr. Kinkaid's working so he could neither accompany his wife, nor baby sit with the younger children. Mrs. Hopkins offered to go with Mrs. Kinkaid for the first trip, and watch the younger children while she and the older ones saw the doctor if no other arrangement could be made. If they decided to continue, Mrs. Kinkaid felt that her neighbor might agree to baby sit when needed. They discussed the kinds of information the doctor required and the questions they wanted to ask.

ACTION: Mrs. Hopkins called the clinic, referred the Kinkaid children, and sent the school reports. She phoned Mrs. Kinkaid the day before the clinic visit. As she had anticipated, Mrs. Kinkaid had had second thoughts and was dwelling on the problems involved in getting there. Mrs. Hopkins recognized how hard it was for her to mobilize the impetus and energy for new undertakings but encouraged and supported her real desire to give the children the care they needed.

When they arrived at the clinic, Mrs. Hopkins remained only long enough to get her client through the first stages and then excused herself to do some errands elsewhere in the building. She did this purposefully. The clinic waiting room was friendly and cheerful, with a coffee urn and a volunteer helper who worked with the younger children as they waited. The twins gravitated very naturally to this group. Other young mothers were there, and Mrs. Hopkins hoped that without her presence, Mrs. Kinkaid would begin to interact with them. If this did not occur naturally, it was the clinic worker's job to attempt to facilitate it.

On the way home Mrs. Kinkaid talked about how she had enjoyed being out. The doctor had prescribed vitamins for both the older children, had complimented her on how well they behaved and seemed particularly interested in their eating and sleeping patterns. He had suggested that Mrs. Kinkaid might want to talk with the nutritionist about how to serve more balanced meals and had said an aide would come to the house if she couldn't get down to the clinic. He had started shots for the twins and the baby and made an appointment for follow-up care.

EVALUATION: Mrs. Kinkaid felt that, on the whole, the clinic was a good resource that she and her family could use. She wanted to take her husband with her next time. Mrs. Hopkins, recognizing the sometimes transitory ebullience that results from doing something about a problem and knowing how difficult it was going to be for the Kinkaids to maintain the motivation to act, supported and encouraged as much as she could and agreed to keep in touch.

In looking at her initial intervention Mrs. Hopkins decided that it had been a good beginning. In addition to providing the vital medical care, the clinic offered opportunities for learning and for meaningful relationships that could help to ease the pressures on this family—provided the workers in the various areas involved were skillful enough to keep them involved, and they were sufficiently motivated to use the service.

This intervention, however, left the broader and more basic social problems untouched. Society faces the clear issues of guaranteeing an adequate income to families such as the Kinkaids whose earnings are too small, providing free the essential services necessary to meet their basic human needs, or dealing with the endless series of problems of increasing severity that result from this semi-poverty. In the final analysis, the economic cost of the latter alternative is much greater than that of the first two, to say nothing of the human suffering involved.

Where, then, does the responsibility of the individual worker lie? How can Mrs. Hopkins intervene effectively to help deal with these basic problems, to do more than merely palliative work, and to bring about the changes in the total social system that are essential in order to ensure that this family become and remain a healthy unit in the total society?

Social change on so broad a scale cannot be effected by one individual working alone. It requires the strength of many people working together and utilizing the tools that a democratic system provides. In her role as a social changer, Mrs. Hopkins can use specialized knowledge of and experience with the inadequacies of the total system and their effect upon both individuals and the society. She has recourse to the various groups to which she belongs by virtue of her work; those of teachers or health workers; those to which she belongs by virtue of her role as a citizen; and those which she helps create with her clients and colleagues to deal with specialized situations.

The two former categories are ones through which she could work for the necessary legislation and the enforcement of that legislation. The two areas of basic need in this family—adequate wages and health care—are ones to which the country as a whole is already committed, and the questions that need resolution now deal with how this can be achieved. Mrs. Hopkins can contribute knowledge and strength to this resolution.

One of the major problems of the Kinkaids was their feeling of helplessness and hopelessness, and an excellent tool in overcoming this problem was involving the clients in ways to change their own situation—in the struggle for self-realization. The Parents' Group at the clinic, developed out of a common interest in the needs of families and children, need only take one further step to start moving actively to secure the resources to meet these needs. Opportunity for personal growth as well as necessary social action can be achieved through use of this medium. We can see concrete evidence of this in the vastly changed attitudes toward and improved care for retarded children through group efforts of both lay and professional people; for the elderly through their own group efforts; for children in foster care through foster parents' groups; for a multitude of various special interest groups. When individuals band together in a common interest and acquire the knowledge of how to tackle the system, they can develop the necessary power to effect change. The worker, by virtue of specialized knowledge and skill, can provide the catalytic action often needed to get this process started and serve as consultant, resource person, enabler and, when necessary, advocate.

CONTINUATION: The outcome of Mrs. Hopkins' evaluation with the Kinkaids of the results of their initial clinic visit would be a continuation of the process well begun. The worker's efforts would focus on providing the essential personal support to keep their courage high, and to work toward changing the basic social conditions that create problems for this family.

BASIC PROCESS—II

The second example of application of this overall process is that of a neighborhood organizing to save itself through a coalition of the residents. Hillcrest is an old section of a city with big homes and wide lawns, good schools, and moderate business development. It is close to the city, with good access to jobs and the downtown facilities. It is a pleasant, convenient place to live.

With the adoption of open housing ordinances, black families began to move into the neighborhood which had previously been all white. Panic developed among the residents and a few hastily sold their homes and moved. Thus encouraged, "block busters" appeared and a state of near crisis evolved. In addition, newspapers reported discussion by the city council of a proposed expressway to go down one of the wide old streets.

The Hillcrest Neighborhood Association actually started in the liquor store on Wendell Street late on Friday night when young Bill Adams, a research chemist at the hospital, stopped in to buy a couple of bottles of Chianti for his weekend cookout. Few customers came in, and he and Tony talked about the neighborhood's problems and how they wanted to go on living in their homes. They decided to do something about it, and by the time Bill left Tony's, the initial process of planned change was underway.

Engagement took place when they jointly decided that there was a problem about which something needed to be done, and that they were motivated to do it. In this preliminary step, they saw the problem as the threatened destruction of their neighborhood because of the social changes that were taking place. Their *assessment* could, at this point, only be based on a few facts—the new ordinance had been passed, some black families had moved in, there were unethical real estate operators working in the neighborhood, and many unsubstantiated rumors were being circulated. They *defined the immediate problem* as the need for more facts and the development of an approach to influence the situation. Their *goal* was to keep their neighborhood a good place in which to live. Their *mode of intervention* was to bring the residents of the neighborhood together and try to develop an organization to deal with the immediate crisis. They agreed (*contract*) to talk with as many people as possible and set up a meeting. Tony agreed to bring up the problem at the parochial school PTA meeting on Monday night and thought Father Minelli would let them use the parish hall for meeting. Bill agreed to talk it over with the people at the cookout and try to arrange for someone from the Mayor's Housing Committee on the Real Estate Board to attend the meeting to answer questions and lend professional know-how. Recognizing the difficulties that fear and prejudice on both sides were creating, they decided to attempt to get a black resident, Mrs. Niles, who lived near Bill, to help in planning. They decided to ask the young minister of the local Unitarian church, which was particularly active in social issues, to chair the meeting which they feared might be a difficult one.

In the ensuing two weeks of *action* before the neighborhood meeting took place, Bill and Tony commented frequently that had they known what they were undertaking, they would probably never have started. Organizing a neighborhood or community is a demanding, almost full-time job. Their phones rang constantly and they had to cope with fears, misunderstanding, anger, and frustrations as well as arrangements that broke down. Mrs. Niles, an experienced precinct worker for her party, did not take them seriously. It was she who suggested that education was a major need and enlisted the support of the editor of the *Evening News* to run a series of articles on blockbusting tactics in general and the utility of neighborhood associations in combating them for the week immediately prior to the planned meeting.

The meeting at the Parish Hall was well attended. The newspaper publicity, a calling campaign set up by Bill's wife, Mary, and Tony's wife, Joan, and word of mouth advertising, as well as the strong feeling about the situation, had brought out a large crowd. The chairperson set the tone by defining the boundaries of the neighborhood using city maps, and pointing out its strengths: the absence of pockets of extreme poverty, the good balance of business and residential property, the three small parks and adjacent larger one with a good-sized lake, the resources such as schools, a hospital, churches, and a branch library; and its problems: the proposed expressway that would run through a predominantly residential section, a decaying warehouse area, and the current reaction to the influx of black families to the area.

The Housing Authority representative talked about the need for and development of open housing and the general laws relating to housing. He ended by saying that what occurred in the neighborhood would depend on what the residents allowed to happen.

Bill told how he and Tony had gotten involved, their concern and desire to remain in their homes and preserve the stability of the neighborhood. They hoped that the residents would be willing to work with them to accomplish this.

Discussion, at first, was stilted and limited. Then one angry white man rose and voiced the widely held feeling that when black people moved into a community, it deteriorated. He pointed to other sections of the city to prove his point that homes were neglected, property values went down and crime went up. Others echoed his comments.

Mrs. Niles, calmly and undefensively, replied that this was not necessarily so and pointed to other cities in which integrated neighborhoods did not have these problems, and she stated that other factors besides race were involved. The representative from the Real Estate Board supported her and added bluntly that the basic issue was not only economic, but also bias and fear of change. He recognized that attitudes and feelings do not change overnight but stated that integrated housing was coming and the vital decision was how people were going to live with it.

There was a silence after this and Tony proposed a neighborhood coalition to encourage people not to sell their homes in a panic and to work toward retaining the health and strength of the neighborhood. He suggested a committee of twelve be formed to study the question and recommend procedures. Bill suggested that because time was important, the committee also be empowered to act. There was considerable discussion pro and con but finally the proposal was accepted, an *ad hoc* committee of volunteers was formed and a second general meeting date was set. The committee members got together at the end of the meeting and agreed to meet the following night at Bill's house.

Because the twelve committee members had been selected from varying geographical areas within the neighborhood, it was necessary for them to get acquainted. Mary served coffee and cookies to help in this, and there was general conversation. During this period and the initial stages of the formal meeting, which began with the election of Tony as chairman and Mary as recorder, *evaluation* of the general meeting was taking place. All agreed that it had been too large for good discussion and the formation of the *ad hoc* committee had been railroaded through by the people who were strongly motivated to act. Mrs. Niles reported that the black people were saying that the real purpose of the Association was to keep black families out of the neighborhood, and the other black member of the committee supported this view.

There was considerable discussion as to whether small neighborhood meetings, or breaking the next general meeting down into small discussion groups, should be the way of developing a more democratic base for action. Without ruling out neighborhood meetings indefinitely, it was decided to opt for small group discussion within the general meeting to serve as an opportunity to express feelings and to develop ideas for action.

To deal with the rumor that the Association was segregationist, it was suggested that black and white co-chairpeople be appointed, and this was agreed upon as a temporary expedient. Mrs. Niles, very naturally, was chosen. She assumed the chair of a task force of three to draw up a statement of purpose and plan of organization for the Association. The task force agreed to have the outline ready to present to the committee for adoption three days before the next general meeting so it could be duplicated for distribution, discussion, and adoption at the meeting.

The emergency nature of the situation in the Southeast section of the community was also discussed. Al Federson, a committee member from there, reported on many For Sale signs on houses and tension among the residents. A suggestion was made that the Federsons invite their neighbors to a meeting at their home to talk about what the Association was trying to do or that two or three people visit each of these families and try to allay some of their fears and concerns and invite them to the next general meeting. It was agreed that the most pressing general concerns were fear of devaluation of property, increased crime, and prejudice toward neighbors who were different from themselves. After considerable discussion, it was decided that one person would visit each of these homes taking reprints of the *News* article on blockbusting, and try to open lines of communication with the householders. It was agreed that in some cases, the biases could be altered by dealing with the economic fears. A task force with Al Federson as chairperson was appointed to develop and carry out plans for these visits and various committee members volunteered for the job. A second committee meeting was set for three days before the general meeting to act on the report of the task force on organization.

Throughout this meeting, the basic process for planned change was taking place. The members of the committee had engaged themselves individually with the situation when they volunteered. In this meeting, they were engaging themselves as a group with all the strengths that arise through such a coalition. Assessing the situation, they arrived at a definition of both an overall problem and goal and many subsidiary problems and goals. In so doing they established priorities and selected modes of intervention from the various alternatives available to them, arriving at a series of contracts and agreed upon action. They built into their deliberations and actions provisions for evaluating and continuing or changing the process being used as indicated by subsequent results of the interventions.

C

Interviewing, Discussion, and Making Referrals

INTERVIEWING

There are so many different kinds of interviews that it is difficult to select any one that is illustrative of the total process. Workers' roles will vary according to the personality theory they adopt and the mode of interviewing it dictates, the needs of the clients and the way in which they respond to the workers' efforts, the purpose and goal of the interview, and to some extent, the setting in which it occurs.

The one that follows is an excerpt from a simple, purposeful conversation which begins between two people in the presence of a third and ends as a discussion among three people.

William Bingham, minister of the Glenview Church, had been asked by Mr. and Mrs. Woodford to persuade her parents to accept nursing home care. Mr. and Mrs. Anderson were both in their eighties. While Mrs. Anderson was still able to putter around and do a few things in the house, Mr. Anderson was totally deaf, and a recent stroke had left him incontinent so that his care was more than she could manage alone. The Woodfords had only limited income and four small children, but with the various care programs for the aged for which the old couple were eligible and the proceeds that could be realized from the sale of the Andersons' house, they could manage to pay for their parents' care. Mrs. Anderson would not go unless her husband was willing, and Mr. Anderson clung with stubborn and desperate fear to his home and the last vestiges of independence available to him. Rev. Bingham agreed to talk with them when, in the course of his pastoral duties, he made a call at the home.

Mrs. Anderson met Rev. Bingham at the door and invited him in.

"Here's Mr. Bingham, Dad," she called to her husband, who was sitting huddled in a chair before the fire. Mr. Anderson responded minimally and then withdrew into silence, while the minister and Mrs. Anderson talked about the weather, her health, what was happening in the church, and so on. Finally Rev. Bingham brought the conversation around to the business of the interview.

Rev. Bingham: I had a purpose for coming today, Mrs. Anderson. Mary asked me to talk with you about your plans. She's worried about you and her dad.

Mrs. Anderson: I know. She told me you were coming. (Tears welled in her eyes.) We've got to do something. I just can't do the work anymore.

Rev. Bingham: I know—you've done the best you can, and it hasn't been easy.

Mrs. Anderson: Doctor Rogers says he has to have a nurse to take care of him—and wants him to go to Elm Hill but he won't consider it. He's mad now because Mary told him she asked you to see us.

Rev. Bingham: Maybe I better tackle him directly then. (He turned to the silent figure in the chair.) How are you feeling today, Mr. Anderson?

Mr. Anderson: What'd you say?

Mrs. Anderson: He doesn't have his hearing aid on. Want your hearing aid, Dad?

Rev. Bingham: HOW—DO—YOU—FEEL?

Mr. Anderson: Feel all right.

Rev. Bingham: GOOD! MARY ASKED ME TO TALK WITH YOU.

Mr. Anderson: No use in it. I'm not going.

Rev. Bingham: NOT GOING WHERE?

Mr. Anderson: What?

Rev. Bingham: WHERE ARE YOU NOT GOING?

Mr. Anderson: (Angrily) I can't hear a word you're saying. Get my hearing aid, Sallie.

(The hearing aid was produced and adjusted with considerable normal bickering, which, however, held an edge of anxiety and fear.)

Mr. Anderson: Now, what did you say?

Rev. Bingham: I asked where you weren't going.

Mr. Anderson: I'm not going to Elm Hill. I don't need a nursing home.

Rev. Bingham: (Gently) I didn't come to try to force you to go to Elm Hill, if that's what you're worried about Mr. Anderson. You have to make your own decisions.

Mr. Anderson: (Fiercely) What did you come for then?

Rev. Bingham: I came because I'm your minister and Mary's and Alton's. I came because they are worried about both of you, and because I know you're having a hard time. You're at the place where you have to make some decisions that are really important, and I thought perhaps I could help.

Mr. Anderson: I've already made up my mind what I'm going to do. I'm going to stay right here.

Rev. Bingham: I know that's what you'd like to do, and I can sure understand it, but for how long?

Mr. Anderson: As long as I can.

Rev. Bingham: But the time is very close when you can't. All I'm asking you to do is to think about that and start planning for it so you can make a decision without being forced to do it hastily without proper consideration of everything involved. Dr. Rogers says . . .

Mr. Anderson: Dr. Rogers is a young fool!

Rev. Bingham: (Grinning) Depends on where you sit. To me, if he's a fool he's an old one.

Mr. Anderson: (Smiling in spite of himself) I guess that's true. He must be about fifty-five.

Rev. Bingham: Young or old, he knows his medicine. You couldn't have a better doctor, and he says you have to have nursing care, and he says this whole thing is too much for Sallie.

Mr. Anderson: (Turning to his wife) Can't you get that woman to help you again?

Mrs. Anderson: There just isn't anybody anymore, period! Mary keeps coming over, and with the baby she shouldn't be doing anything extra. She's too thin.

Mr. Anderson: You don't have very much to do. Just keep the house and take care of me.

Mrs. Anderson: I'm eighty-four-years-old, Billie, and I'm tired. I can't cook and clean and shop and take care of you at night. This house is too big, and we can't do the yard anymore. Alton doesn't complain, but they've got their own home to take care of.

Mr. Anderson: They're just putting me out to die like an old horse.

Rev. Bingham: I think all older people feel that way sometimes, but it just isn't true with you. Everybody has to accept inevitables and age is one of them. No matter how old we are, however, our choices are limited.

Mr. Anderson: It's easy for you to sit there and say that.

Rev. Bingham: I know, but not completely easy. Its ahead of me, too.

Mrs. Anderson: (Desperately) Billie, we just got to do something.

Mr. Anderson: All right go ahead, take me out and put me away.

Rev. Bingham: Nursing homes aren't putting people away. They're especially designed to meet the need of many different kinds of people. Have you ever seen Elm Hill?

Mr. Anderson: No, and I don't want to.

Rev. Bingham: There are others beside Elm Hill. The only thing is, it's close to Alton and Mary, and in good weather you could probably even walk down to their place. There's Rest Haven out on Cortland Road which is close to the reservoir, and lots of people from there go fishing. Both of these have the three different facilities—apartments, rooms, and hospital beds—but all three afford the nursing care you need. I think you can take some of your own furniture with you so you can still have your own bed which is real important.

Mrs. Anderson: I'd like to be close to Mary and the children.

Mr. Anderson: (Defiantly) And I'd rather have the fishing!

Rev. Bingham: Why don't you look at both of them—and any of the others you'd like and see what alternatives are open to you.

This interview, while only a skirmish in the total campaign, was successful in that it moved Mr. Anderson from an immovable position to the point where he was thinking about alternatives. Rev. Bingham used *support, confrontation, universalization,* and *presentation of alternatives* in a manner characterized by empathy and compassion, but with understanding and acceptance of an unpleasant reality. His use of humor to relieve the tension was deliberate and in keeping with his character and struck a responsive chord in a frightened, sick old man. The lines of communication, initially between two individuals, at the close of this interview had enlarged to encompass communication among the three. In the final moments, this became a discussion.

DISCUSSION

At best, discussion is a democratic growth experience for the participants. Like the other skills upon which this most difficult form of self-government rests, it must be learned. More and more families and schools are attempting to teach the knowledge and techniques upon which its successful use depends. It can be usable in any life area and in any context by any combination of persons.

The following excerpts are from the meetings of a club group of a dozen boys between the ages of twelve and sixteen. They took place in a settlement house in the ghetto area of a midwestern city. The boys were from the three major racial groups in the city, black, Chicano and white. The group was formed by the center to provide recreation and a growth experience in group interaction. Harry, the leader, was a staff group worker. Originally this had been thought of as a coed group, but the girls who responded to the initial invitation did not return, and the boys decided to make this their own club and invite girls only to special events. With the girls' departure, three older boys left also, and those who remained were younger and less mature, but had a fairly common span of interests.

At the first meeting, the boys and the worker talked about what the group's function should be. At this point they seemed mainly interested in the worker and his role, finally deciding that he would be a group member and adviser. They decided to select a project later, to concentrate on getting an organization underway, and to discuss structure at the next meeting.

As the second meeting began, the group became interested in the tape recorder the worker had brought. It wasn't long before imitations and songs began to burst forth as each member added his particular talent to the swell of sound. The worker suggested that if they would all like to record, each could have a turn. First, each was given a chance to say something about himself. Then Mike volunteered to do an imitation of Flip Wilson and Sam did the introduction. After that an impromptu skit developed based on a current rock group with Mike, Sam, and Bobbie in the major roles. Following the skit and the playback, the group was ready for the business meeting.

The decision was made that the group should have a president, vice-president, secretary, treasurer, and sergeant-at-arms. Once this was agreed on, they considered the business of voting. It was decided that nominees could not vote and that in case of a tie, there would be a new vote until one candidate received a majority. Sam was elected president; Andy, vice-president; Mike, treasurer; Bill, secretary; and Leon, sergeant-at-arms. (Almost every group has within itself an indigenous leader who arises in the normal process of group development, usually as a result of personality or group selection. Often two strong persons will compete for this role and the struggle will go on throughout the life of the group unless one chooses to withdraw. In this instance Sam and Mike appeared to be those persons, but Mike accepted his defeat with little apparent dejection.) The boys decided to call themselves the Kool Kats.

During the election, interest and participation were high and at several points the worker intervened when the boys attempted to coerce each other, by reminding them they had decided to use parliamentary procedure, consisting of nomination, discussion, question, and vote. They responded to this control and finished the business at hand.

After his election, Sam took over the meeting and the boys decided to spend their next meeting discussing an overnight camp-in in the center's gym and to have refreshments at this meeting. Mike volunteered to bring doughnuts, Eddie and Leon to make punch.

The worker began the next meeting with a game designed to afford expression for some of the accumulated energy the boys brought from school and to provide opportunity for interaction before the more demanding task of discussion was undertaken. The boys were asked if they wished to play and although there was some grumbling, participation was wide. A Ping-Pong ball was placed in the middle of the table with a team positioned on either side of the table. Each team attempted to blow the ball to the other side. There was a lot of kidding about this in terms of the team with the worse smelling breath having the advantage. After about fifteen minutes of intense activity, play was terminated.

The meeting was called to order by Sam, no mean feat as the boys tended to run around or converse loudly, and Sam sometimes forgot the purpose of the group. Discussion centered on the camp-in. Bill, the secretary, suggested he use the blackboard to write down details. This was agreed on, and he recorded the items discussed.

The first order of business was to determine a date. Andy suggested the same week, but Ralph pointed out that this would not allow enough time to make all the necessary plans. The worker requested that it be on a weekend because of his own schedule and after much debate Friday, April 10, was selected. Sam suggested that he be the one to confirm the date with the director, Miss Marcusson, and was excused to do so. The group decided that the camp should extend from 7 p.m. Friday to 10 a.m. Saturday.

Food was the next item on the agenda and was discussed enthusiastically by all the boys. There was quick agreement about eggs and sausage, strong difference over pop or juice and toast or pancakes. Pancakes and juice won by vote. Agreement was unanimous on one dollar per person for food, and Max suggested that any left over money be given to the worker who thanked him, but suggested that any leftovers be returned to the treasury or prorated among the members. The decision was that it go to the treasury.

The next two meetings were devoted to planning details of the camp-in. During this time, structure was emerging, and the boys assumed responsibility for planning the game that had become the opening part of each session and accepting the discipline of discussion. A combination of play and work emerged and the chaos that so often seemed about to take over never really materialized. Three boys, Sam, Mike and Max, all fourteen-year-olds, were vying for the position of leader, but there was little real animosity among them. The younger boys formed their own subgroup, but accepted any of the three leaders, probably because there was good acceptance and interaction among the older and younger members. Sometimes tensions arose when a proposal was modified or defeated by vote, but they apparently were resolved as the further business took place.

At the fourth meeting decisions were made as to who was to cook and clean up (nomination and vote); who was to buy the food (worker, by unanimous vote as it was agreed he would know where to get the best buys); who was eligible to attend the camp-in (all who had attended at least two planning meetings, paid their dollar, and gotten a permission slip); and what acceptable behavior was to be. ("It was agreed that open quarreling and fighting would not be tolerated. The general behavioral mode was to be 'civilized' behavior. If anyone started fighting or was uncooperative he would have to go through a paddling line. The worker asked for an example of just what kind of paddling would be administered. After discussion it was agreed that this should be paddling with the hand on the rump. This seemed reasonable and acceptable to all.")

At the final meeting before the camp-in, fees and permission slips were gathered and plans were made for games, films, and division of activity and quiet games. Movies were planned for a part of the time and hit-the-sack hour agreed on.

Eight members of the Kool Kats attended the camp-in, which was voted an unqualified success. Al was late, and Max was forbidden to attend by his parents because he had been caught shoplifting earlier in the week. After an evening of games, movies, and snacks "gym mats were unrolled on the floor, and everyone got into pajamas. Spiders ran out of the mats and the boys pretended fear, but enjoyed chasing and squashing them. There was an ongoing exchange of jibes, but they seemed well tolerated and there seemed no concentrated scapegoating." The boys, exhausted, fell asleep around three, were up at seven, cooked breakfast and cleaned up to the satisfaction of Miss Marcusson.

This experience in group interaction was judged to be a constructive one by both the boys and the worker. The club continued and was a meaningful part of their lives during the year. In analyzing it, the worker thought that the original goals were achieved through the following developments: (1) the boys learned to work together, to develop and enjoy a give-and-take relationship with others, and to draw strength from the bond that developed from shared experiences and feelings; (2) they created and worked within a structure of their own making, participated in the decision-making process, and learned the satisfactions and difficulties of creating and carrying through on a project; (3) they experienced the strength of the group which grew from use of the capacities of the individuals and the solidarity of the whole; (4) they learned to deal with their own feelings toward both themselves and others in a group situation.

The worker's role here demanded that he facilitate the development of these experiences, and a major tool was discussion which the boys had to learn to use, in order to compromise, to arrive at a decision, and to abide by the decisions of the majority. A good example of this occurred in dealing with the touchy subject of discipline during the camp-in. Miss Marcusson was a strong executive who ruled with an iron hand; but she was respected by the neighborhood kids, so the rules laid down by the center for use of its facilities were accepted fairly readily. The discipline that the boys had to decide on was that relating to their own individual and group behavior within these rules. The worker brought up the subject, pointing out that it was well to agree in advance on what expected behavior was and how it would be enforced.

Sam: (Self-righteously) No fighting, no swearing, no goofing off. . .

Mike: (Quickly) No ripping off. . .

Allen: (One of the younger boys, bravely). . . and we'll kick out anybody who does!

Max: (Defensively) Nah, that's no good . . .

(Chaos of voices agreeing, protesting, offering other suggestions)

Sam: (Yelling) Shut up, you guys. We ain't gettin' anyplace, and I gotta go deliver my papers.

Worker: The idea's to have fun, so we don't want to make it too strict. You've all been coming to the center long enough to know what's expected here, and we get along pretty well with each other.

Leon: Yeah—let's just say civilized behavior like at the meetings, and Harry will make like the fuzz.

(Chorus of protests, including one from Harry)

Allen: Why can't we kick anybody out?

Worker: In the middle of the night and your parents expecting you to stay here? Isn't it better to work things out among ourselves anyway?

Ralph: We could paddle anybody who got out of line.

Mike: (With relish) Yeah, I'll bring the paddle.

Sam: (Sensing a threat to his leadership) That's no good. How about just a slap on the rump by hand.

(This brought a chorus of agreement from the subgroup of younger boys—Bobbie, Leon, Bill, Ralph and Eddie.)

Allen: (A younger boy who saw the way the wind was blowing and changed sides quickly) I move we say civilized behavior and anybody who gets out of line get a swat on the rump.

Sam quickly called for a second and a vote, and the motion carried.

The process that took place with the Kool Kats is duplicated in all groups, regardless of how simple or sophisticated. The decisions of workers as to how they utilize themselves rest on the basic process that underlies all work with people. In this simple and brief example of decision making as a group, the worker employed the total process from an initial assessment of what was involved, to a final evaluation of the results of his intervention and a decision as to how to proceed.

MAKING REFERRALS

What resources are available? How much can clients do for themselves? What is the role and task of the worker in making and of the client in using a referral?

For the Raphaels, a good resource existed and the worker's activity was clearly defined and structured. The Raphaels were quite capable of using the referral successfully once they were able to accept the necessity for it.

In a play situation, Sally Raphael looked like almost any other six-year-old—a little more active perhaps, and less able to concentrate on what she was doing. It was only in the classroom that her hyperactivity and almost nonexistent attention span became apparent. At the end of the first semester, her concerned teacher asked that she be evaluated by the school psychologist. Dr. Bernard administered individual tests which indicated the extent of Sally's inability to function and pointed to the possibility of brain damage. He asked Mr. and Mrs. Raphael to come in to discuss the findings and his recommendation that Sally be further studied at the Children's Clinic and that she be placed meanwhile in a special education class at school.

The report of these findings came as a shock to the parents. Sally's behavior had gone unnoticed in a family of three children. She was "just a little more difficult than the others," and when her mother had mentioned to her doctor that she was harder to manage, the physician assured her that, with firmness on her part, Sally "would grow out of it." They were overwhelmed by their own feelings and had difficulty comprehending what the psychologist was saying. Dr. Bernard told them about the classroom experience, his own observations, and the test findings. He encouraged them to talk about their feelings of disbelief, anger, fear, and pain and answered any questions directly and honestly, emphasizing that Sally could be helped with the right program but that the usual school routine demanded more than she was capable of, and this failure was having a destructive effect on her. He then suggested that they take a week and observe Sally at home with the test results in mind, that they visit the classroom and talk with the teacher, and that they then come back and talk with him again. He encouraged them to call him during this time with any questions and to think over and talk with each other about what they saw and learned. He strongly recommended, as a first step, a thorough study of Sally by specialists in the area of child development.

In assessing the Raphaels' capacity to make use of a referral at this point, Dr. Bernard considered the impact of his findings which verified their greatest, almost unconscious fears, and the necessity of dealing with them. They possessed strength both individually and as a couple and were perfectly capable of carrying through on the tasks that the referral would involve—making and keeping appointments, participating in history taking and planning, following through on recommendations. The immediate task of mourning for themselves and for the child and of adjusting to the initial shock was one that he hoped to help them begin to deal with during this interim. The Children's Clinic was the only resource available in the community but was a well-functioning institution with competent staff. As a worker he had to enable them to use this or a comparable resource to help both themselves and Sally. Once this was achieved, as school psychologist, he would continue to work with the teachers toward carrying out the clinic's recommendations. Opportunity for ventilation of feeling, support in accepting the need for and working toward the next step, and giving of specific and concrete information about how to go about taking it were Dr. Bernard's main tasks at this point.

Before the end of the week, the parents called to say that they were ready to proceed with the study at the clinic and asked that the transfer to a special education class be held up pending the results of this. This request was not unreasonable or uncommon; perhaps it was indicative of their continuing inability to accept the reality of the current test findings and their hope that further study would negate them. They took the name of the intake worker at the clinic and asked Dr. Bernard to send a copy of the test results to him before their appointment.

In contrast to this formal referral procedure, the second example involves bringing in another person in an informal way. In this instance the original worker delegated responsibility for the actual process to another, and several resources were available. The client was able to choose among a variety. Mr. Crocker, age eighty-seven, lived in a decrepit old trailer at an intersection of the new interstate highway. As the road building progressed he was isolated between various lanes of the highway. In addition, he had a history of heart disease with attendant swelling of his legs and feet that made it difficult for him to get around. He did not eat properly, and the doctor whom he would visit only occasionally was concerned about malnutrition. He was reluctant to leave his home because he had a goat and two cats that would be unwelcome elsewhere.

The Old Age Assistance worker had been concerned about his living alone and from time to time had raised the question of possible nursing home care, but Mr. Crocker would not even consider it. When it became essential that he find another place to live, there were only limited alternatives. He had no relatives or close friends and his sole acquaintances centered in the small grocery in the neighborhood where he shopped. This, too, was being displaced by the interstate. He could (1) find a place to continue to live alone in either public or private housing; (2) live with another family; (3) live in a nursing facility where he could have care suited to his individual need and still have considerable freedom.

Mr. Crocker had no means of transportation, and the worker was anxious that he personally survey what was available and be able to choose between alternatives, however limited. He was an independent, rather irritable old man, accustomed to living alone and to his own life style, and any change would be difficult. The worker, therefore, prevailed on him to accept the services of a young man who, as a part of his class work, was serving as a neighborhood aide. After considerable discussion of the laziness, long hair, drugs and general uselessness of the young, Mr. Crocker reluctantly agreed to use him as a driver.

The OAA worker first met with the student, Fred Carpenter, explaining the needs and the limitations on income, and providing him with lists of approved nursing homes, public housing facilities, and suggested areas in which to search for private ones. The three of them then met and Mr. Crocker added his suggestions to the list. They talked about his pets and the problem they would pose, but as he naturally wanted to keep them, both Fred and the worker promised to make every effort to make this possible.

Although Mr. Crocker was irascible, frequently snarled at his young companion when tired or discouraged, and continually made disparaging remarks about people and the world in general which Fred found difficult to take, they seemed to get along fairly well. When the student became too discouraged, he would come in and talk with the worker thus ventilating his own feelings. They searched for three weeks and finally settled on a boarding situation with an old couple who lived on the edge of town in a ramshackle home and had a little land and were anxious to supplement their own income. They did not mind the pets, and Mr. Crocker could either eat alone in his room or with them. He could bring his own few pieces of furniture.

While this was not the solution that seemed most desirable to the worker, who recognized that another move would probably have to come in the near future, it represented what Mr. Crocker was able and willing to do at this point. His newly acquired knowledge of available facilities could help to make the next move easier. He was perfectly capable of making his own decisions and had made good use of the help of the neighborhood aide. The OAA worker's ongoing responsibility would be to keep in touch with him in the new living situation and try to help make it work so long as it met his needs. In this referral, the worker's task was selecting a resource, providing ongoing supervision and support and participating in planning and carrying out the work.

The final example illustrates a situation in which the resources are quite limited, the client is so damaged by his life experience that he has great difficulty in using even what is available, and the worker's role demands activity in both manipulating the environment and using a strong supportive relationship. Some of the most difficult of all referrals are those faced by social workers and employment counselors in placing clients with limited capacity in jobs. Finding work in a complicated, competitive society when unemployment is high, particularly among unskilled workers and minority group members, can be extremely difficult. Persistence and optimism are potent factors in determining success. The competent counselor anticipates this and copes with it insofar as possible by (1) prior spadework with prospective employers so that they have common agreement of what the job both provides for the employee and requires of him; (2) not making blanket referrals with the resulting high chances of failure; (3) knowing the client well enough to match him to the job; and (4) providing the support necessary to maintain the essential, reality based optimism that is so crucial in motivation.

Tony Morales was laid off when the packing plant for which he worked was automated. At fifty-five, he was married, the father of four and had held his present job for ten years, longer than any of his previous ones. Although the work was steady and paid enough to support the family, he disliked it intensely but was afraid to quit. He was one of the many who "lead lives of quiet desperation" and over the years had acquired the habit of drinking before work and at lunch to mask his unhappiness. During the long months of idleness while the family lived on unemployment insurance, and afterwards when his wife took a job and they applied for public assistance to supplement her inadequate wages, he felt even less adequate and started drinking more heavily. At first he had made the rounds of the employment agencies and been sent out on jobs, but he experienced failure after failure, either not being hired or getting only short-term work.

Al Roberts, the family assistance worker, set two related goals—to try to help Mr. Morales deal with his own feelings of inadequacy and worthlessness and to help him find employment. He felt that time was of the essence because his client was rapidly developing attitudes and a way of life characterized by apathy and indifference. He worked with the counselor at the State Employment Service in assessing both the availability of jobs in the area and the basic capacities of Mr. Morales. Based on the findings of these two undertakings, they utilized a federally funded program to retrain him for work in maintaining and servicing laundromat machines. As he possessed good manual skills, he was capable of doing this work and obtaining satisfaction from it.

This process required of Mr. Morales the motivation and capacity to use referrals to the training program and the employment agency as well as prospective employers, no easy task for a badly demoralized man. A strong, reality-based relationship with his worker was of vital importance in developing and maintaining this ability and success was a fragile thing, for at best, he was a highly vulnerable employee in a shaky labor market.

Index